Palgrave Macmillan Studies in Banking and Financial Institutions

Founding Editor
Philip Molyneux

Series Editor
Jon Williams, Surrey Business School, University of Surrey, Guildford, UK

The Palgrave Macmillan Studies in Banking and Financial Institutions series is international in orientation and includes studies of banking systems in particular countries or regions as well as contemporary themes such as Islamic Banking, Financial Exclusion, Mergers and Acquisitions, Risk Management, and IT in Banking. The books focus on research and practice and include up to date and innovative studies that cover issues which impact banking systems globally.

Greta Benedetta Ferilli

Bank-FinTech M&As and Banking Innovation

A Performance Assessment of the Global Banking System

palgrave
macmillan

Greta Benedetta Ferilli
Department of Economic Sciences
University of Salento
Lecce, Italy

ISSN 2523-336X ISSN 2523-3378 (electronic)
Palgrave Macmillan Studies in Banking and Financial Institutions
ISBN 978-3-031-84447-8 ISBN 978-3-031-84445-4 (eBook)
https://doi.org/10.1007/978-3-031-84445-4

This Palgrave Macmillan imprint is published by the registered company Springer Nature Switzerland AG
The registered company address is: Gewerbestrasse 11, 6330 Cham, Switzerland

Foreword

The banking industry has undergone transformative changes over the past two decades, driven by the convergence of technological advancements, regulatory shifts, and complex market demands. Against this background, characterised by increased competition from financial technology (FinTech) firms and other non-bank financial institutions, incumbent banks are encouraged to rethink their strategies in order to maintain competitiveness, financial stability, and relevance in the evolving market. Among these changes, mergers and acquisitions (M&As) between incumbents and FinTech firms have emerged as a critical strategy for addressing competitive pressures, fostering innovation, and ensuring adaptability and business sustainability in an increasingly dynamic financial environment.

The book, authored by Greta Benedetta Ferilli, provides a timely and insightful analysis of this phenomenon, assessing its impact on banks' performance metrics and the implications for the dynamics of business model evolution. The book's relevance lies in its focus on the intersection of two key drivers of the contemporary financial industry: the rise of FinTech and the ongoing restructuring of banking business models. The advent of FinTech firms, defined by the Bank for International Settlements (BIS) as *"technology-enabled innovation in financial services"*, has prompted a rethinking of traditional banking practices, with incumbent institutions seeking to integrate advanced technologies to remain competitive. This study assesses the role of M&As as a mechanism for banks to acquire technological capabilities, improve performance, and reposition their business models in order to align with the demands of the digital era.

The author adopts qualitative and quantitative approaches to assess the impact of FinTech M&As on banking institutions' financial and non-financial performance. The analysis draws on a global sample of listed banks that have engaged in FinTech M&As for over 25 years, assessing a range of banks' performance indicators, including profitability, efficiency, risk, and ESG score. The inclusion of financial and non-financial metrics reflects the comprehensive approach adopted in this book, which captures the manifold effects of FinTech-Bank M&As.

The book's main contribution is a detailed examination of how the business models of both banks and FinTech firms influence the outcomes of M&As. By focusing on business model heterogeneity, the author offers practical guidance for decision-makers in tailoring M&A strategies to optimise their outcomes, thus filling a crucial gap in the literature.

The book represents an important reference in the financial economics literature targeting a broad audience ranging from practitioners in the finance and banking sectors to policymakers, academics, and students involved in finance and law. Through a rigorous discussion of their study's findings, the author also contributes to the debate on financial innovation and its implications for the banking industry. In summary, the book bridges the gap between theory and practice in financial economics, offering a forward-looking perspective on how banks can harness M&As to remain competitive and improve performance in an evolving environment.

Professor Yener Altunbaş
Bangor Business School
Bangor, UK

Contents

List of Figures

List of Tables

CHAPTER 1

Introduction

Abstract This chapter highlights the strategic faction assumed by mergers and acquisitions (M&As) in the banking sector, emphasising their role in fostering innovation, improving operational efficiency, and broadening market reach. It focuses on M&A operations involving financial technology (FinTech) firms, which are identified as significant innovation drivers of traditional business models. According to this perspective, this chapter examines the evolution of banking business models (BBMs), emphasising their adaptation to digitalisation, regulatory changes, and competitive pressures. Finally, this chapter delineates the research objectives and provides a briefly description of the book's structure.

Keywords Mergers and acquisitions · Banking · Financial technology · FinTech · Innovation

1.1 Mergers and Acquisitions (M&As) in the Banking Industry

The rise of digitalisation and technological advancements has transformed the business environment. In the banking sector, mergers and acquisitions (M&A) have been a significant building block in the evolution

G. B. Ferilli, *Bank-FinTech M&As and Banking Innovation*, Palgrave Macmillan Studies in Banking and Financial Institutions, https://doi.org/10.1007/978-3-031-84445-4_1

of the banking industry, offering credit institutions a strategic opportunity to pursue innovation integration processes, expanding their portfolio activities, and safeguarding their market relevance and competitiveness (Altunbaş & Marqués, 2008; Beccalli & Frantz, 2009; Caiazza et al., 2012).

However, macroeconomic and geopolitical factors and the emergence of new technological paradigms at the global level have impacted the dynamics of M&A activities in the banking sector over the past year. Despite the slowing of cross-border M&As across industries since 2022, the most recent *PWC Mid-Year Outlook 2024* suggests that the banking sector continues to pursue a strategic purpose through such activities, mainly due to the integration processes established with the involvement of FinTech players (PWC, 2024).

In a highly competitive banking environment, where conventional banks face pressure from BigTech and FinTech firms (BIS, 2023; World Bank, 2023), M&As have emerged as a critical strategy for traditional financial institutions to acquire capabilities and enhance their existing value-creation policies. The most recent data indicate that, despite a decline in the overall volume and value of M&A transactions, these activities remain consistent in the banking sector, as they are able to bring a wide range of benefits to the banking industry (Elsas et al., 2010; Caiazza et al., 2012). As a strategy for internalisation, cross-border M&As have been employed by banking institutions to acquire overseas strategic assets, enter foreign markets, and enhance operational efficiency (Luo & Tung, 2007; Wang et al., 2023). The existing literature has highlighted the benefits of acquisition strategies for banks, demonstrating how they can facilitate the rapid internalisation of new capabilities and the expansion of customer reach (Dezi et al., 2018; Hornuf et al., 2021; Shin et al., 2017). Additionally, the potential for banks to enhance their resilience in the face of macroeconomic shocks has been emphasised by Markman and Venzin (2014).

In the current economic context, characterised by elevated interest rates and geopolitical uncertainty (e.g., the Russia-Ukraine conflict), M&A transactions in specific sectors, including technology and finance, continue to demonstrate considerable dynamism (PWC, 2024). Banks that have previously demonstrated high returns on their investments have continued to pursue corporate mergers and acquisitions as a crucial strategy. This approach may assist them in strengthening their positions, optimising operational activities, and achieving higher levels of economies of scale. For example, megadeals have contributed to a notable increase in transactions within the global financial services sector, with a particularly pronounced growth in the US banking industry. Thus, this trend underscores the ongoing relevance of M&As as a strategic option for banks oriented to compete in an increasingly complex financial environment and a global market characterised by high uncertainty.

1.2 The Evolution of Banking Business Models in the Open Innovation Era

The evolution of banking business models (BBMs) in the open innovation era reflects a broader transformation driven by technological breakthroughs, regulatory shifts, and evolving market demands (EBA, 2018).

Historically, banks have assumed central roles within the financial system, fulfilling a range of functions, including the provision of liquidity, risk management, and the optimisation of capital allocation (Ayadi, 2019). This perspective is supported by a consolidated literature field (Aghion & Bolton, 1997; Berndt & Gupta, 2009; Holmström & Tirole, 1997), which highlights the critical role that banks play in addressing information asymmetries, adverse selection, and moral hazard issues. Scholars have also emphasised a shift in the operational approach of the banking industry prior to the global financial crises. This change involved banks expanding beyond their traditional activities (e.g., lending and deposit-taking) towards a more pronounced activity in global financial markets, assuming short- and long-term liabilities and participating in the interbank market. Established incumbent credit institutions began acting as both buyers and sellers of third-party risk through credit derivatives, indicating the advent of a more integrated approach that combined traditional banking roles with market-oriented functions (Boot & Thakor, 2010).

Other factors, such as the emergence of non-bank financial institutions (NBFIs) (such as new digital-based institutions or challenger banks, technology providers or ICT companies) and the progressive advent of the financial technology infrastructure, have supported the spread of *digital disruption* processes in the banking industry. This challenging scenario has pushed banks to rethink how they offer core banking services and adjust their business models and operational strategies. According to EBA (2018), (i) customer expectations and behaviour, (ii) profitability concerns, (iii) competition forces, and (iv) regulatory framework are the broad drivers that have shaped and induced changes in incumbent's business models. Literature has emphasised that financial innovation processes have led incumbent banks firstly to embrace a *one-stop shop* model (Ayadi, 2019) and secondly to evolve from a *universal* banking model (Morrison, 2010) towards a banking *verticalization* model (Ferrari, 2016). FinTech players are able to leverage cutting-edge innovation to provide novel and efficient customer solutions. Besides, other FinTech players try to compete and scale incumbents through re-building processes. In this context, banks are encouraged to adjust their operational frameworks to remain competitive and safeguard their dominant role in the market. In alignment with this viewpoint, literature provides evidence that incumbents have started to collaborate and establish relationships with FinTech firms (Drasch et al., 2018; Hornuf et al., 2021) to enhance customer engagement and operational efficacy, while concurrently mitigating the emerging risks associated with the digitalisation of finance (Elia et al., 2022).

Based on these drivers that have impacted the banking industry, evaluating BBMs' adaptability within the open innovation framework becomes crucial. Literature highlights the role of business model analysis (BMA) as a critical tool for tracking changes within banking institutions, providing data-driven insights and assessing the effect of technological innovation on the banking industry and financial stability (Ayadi et al., 2011; EBA, 2018). By examining the evolution of banks' business models, researchers and practitioners can better understand how banks address external pressures, manage risk, and pursue profitability and operational efficiency. Consequently, assessing business models in the banking sector is crucial for understanding how banks adapt to the accelerated integration of financial technology.

1.3 The Spread of FinTech Firms and Their Strategic Relationship with Banks

The spread of FinTech firms has led to the transformation of the financial industry, giving rise to new market dynamics and triggering strategic adaptations within established banking institutions (EBA, 2018). The term "FinTech", short for *"Financial Technology"*, describes a range of technological developments in the financial services sector. According to the Financial Stability Board, FinTech is a "*technologically enabled innovation in financial services that could result in new business models, applications, processes or products with an associated material effect on financial markets and institutions and the provision of financial services"* (FSB, 2017). Although FinTech is defined as a broader and blurred phenomenon by Friedline (2020), the evolution of FinTech is commonly divided into three stages, each reflecting a substantial change in how financial services are delivered, used, and integrated with technology. The initial phase, *"FinTech 1.0"*, marked the transition from analogue to digital financial systems, characterised by digitalising financial products and processes. This stage established the foundation for subsequent innovations by facilitating electronic transactions and expanding digital access (Murinde et al., 2022). The advent of "*FinTech 2.0*" represented a further advance in digital integration, with finance becoming embedded in daily activities using mobile banking, online payments, and other digital platforms able to provide financial services (Puschmann, 2017). The current era, known as "*FinTech 3.0*", emphasises the concept of *decentralisation*, with blockchain technology and decentralised finance (DeFi) facilitating access to financial services without the involvement of traditional intermediaries (Bok, 2024).

As FinTech firms developed, their relationship with traditional banks shifted from *competition* to *collaboration*. As configurated by the Basel Committee on Banking Supervision (BCBS), in the early stage of development, FinTech star ups posed a competitive threat to traditional banking institutions (i.e., *"disintermediated bank scenario"*) by offering streamlined and low-cost services which directly challenged banks in core areas such as payments, lending, and asset management (Stulz, 2019). Banks subsequently recognised the strategic value of cooperation, perceiving the flexibility, technological expertise, and innovation knowledge that FinTech firms could share in an increasingly dynamic banking system (Drasch et al., 2018). From this perspective, the EBA (2018) identified four distinct approaches that incumbent institutions adopt in their engagement with FinTech firms. These approaches range from investing directly in FinTech players (e.g., merger, acquisition, incubation) to in-house development of technological solutions; in the middle, there are partnering approaches with new entrants and product-based collaboration with other stakeholders (Hornuf et al., 2021).

A growing body of literature emphasises the improvements arising from strategic relationships between banks and FinTech (among others, Li et al., 2023; Wang et al., 2021; Zhao et al., 2022). Specifically, banks cooperating with FinTech could enhance operational efficiency (Lee et al., 2021) profitability (Akhtar & Nosheen, 2022) and optimise customer service. For FinTech firms, establishing a partnership with an established bank can facilitate market entry, enhance credibility, and expand customer reach (Puschmann, 2017). Additionally, Fintech startups may engage in alliance with incumbents to obtain quicker access to a banking licence or leverage the extensive financial resources of banks (Bömer & Maxin, 2018). Thus, literature is gradually shifting towards emphasising how Bank-FinTech relationships can foster innovation and promote stability and resilience within the financial system (Daud et al., 2022; Fung et al., 2020).

1.4 Research Objective

This book investigates one of the key innovation strategies that incumbent banks employ to ensure their resilience and adaptability within an evolving financial environment. The book specifically examines the impact of FinTech-driven advancements on the banking industry, focusing on the strategic interactions between traditional banks and emerging FinTech firms. These relationships are formalised through mergers and acquisitions (M&A), a well-established subject in banking literature (Altunbaş & Marqués, 2008; Hankir et al., 2011; Caiazza et al., 2012; Zheng & Mao, 2024).

According to the book's perspective, the entity undertaking the acquisition is a listed bank, whereas the entity being acquired is a financial technology (or FinTech) firm. Consequently, the book aims to examine the impact of bank equity investments in FinTech firms (i.e., bank-FinTech M&As) on the performance of traditional financial institutions. Bank-FinTech M&As contribute to the ongoing transformation of traditional banking models. This is in line with the current literature, which emphasises the requirement for banks to adapt to financial innovations and engage proactively with new market entrants in order to maintain competitiveness. (Collevecchio et al., 2024).

To comprehensively assess the impact of FinTech M&As on bank performance, a set of ***financial*** and ***non-financial*** metrics are considered. Financial metrics are employed to assess the profitability, efficiency, and stability of banks, whereas non-financial metrics are used to evaluate the probability of default and ESG (Environmental, Social, and Governance) scores. The empirical analysis is applied to a global sample of listed banks that have engaged in domestic and cross-border FinTech M&As over an extended period from 1997 to 2022.

As an element of novelty, the study enriches the knowledge in the reference field of literature considering the heterogeneity of banks and FinTech firms (in terms of the business model adopted) to assess different impacts on bank performance.

In order to achieve the book's aim, a bottom-up approach is employed to explore the following research questions (R.Q.s):

RQ1 Do FinTech M&As affect bank performance?
RQ2 Do time factors affect the impact of FinTech M&As on bank performance?
RQ3 Do banks' business model affect the impact of Fintech M&As on bank performance?
RQ4 Do FinTech and Bank business model affect the impact of Fintech M&As on bank performance?

1.5 Structure and Chapters

This section briefly illustrates the book's structure and offers information about the main contents discussed in each chapter.

Chapter 2 provides a theoretical analysis of the impact of the bank and FinTech relationship, with a review of the existing literature. Specifically, it examines the key motivations, trends, and challenges that may affect banks' performance post FinTech M&As. Furthermore, the chapter analyses the rationale behind banks' investments in financial technology, emphasising the strategic advantages gained by incumbents (e.g., access to innovation, customer base expansion, and competitive positioning). Cultural integration is also a crucial element of FinTech-Bank M&As, emphasising the need to align business styles, regulatory practices, and core values. In this regard, the chapter emphasises that effective and sustained integration efforts are essential for optimising the strategic benefits of FinTech-Bank M&As within an increasingly digital-first financial environment.

Chapter 3 examines the development and the impact of FinTech on the financial industry, focusing on the key drivers and regulatory challenges associated with this *disruptive* phenomenon. Specifically, the chapter outlines three distinct phases of FinTech's evolution: *FinTech*

1.0, the initial digitalisation of financial services; *FinTech 2.0*, the emergence of embedded finance; and *FinTech 3.0*, the rise of decentralised finance. These brief examinations are able to illustrate the effects of technological innovation on financial services. Moreover, the chapter examines the different definitions and taxonomies of FinTech proposed by regulatory bodies and supervisory banking authorities, thereby underscoring the inherent complexity of the sector. Furthermore, it draws attention to the discrepancies in regulatory approaches across different jurisdictions, underscoring the necessity to delineate regulatory frameworks that facilitate innovation while guaranteeing financial stability and consumer protection. Overall, the chapter establishes a foundation for understanding the global challenges and opportunities of FinTech, providing theoretical support for Chapter 5 of this book.

Chapter 4 provides a comprehensive analysis of Banking Business Models (BBMs) and theoretically examines their evolution in response to current technological, regulatory, and market dynamics. It begins by exploring the transformation of banks from traditional financial intermediaries to more complex structures, the growing influence of non-bank financial institutions, and the development of the universal banking model. The chapter then defines and categorises BBMs (i.e., *Retail*, *Investment*, and *Diversified Assets* model), applying a cluster analysis on a sample of worldwide listed banks. The chapter concludes with an overview of the impact of digital transformation on the banking business model. This includes a discussion of the competitive pressures and consumer-driven challenges that FinTech represents, as well as the opportunities and threats that banks face as a result of these innovation processes.

Chapter 5 presents the empirical analysis conducted to examine the impact of FinTech M&As on the performance of acquiring banks. The analysis considers the heterogeneity of banks and FinTech firms involved in the investment operation, in terms of their respective business models. The analysis assesses a range of performance metrics, including *financial* (i.e., profitability, efficiency, risk) and *non-financial* (i.e., probability of default and ESG scores) indicators. The chapter outlines the research design and the methodology applied, thereby ensuring a robust and rigorous approach. The process of selecting the sample and collecting the data is described in detail, ensuring transparency regarding the data sources and guaranteeing the reliability and representativeness of the study's empirical findings.

The chapter employs a bottom-up approach to address four research questions (RQs) that have been outlined. *RQ1*, serves as a baseline analysis, examining the impact of FinTech M&As on a series of performance indicators to identify possible areas of enhancement among incumbents engaged in equity investments. The *RQ2* assesses the impact of lag effects on incumbents' performance indicators, identifying the delayed effect of FinTech M&As on market-based financial and non-financial metrics of the sampled banks. The *RQ3* and *RQ4* originally assessed the impact on performance metrics by considering the heterogeneity of the banks and FinTech firms involved in M&As. Specifically, *RQ3* discriminates the impact according to the business model of the acquiring banks, previously identified through a cluster analysis (Chapter 4). In contrast, *RQ4* jointly considers the business models of banks and FinTech firms to assess their combined impact on incumbents' performance, providing a detailed framework for identifying potential areas of performance enhancement following M&As with FinTech firms. A series of robustness checks have been conducted to validate the empirical results. The analysis has a global perspective; thus, as a final step, a cross-jurisdictional comparison has been performed to take into account any possible divergences impact on banks' performance arising from regulatory frameworks adopted by countries.

Chapter 6 concludes the book, summarising the study's aim and main findings. The chapter also highlights the study's contributions and elements of novelty, outlining theoretical and managerial implications for bank industry, policymakers, and stakeholders.

References

Aghion, P., & Bolton, P. (1997). A theory of trickle-down growth and development. *Review of Economic Studies, 64*(2), 151–172.

Akhtar, Q., & Nosheen, S. (2022). The impact of fintech and banks M&A on Acquirer's performance: A strategic win or loss? *Borsa Istanbul Review, 22*(6), 1195–1208.

Altunbaş, Y., & Marqués, D. (2008). Mergers and acquisitions and bank performance in Europe: The role of strategic similarities. *Journal of Economics and Business, 60*(3), 204–222.

Ayadi, R. (2019). *Banking business models. Definition, analytical framework and financial stability assessment.* Springer.

Ayadi, R., Arbak, E., & Pieter De Groen, W. (2011). *Business models in European banking: A pre-and post-crisis screening.* Center for European Policy Studies.

Bank for International Settlements (BIS) (2023, October). *Big tech in finance* (BIS Working Papers, No. WP1129).

Beccalli, E., & Frantz, P. (2009). M&A operations and performance in banking. *Journal of Financial Services Research, 36*, 203–226.

Berndt, A., & Gupta, A. (2009). Moral hazard and adverse selection in the originate-to-distribute model of bank credit. *Journal of Monetary Economics, 56*(5), 725–743.

Bok, K. (2024). *Decentralizing finance: How DeFi, digital assets, and distributed ledger technology are transforming finance*. John Wiley & Sons.

Bömer, M., & Maxin, H. (2018). Why fintechs cooperate with banks—Evidence from Germany. *Zeitschrift Für Die Gesamte Versicherungswissenschaft, 107*, 359–386.

Boot, A., & Thakor, A. V. (2010). The accelerating integration of banks and markets and its implications for regulation. In *The Oxford handbook of banking* (pp. 58–90).

Caiazza, S., Clare, A., & Pozzolo, A. F. (2012). What do bank acquirers want? Evidence from worldwide bank M&A targets. *Journal of Banking & Finance, 36*(9), 2641–2659.

Collevecchio, F., Cappa, F., Peruffo, E., & Oriani, R. (2024). When do M&As with fintech firms benefit traditional banks? *British Journal of Management, 35*(1), 192–209.

Daud, S. N. M., Khalid, A., & Azman-Saini, W. N. W. (2022). FinTech and financial stability: Threat or opportunity? *Finance Research Letters, 47*, 102667.

Dezi, L., Battisti, E., Ferraris, A., & Papa, A. (2018). The link between mergers and acquisitions and innovation: A systematic literature review. *Management Research Review, 41*(6), 716–752.

Drasch, B. J., Schweizer, A., & Urbach, N. (2018). Integrating the 'Trouble-makers': A taxonomy for cooperation between banks and fintechs. *Journal of Economics and Business, 100*, 26–42.

Elia, G., Stefanelli, V., & Ferilli, G. B. (2022). Investigating the role of Fintech in the banking industry: What do we know? *European Journal of Innovation Management, 26*(5), 1365–1393.

Elsas, R., Hackethal, A., & Holzhauser, M. (2010). The anatomy of bank diversification. *Journal of Banking and Finance, 34*(6), 1274–1287.

European Banking Authority (EBA) (2018, July 3). EBA report on the impact of Fintech on incumbent credit institutions' business models.

Ferrari, R. (2016). FinTech impact on retail banking–from a universal banking model to banking verticalisation. *The FinTech book: The financial technology handbook for investors, entrepreneurs and visionaries* (pp. 248–252).

Financial Stability Board (FSB). (2017). Financial stability implications from FinTech. Supervisory and regulatory issues that merit authorities' attention.

Friedline, T. (2020). *Banking on a revolution: Why financial technology won't save a broken system*. Oxford University Press.
Fung, D. W., Lee, W. Y., Yeh, J. J., & Yuen, F. L. (2020). Friend or foe: The divergent effects of FinTech on financial stability. *Emerging Markets Review, 45*, 100727.
Hankir, Y., Rauch, C., & Umber, M. P. (2011). Bank M&A: A market power story? *Journal of Banking & Finance, 35*(9), 2341–2354.
Holmström, B., & Tirole, J. (1997). Financial intermediation, loanable funds and the real sector. *Quarterly Journal of Economics, 112*(3), 663–691.
Hornuf, L., Klus, M. F., Lohwasser, T. S., & Schwienbacher, A. (2021). How do banks interact with fintech startups? *Small Business Economics, 57*, 1505–1526.
Lee, C. C., Li, X., Yu, C. H., & Zhao, J. (2021). Does fintech innovation improve bank efficiency? Evidence from China's banking industry. *International Review of Economics & Finance, 74*, 468–483.
Li, E., Mao, M. Q., Zhang, H. F., & Zheng, H. (2023). Banks' investments in fintech ventures. *Journal of Banking & Finance, 149*, 106754.
Luo, Y., & Tung, R. L. (2007). International expansion of emerging market enterprises: A springboard perspective. *Journal of International Business Studies, 38*, 481–498.
Markman, G. M., & Venzin, M. (2014). Resilience: Lessons from banks that have braved the economic crisis—And from those that have not. *International Business Review, 23*(6), 1096–1107.
Morrison, A. D. (2010). Universal banking. In *The Oxford handbook of banking* (p. 2).
Murinde, V., Rizopoulos, E., & Zachariadis, M. (2022). The impact of the FinTech revolution on the future of banking: Opportunities and risks. *International Review of Financial Analysis, 81*, 102103.
Puschmann, T. (2017). FinTech. *Business & Information Systems Engineering, 59*, 69–76.
PWC (2024). *2024 Mid-year outlook*. Global M&A Trends in Financial Services.
Shin, S. R., Han, J., Marhold, K., & Kang, J. (2017). Reconfiguring the firm's core technological portfolio through open innovation: Focusing on technological M&A. *Journal of Knowledge Management, 21*(3), 571–591.
Stulz, R. M. (2019). Fintech, bigtech, and the future of banks. *Journal of Applied Corporate Finance, 31*(4), 86–97.
Wang, Y., Hu, J., & Chen, J. (2023). Does Fintech facilitate cross-border M&As? Evidence from Chinese A-share listed firms. *International Review of Financial Analysis, 85*, 102435.
Wang, Y., Xiuping, S., & Zhang, Q. (2021). Can fintech improve the efficiency of commercial banks? An analysis based on big data. *Research in International Business and Finance, 55*, 101338.

World Bank. (2023). Fintech and the future of finance: Market and policy implications (by Feyen, E.H.B.; Natarajan, H., and Saal, M.). World Bank Group. http://documents.worldbank.org/curated/en/099450005162250110/P17300600228b70070914b0b5edf26e2f9f.

Zhao, J., Li, X., Yu, C. H., Chen, S., & Lee, C. C. (2022). Riding the FinTech innovation wave: FinTech, patents and bank performance. *Journal of International Money and Finance, 122*, 102552.

Zheng, H., & Mao, M. Q. (2024). Fintech mergers and acquisitions. *Journal of International Money and Finance, 143*, 103076.

CHAPTER 2

Banks' Performance and FinTech M&As: A Theoretical Perspective

Abstract This chapter, adopting theoretical approach, reviews the existing literature of FinTech-Bank M&As, assessing their impact on bank performance and highlighting the integration challenges linked to these operations. This chapter briefly examines global M&A trends in the banking sector, exploring the rationale behind banks' investments in FinTech firms. Additionally, this chapter addresses cultural integration challenges, emphasising the need for sustained efforts to align different organisational structures, technological assets, and regulatory frameworks that characterised incumbent and newcomer operators.

Keywords FinTech M&As · Bank Performance · Cultural Integration · Banking Business Models · Regulatory Challenges

2.1 M&As Trends in Banking

Pursuing mergers and acquisitions (M&A) remains a significant priority for financial services firms, given the extensive range of benefits identified as potential outcomes of these strategic operations (PWC, 2024). According to PWC's Mid-Year Outlook 2024 *"Global M&A Industry Trends"*, in the first half of 2024, the value of overall M&A deals fell

G. B. Ferilli, *Bank-FinTech M&As and Banking Innovation*, Palgrave Macmillan Studies in Banking and Financial Institutions,
https://doi.org/10.1007/978-3-031-84445-4_2

by 25%, continuing the downward trend started in 2022 (deals volume over 23,000, and deal values reached $1.3tn) (Fig. 2.1). Several factors have contributed to the decrease in M&A activity, such as (i) elevated interest rates that have constrained returns, making potential deals more reliant on value creation; (ii) high valuations which create significant gaps between buyer and sellers; and (iii) political uncertainty and geopolitical tensions (e.g., Ukraine's conflict, the Middle East and strained US-China relations), which have characterised the global scene (PWC, 2024).

However, despite the decreasing trend observed in M&A operations, some sectors, such as technology and financial services, exhibited a growth of their transaction volumes partially due to some "*megadeal*" activity performed by sector players. In this context, the latest data indicates that banks with solid returns pursue M&As to enhance their positions and gain scale, thereby boosting efficiencies. Coherently, McKinsey & Company's latest report indicated that following the spike in large deals and bank failures in 2023, interest in M&As in the financial services sector has returned to grow (McKinsey & Company, 2024).

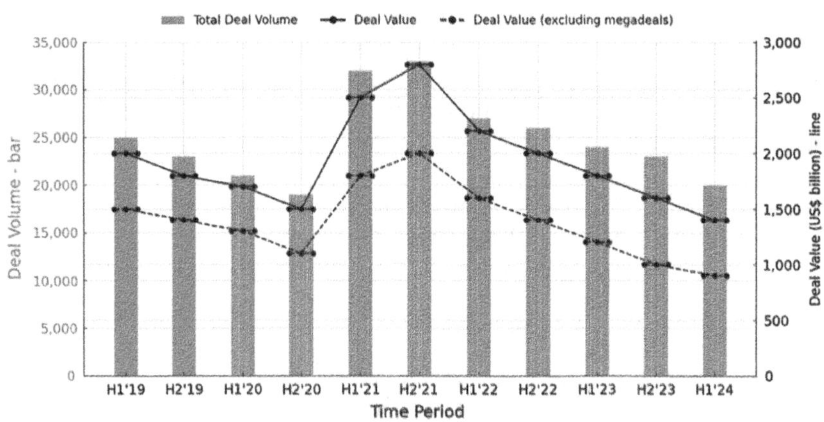

Fig. 2.1 Global banking deal volumes and values over time (*Note* The figure illustrates the global trends in total deal volume (represented by bars) and deal value (represented by lines) in the global banking sector from the first half of 2019 to the first half of 2024. Specifically, the figure differentiates the total deal volume, the total deal value excluding megadeals, and the total deal value, highlighting transaction fluctuations over a long time of observation. *Source* Author's elaboration based on data from PWC)

However, the M&A activity exhibits specific dynamics according to the geographic area of interest. For instance, in the European context, large-scale transactions remain limited, particularly in the case of cross-border deals. This trend can be attributed to the overall complexities associated with local licensing regulations, liquidity issues, accounting implications, and fair value adjustments. Consequently, all these factors push the European banks to pursue organic expansion over inorganic growth. However, forecasts indicate that a large volume of M&A activity will be focused on domestic targets in the E.U. context. From a global perspective, the considerable benefits arising from the evolving dynamics of the banking business model (such as technological innovation and the spread of FinTech) may enhance the value of a bank's cross-border transactions. Against this backdrop, leading banks are moving to address many challenges linked to these operations to benefit from diversification, immediate access to local talent, and the realisation of value more expediently.

Looking at the FinTech sector, according to *Norton Rose Fulbright's* latest report, 2023 was a challenging year for global FinTech M&As and investment activity, which have exhibited the lowest levels of M&A since 2017 due to a period characterised by higher interest rates, inflation, decelerating economic growth and geopolitical tensions. Although investment activity has slowed down notably in recent years, according to *Statista's outlook*, the growing number of financial technology players and the expanding user base portend that FinTech M&A and investment activity are expected to pick up in 2024 on the back of improving macroeconomic conditions worldwide. Reopening the IPO market and adjusting to a more subdued valuation environment will be key drivers of this anticipated rebound. As Norton Rose Fulbright (2024) reported, the early months of 2023 witnessed a notable decline in both the value and volume of deals, compounded by the unexpected collapse of several US banks. The total value of deals fell from $63.2 billion across 2885 deals in the second half of 2022 to $52.4 billion across 2153 deals in the first half of 2023. Furthermore, annual equity funding decreased to $39.2 billion, representing its lowest level since 2017 and indicating a notable shift towards early-stage funding rounds.

On the other hand, the combined value of M&A and investment transactions in the Americas increased from $28. 9 billion in the second half of 2022 to $36. One billion during the first half of 2023. This trend was observed in the year's first and second halves. Notably, the United States emerged as the leading contributor to global fintech investment deals, accounting for 41% of the total in the second half of 2023. FinTech firms also rose to unicorn status in the Asia–Pacific region, particularly in the payments sub-sector of the industry, which proved relatively resilient in the year.

The FinTech sector of the Americas remained active, with the highest transaction value witnessed in the United States. This is well illustrated by the payments sub-sector, where Thomas Bravo acquired Coupa in an $8 billion deal, including the $5 billion acquisition of a controlling stake in the Worldpay group, among others. Furthermore, the Insurtech sector experienced a relatively high level of merger and acquisition, the most famous of which was Vista Equity Partners' $2.5 billion deal on Duck Creek Technologies.

The adverse macroeconomic environment affected the EMEA region, and challenges were present, as shown below. However, it completed several significant deals, mainly in the United Kingdom, representing the most significant proportion of the global M&A and FinTech activities. Data shows that Europe outperformed the United States regarding M&A activity during the fourth quarter of 2023. Some transactions that defined the market include where Deutsche Börse acquired Simcorp for €3.9 billion, among others. Nevertheless, while the M&A and investment deals are at near-independent decade lows, APAC has had some noteworthy deals in the banking and lending tech subsegment. Furthermore, regulatory changes in Singapore have focused attention on the practical aspects of the crypto sub-sector, with a significant investment of $300 million in the Series C round of Amber Group.

Hence, investment and M&A activities will increase in 2024 to help the FinTech industry. The use of modern technology and increased demand for internet and mobile banking solutions is expected to propel the FinTech sector forward. However, it should be noted that higher numbers can still be observed in segments where banks have continued to actively search for acquisitions to increase competitiveness by broadening the range of their products. There can be an escalation in the number of seed funding rounds, regardless of the existing constraints true of capital-raising processes. Increased and stable macroeconomic conditions, growing investors' confidence, and a more appropriate valuation environment will generally enhance the fintech M&A activity (Norton Rose Fulbright, 2024).

In light of the shifts mentioned above and the emergence of geopolitical issues during the period under review, it is projected that FinTech-Bank M&A activity will recover by 2024 following the prevailing market trends.

The industry's strengths include increasing the proportion of high-value payment transactions and attracting greater investments in the Americas and the Asia–Pacific region. Optimistic changes in the economic climate and normalised shareholders' values will provide a new impetus for the fintech industry's merger and acquisition activities. This growth will be achieved through investment in technology and acquisitions as part of efforts to improve competitiveness and diversify product portfolios.

2.2 Why Do Banks Invest in FinTech Firms?

Over the last decade, traditional banks have begun to adopt an outward-looking approach to innovate their business models and satisfy customers' new and sophisticated financial needs (Ayadi et al., 2021). The banking industry has also faced increasing pressure to become more digitalised to compete more effectively with external (i.e., *non-banks*) and internal (i.e., *neo-banks*) market players better equipped to leverage technology innovations. In this context, FinTech firms have impacted three product segments directly related to core banking functions (payments, clearing and settlements, credit, deposit and capital-raising services; and investment management services), as well as general market support services (i.e., artificial intelligence, machine learning, blockchain). Consequently, FinTech firms have played a critical role due to their capabilities to offer cheaper and more tailored bank-like products to retail and corporate customers (Stulz, 2019; p. 86). Therefore, FinTech firms have established an image representing *innovation* and *exploration*, whereas incumbent banks represent *continuity* and *seniority* (Bussmann, 2017).

Due to the challenges that have characterised the banking industry, academics, regulators, and practitioners have paid growing attention to the relationship between FinTech and the traditional banking industry, also investigating the multiple approaches in which banks can engage financial technology firms (Hornuf et al., 2021). Among various options related to the "build-partner-acquire" approach (i.e., alliances, in-house development, joint ventures, product-related collaborations), each of these characterised by benefits and drawbacks (see Table 2.1), incumbents can interact with FinTech firms performing an M&A operation.

In this regard, a more recent body of banking literature has examined the main driving forces behind banks' likelihood of acquiring FinTech firms (Cappa et al., 2022; Collevecchio et al., 2024; Kwon et al., 2024; Li et al., 2023; Wang et al., 2023), identifying a range of advantages for both the acquiring banks and the FinTech acquired. In this field, Hornuf et al. (2021) found that banks are more likely to invest in relatively small FinTech (as they need a startup phase to become attractive for financial investments) while engaging in product-related collaboration with large FinTech (as they are established in the market and provide a mature portfolio). Indeed, according to Luo & Tung (2007), cross-border M&As are undertaken to acquire overseas strategic assets and enter a foreign market.

However, considering the new paradigm of open innovation (O.I.) in which FinTech firms operate, the acquisition strategy presents some key

Table 2.1 Comparison of strategic approaches: Build, partner, and acquire

Option	*Advantages*	*Disadvantages*
BUILD	Complete autonomy and control over the process	High financial obligation
	Tailored and bespoke solutions designed specifically for the organisation's needs	Time consuming solution
	Confidentiality protection	High risks associated with integration and execution processes
PARTNER	Access to the expertise, knowledge, and resources of the partner	Reduced organisational control over the project's direction
	Quicker implementation of technologies due to shared responsibilities	Risk of confidential information exposure
		Potential risks in the partnership's successful execution and long-term alignment
ACQUIRE	Full control post-acquisition, ensuring direct management over the acquired capabilities	High costs related to the acquisition process and subsequent integration
	Immediate access to new capabilities, resources, and talent	Significant challenges associated with integrating the acquired company's processes and operations
	Accelerated option compared to building internal solutions	Risks to confidentiality during and after the acquisition process

Note The table compares three strategic options for business expansion: building, partnering, and acquiring. Each option is evaluated based on its advantages and disadvantages. *Source* Author's elaboration advantages: exclusively rapid access to new clients/markets, cross-selling opportunities, strategic value, and synergy achievement by combining their respective strategic assets. These potentially advantageous factors could make the acquisition a preferred strategy rather than internal development when the target resources (e.g., advanced technological assets) are distant from the acquirer's expertise (Lee & Lieberman, 2010). According to Kwon et al. (2024), an acquisition strategy can shorten (costly) in-house development of new solutions and consequently increase the bank's *"digital footprint"*. M&As are also a way to achieve the outside-in typology of open innovation, as they favour knowledge inflows from outside organisational boundaries (Bogers et al., 2017). In this field, some scholars have identified several positive effects of M&As in the banking sector due to knowledge synergies[1] that allow increased operational efficiency, dimensional growth, and improved possibility of creating customer value (Caiazza et al., 2012). In line with this perspective, Oliver Wyman's (2024) latest report (2024) emphasises how banks should primarily identify their most important M&A priorities before undertaking a scan for potential FinTech targets.

Consequently, incumbents should evaluate the potential synergies achieved through a deal instead of partnering or building in-house solutions. For instance, the study of Elsas et al. (2010) shows that M&A operations increase the efficiency of financial intermediaries through organisational restructuring, which can improve revenue flow and minimise costs. Instead, Templeton & Severiens (1992) show that M&As may diversify a bank's activities, reducing the specific risk of the assets owned to just that of holding systematic risk. Incumbent banks involved in Fintech M&As may also benefit from risk diversification (Berger et al., 1999) or an increase in their market share (Hankir et al., 2011) and profits (Turk Ariss, 2010). Some studies (Dezi et al., 2018; Shin et al., 2017) have also identified M&As as a strategy for banks to narrow the *"digital gap"* and avoid perishing through the absorption of technological knowledge, expertise, capabilities, and tacit awareness by the target firms (e.g., FinTech firms). Substantially, according to Stulz (2019) and Vives (2019), traditional banks may strategically take equity stakes in FinTech

[1] Synergy is the incremental value generated by the combination of two companies because it creates opportunities that would not be achievable if the two companies operate independently (Cappa et al., 2022).

operators as a future-proofing strategy in reaction to the competition in the financial industry.

Literature has also highlighted the effects of a partial than a full acquisition of a FinTech firm. Partial acquisitions allow for gradual integration into new technology-based services, minimising risk and complexity while providing greater management autonomy. This approach enables smoother absorption of strategic resources and gradual alignment with FinTech's business model, positively impacting post-acquisition performance and future profits (Folta, 1998; Pinelli et al., 2022; Wang & Larimo, 2020). In contrast, full acquisitions involve higher risks due to substantial investments and technological uncertainties, often leading to misalignment between the bank's traditional business model and FinTech's modern approach, which can hinder value creation (Le Floc'h & Scaringella, 2017). Scholars have also identified the differential effect of FinTech M&As on banks according to the area of operations of financial technology firms (i.e., payments, fundraising, asset management, and others). For example, acquiring a FinTech specialised in payment services may lead to overlaps with existing bank services, resulting in resource redundancy and increased complexity. Specifically, integrating a FinTech's dynamic, digital mindset with a traditional bank's approach can create cultural conflicts, hindering the bank's ability to fully transition to a digital model (Alt et al., 2018; Bauer & Matzler, 2014). These challenges prevent banks from effectively leveraging new technologies and creating value.

2.3 FinTech Opportunities Dealing with Bank M&As

The extant literature on mergers and acquisitions (M&As) between banks and FinTech firms has mainly focused on assessing the benefits for incumbent banks arising from such types of strategic operations (among others, Cappa et al., 2022; Kwon et al., 2024; Li et al., 2023; Zhao et al., 2022; Zheng & Mao, 2024). Limited studies have also emphasised the FinTech perspective, outlining the main motivations that make interactions with banks (e.g., alliances, business collaborations, incubators, outsourcing, co-shareholder, or equity investments—Klus et al., 2019) appealing and favourable to FinTech entities. In this strand, scholars such as Puschmann (2017) and Hornuf et al. (2021) have highlighted how FinTech creating an alliance with an established player in the financial industry, such as a traditional bank, can obtain access to a broader customer base, gain access to knowledge in how to deal with financial regulation and overcome regulatory boundaries. However, they can also improve their digital services and products, renewing their business model.

According to Klus et al. (2019), FinTech startups may engage in alliances with incumbents to obtain quicker access to a banking licence. According to Bömer & Maxin (2018), bank-FinTech partnerships enable new financial operators to leverage the extensive financial resources of banks, which are crucial for scaling operations and developing novel products that may require considerable financial and technical capabilities. In addition to financial support, traditional banks provide valuable support in enabling FinTech firms to "survive" in a complex regulatory environment that can pose significant barriers to the sector's growth. Furthermore, FinTech firms that have formed alliances with banks may benefit from increased credibility and acceptance, enhancing their market reputation and fostering trust and confidence among potential customers and investors.

Collaborations with banks facilitate the transfer of knowledge and mutual learning, enabling FinTech firms to benefit from banks' operational experience and regulatory knowledge. Consequently, scholars have emphasised how this relationship fosters an environment of continuous improvement and innovation, where both partners can adapt to evolving market demands and technological trends (Hildebrandt, 2015). Moreover, these strategic partnerships also lead to enhanced operational efficiency and reduced expenditure for financial technology firms, as banks' back-office processing capabilities and established infrastructures streamline operations and reduce the need for substantial capital investments in these areas.

Additionally, FinTech firms may derive strategic advantages from the stability and continuity associated with traditional banking institutions. By establishing collaborative relationships with banking institutions, financial technology enterprises can effectively mitigate the uncertainties and risks of the financial technology sector. This stability provides a robust basis for FinTech firms to innovate and explore new business models, free from the persistent pressure of market volatility (Nambisan et al., 2017). Based on the current literature, scholars in this field have provided clear evidence that an M&A operation between FinTech firms and traditional banks can create a mutually beneficial framework. Performing M&A operations, FinTech firms gain access to financial resources, regulatory support, enhanced credibility, operational efficiency, and strategic stability. These factors contribute to the growth, innovation, and market success of FinTech firms.

2.4 The Effects of FinTech M&As on Bank Performance Indicators

Prior research has identified several positive effects of FinTech M&As within the banking sector. These outcomes are attributed to the bank-FinTech synergies that allow increased operational efficiency, growth, and value for banking customers (Caiazza et al., 2012). In light of the growing consolidation of the FinTech sector and the concomitant increase in data availability, recent studies have begun to investigate the impact of M&A operations on acquirers' performance. In this regard, scholars have assessed the impact of FinTech investments or alliances with incumbents on several banks' performance metrics, focusing primarily on several proxies for efficiency, profitability, and riskiness (among others, Austin & Dunham, 2022; Collevecchio et al., 2024; Dranev et al., 2019; Li et al., 2023; Wang et al., 2021; Zheng & Mao, 2024).

For instance, in examining the impact on efficiency bank's profile, Lee et al. (2021) have demonstrated how FinTech innovations improve the cost efficiency of Chinese banks. Similarly, Zhao et al. (2022) have revealed how financial technology firms are able to improve capital adequacy and management efficiency. From a more comprehensive standpoint, Wang et al. (2021) have discovered that the advancement of FinTech results in a reduction of bank operational costs, improvements in service efficiency, and an enhancement of risk control capabilities. Instead, the study of Borello et al. (2022), which is focused on the Euro area, has demonstrated that only medium-efficiency banking groups that adopt a more diversified investment acquisition strategy exhibit a positive relationship with FinTech investment aptitude. Otherwise, the relationship between bank efficiency and financial technology investment indicators appears negative.

Other scholars have analysed the impact of FinTech investments on different bank's profitability metrics. In this sub-field, Dranev et al. (2019) have identified significant positive abnormal returns following FinTech firms' acquisitions in the short term and negative abnormal returns in the long term. Akhtar & Nosheen (2022) have documented a positive impact of FinTech M&As on bank operating performance (ROA and net profit margin), liquidity (current ratio), and leverage (total debt on shareholders' equity). However, they also reported a negative impact on banks' long-run market performance (average share price). Using similar metrics, Cappa et al. (2022) have examined the impact of FinTech M&As on stock market performance, finding that investors tend to react negatively to the FinTech M&As when the acquirer bank engages in a full acquisition or when the FinTech acquired operates in the payment sector. Li et al. (2023), exploring the long-run impact of FinTech entrants on the banking industry, have found that banks which invest in a larger proportion of financial technology startups are able to achieve a higher IPO exit rate. Specifically, the authors highlight how banks' outperformance is mainly concentrated in *fin-native* firms and those whose business operations overlap with banks' core business segments.

Looking at alternative metrics, Collevecchio et al. (2024) have analysed the impact on expected performance (cumulative abnormal returns—CARs), finding that three factors can optimise the expected performance of the bank in question:(i) the sustainability profile of the acquirer, (ii) the minority acquisitions, and (iii) the institutional distance between the FinTech and the bank's country of incorporation. Similarly, the recent study by Zheng & Mao (2024) has examined the value of FinTech M&As, measuring their impact through CARs. The empirical findings suggest that M&As improve acquirers' subsequent operating performance and business diversification strategies.

Other scholars have evaluated the impact of FinTech innovation on the more usual banks' balance sheet metrics, highlighting mixed findings (Haddad & Hornuf, 2023; Katsiampa et al., 2022; Zhao et al., 2022). In this field, Katsiampa et al. (2022) analysed traditional Chinese established banks' *financial* and *prudential* performance. They found that they experienced increased risk-operating costs, a decline in profit margins and a softening of loan quality. Zhao et al. (2022) empirically demonstrated how FinTech development improves capital adequacy and management efficiency but lessens banks' asset quality and earning power. The study also revealed how such impacts became more significant after 2011 when the FinTech industry overgrew. The authors also found non-linear effects on the relationship between FinTech rise and bank performance. Large banks benefit more from FinTech under the profitability (ROA) and risk control (profiles while leverage and liquidity risk (liquid assets to total deposits ratio) are also lower in these banks' categories. Credit risk (non-performing loans-NPL) increases in large and small banks.

Investigated the same relationship but on a large sample of banks from 87 countries, the study by Haddad & Hornuf (2023) used a set of consolidated measures to assess the impact on financial institutions' performance. The study's findings provide a positive and robust effect of FinTech firms' development on banks' ROA, ROE, and annual stock return. Li et al. (2023), with similar results, found that FinTech significantly contributes to improving business performance by enhancing information transparency, alleviating financing constraints, and improving the efficiency of corporate investment environments. Conversely, Phan et al. (2020) show that the growth of FinTech firms negatively influences bank performance. Specifically, it reduces net interest income to total assets (NIM), return on equity (ROE), return on assets (ROA), and yield on earning assets (YEA). The IMF (2023) has also reported a negative impact on bank performance. The study's findings point to a negative impact on profitability metrics (ROA and ROE), primarily due to a reduction in interest income and operational costs. This evidence suggests that, although established banks have tried to diversify their revenue streams, the efforts have proven inadequate to offset losses associated with increased market competition from financial technology firms. The IMF study also revealed how FinTech specialising in *peer-to-peer lending* and *balance sheet lending* produced a profit deterioration in the sub-category of cooperative banks. In contrast, commercial banks seem to benefit from this type of FinTech partnership.

On the riskiness side, the study of Haddad & Hornuf (2023), mentioned above, has also assessed the impact on banks' risk-taking (measured by Z-score, stock return volatility, and marginal expected shortfall) and found that the relationship with FinTech firms decreases the stock return volatility of incumbents and decreases the banks' systemic risk exposure. These findings are corroborated by the study of Austin & Dunham (2022), which examined the long-term impact of FinTech acquisition, revealing that the risk profiles of acquirers (i.e., traditional banks) significantly improve in the post-acquisition period. In the same stream, He et al. (2023) have examined the impact of FinTech on banks' risk management practices. Their findings indicate that the adoption of FinTech by incumbent banks has led to a notable reduction in risk-taking behaviour, attributed mainly to enhancing internal control systems by integrating FinTech assets and capabilities. However, the study also highlights that this effect has been particularly pronounced among state-owned banks, smaller institutions, and those with a significant proportion of non-interest income. Conversely, Chen & Shen (2024) found that FinTech increases both banks' exposure and their contribution to systemic risk, highlighting how these effects only occur in local commercial banks, less profitable banks, and banks in regions with less developed FinTech industries.

The review of the current studies, summarised in Table 2.2, reveals a mixed and often inconclusive impact of FinTech M&As on bank performance indicators. In this literature body, some authors indicate substantial benefits in efficiency, profitability, and risk management, while other scholars highlight challenges and crucial trade-offs in the bank-FinTech relationship. This discrepancy in outcomes indicates that the efficacy of FinTech M&As is contingent upon a multitude of contextual factors. These include the distinctive attributes of the financial institutions and FinTech entities involved, the nature of their integration, and the regulatory and market context in which they operate.

2.5 Cultural Integration Challenges for Banks Post FinTech M&As

The cultural integration challenges that banks face in the process of FinTech M&As are complex and many-sided, posing considerable risks to the success or failure of M&A operations. One of the primary challenges highlighted by the literature is the alignment of traditional banking and innovative FinTech organisational cultures (Panibratov, 2017; Reghezza et al., 2024; Stahl & Voigt, 2008; Teerikangas & Very, 2006).

Several scholars (Marks & Mirvis, 2011; Shahzad et al., 2012) have defined *"organizational culture"* as the divergent values and beliefs, histories, products, operating styles, and business philosophies among the entities and members involved in M&As. Among various theories and models developed over time to explain the crucial role of culture in M&As and how cultural differences may affect the integration process, Stahl & Voigt (2008) have identified three main elements able to affect the integration processes, which are (i) *cultural fit*, (ii) *acculturation*, (iii) and *social constructivist*. Specifically, in the context of banking innovation, traditional banks typically operate with established, hierarchical structures characterised by a risk-averse approach and a strong emphasis on regulatory compliance. Conversely, FinTech firms, defined as *"newcomers"* in the banking environment (Alaassar et al., 2022 and 2023), are generally more agile, entrepreneurial, and focused on more rapid innovation and growth.

Table 2.2 Summary of main proxies used by scholars to assess the impact of FinTech on banks' performance

Author(s)	*Efficiency metrics*	*Profitability metrics*	*Risk metrics*
Phan et al. (2018)		Reduces NIM, ROE, ROA, YEA	
Dranev et al. (2019)		Increases short-term abnormal returns; decreases of long-term abnormal returns	
Akhtar & Nosheen (2022)		Improves ROA, Net profit, Liquidity, and Leverage; reduces long-run market performance	
Cappa et al. (2022)			Negatively impacts stock market performance
Zhao et al. (2022)	Improves capital adequacy and management efficiency		Enhances risk control
Katsiampa et al. (2022)	Increases operating costs	Reduces profit margin	Raises risks
Wang et al. (2021)	Reduces operational costs Improves service efficiency		Enhances risk management
Lee et al. (2021)	Improves cost efficiency		
Borello et al. (2022)	Reduces efficiency		
Austin & Dunham (2022)			Improvement of risk profile
Li et al. (2023)		Increases IPO exit rate	
Collevecchio et al. (2024)		Optimises performance	
He et al. (2023)			Reduces risk-taking behaviour
Chen & Shen (2024)			Increases bank's risk exposure and systemic risk
Haddad & Hornuf (2023)		Increases ROA, ROE, and stock return;	Reduces stock return volatility and systemic risk exposure

(continued)

Table 2.2 (continued)

Author(s)	*Efficiency metrics*	*Profitability metrics*	*Risk metrics*
Zheng & Mao (2024)		Improves CARs	
Li et al. (2023)	Improves corporate efficiency	Improves corporate profitability due to the enhancement of information transparency and alleviation of financing constraints	

Note The table offers a summary of the main proxies used in academic literature to assess the impact of FinTech on banking performance metrics. The metrics are classified according to three dimensions of analysis: (i) efficiency, (ii) profitability, and (iii) risk profile. Each study offers unique contributions to understanding different facets of banking performance. The findings illustrate the complex and multifaceted impact of FinTech innovations on the banking sector. *Source* Author's elaboration

Consequently, the divergences in corporate cultures highlighted by the current literature can lead to conflicts and inefficiency in decision-making and operational execution. For instance, the hierarchical structure of incumbents may conflict with the flat, specialised, and more flexible structures of FinTech firms (Boot et al., 2021). This disparity may generate tensions between employees and management, potentially impacting the speed and efficiency of decision-making processes. Employees who joined FinTech startups, and thus choosing organisations that offer a more flexible and adaptive environment than traditional financial institutions, clash with the bureaucratic procedures of banks. Conversely, bank employees may perceive the FinTech approach as one that affords less control and rigidity.

Economic conditions and regulatory changes may further complicate the integration efforts. The uncertainty that has characterised the latest years and the recent banking crises can lead to a shift of focus away from strategic growth initiatives like FinTech acquisitions. This can hinder the integration process and increase pressure on the combined entity. Furthermore, the regulatory environments differ between banks and FinTech, thus introducing an additional layer of complexity in the integration process. As highlighted by BIS (2018), banks are subject to rigorous regulatory scrutiny, the objective of which is to guarantee financial stability and safeguard consumers. Despite the increasing regulation of FinTech companies, they frequently operate under disparate or more tolerant regulatory frameworks. Aligning these disparate compliance standards and operational practices can be challenging and time-consuming, necessitating significant adjustments from both parties.

Existing literature (Chatterjee et al., 1992; Schweiger & Goulet, 2000; Teerikangas & Very, 2006) has also emphasised how, in cross-border M&As, the challenges associated with cultural integration are particularly pronounced. The corporate cultures of companies from unequal national backgrounds are shaped by the social norms, business practices, and regulatory environments of their respective countries of origin. This introduces an additional layer of complexity to the integration process, as these differences have the potential to result in misunderstandings and conflicts if not managed effectively. Effective integration necessitates addressing these cultural differences through coordinated efforts, including communication and harmonising corporate values and practices (Schein, 2010). Scholars have also highlighted how the historical background and experiences of the companies involved also influence the process of cultural integration in M&As. For example, organisations that have experienced mergers and acquisitions in the past may already have the best practices and critical activities for dealing with culture clashes, helping a faster change process.

On the other hand, low-experience firms engaged in M&A activities might observe higher difficulties when addressing critical aspects of culture integration, thus meaning that experience is prone to slow down the process and hit barriers. Schein (2010) also stresses that cultural integration involves not only the match of corporate values with organisational practices but soft aspects such as behaviour, attitude, and interpersonal relationships of people at the workplace. Elements like these are often embedded in an organisation and may be relatively complex and challenging to change significantly in highly bureaucratised industries such as banking. Regarding the interaction between bank and FinTech entities, integrating heterogeneous technological systems and platforms is a further challenge. Banks and FinTech firms utilise different technologies and legacy systems to oversee their operational activities. Due to the digital innovation in the banking industry, integrating new and advanced systems can present technical challenges and require a substantial investment of time and resources.

Furthermore, banks' employees must undertake specific training to employ the new systems and adapt to the altered workflows, which can engender additional resistance to change. Oliver Wyman's latest report reported that merging companies' leadership styles and management practices may also present challenges. Effective leadership is crucial in successfully integrating cultures, but differences in leadership styles can give rise to friction. Thus, the leadership teams of a traditional banking institution and a financial technology company may exhibit conflicting characteristics. The former can be more cautious and avoid taking certain risks, whereas the latter may show more inclination towards innovation and risk. Therefore, ensuring that all these dissimilar ways of leadership or management mesh so that they support a coherent and efficient work climate is critical.

Effective communication represents a further crucial element in the process of cultural integration. The implementation of clear, consistent, and transparent communication strategies at the leadership level can assist in the mitigation of employee concerns and the establishment of trust. This necessitates top-down executive communication and the establishment of transparent and open communication channels throughout the organisational structure. Thus, organisations should develop a sense of inclusion and engagement, which are crucial for successful cultural integration (Schein, 2010).

In addition to all the factors mentioned above, the success of a cultural integration process requires an *ongoing* process. The process of cultural integration is not complete once the initial integration phase has been concluded. Implementing a sustained effort to maintain and reinforce the integrated culture over time is essential. Especially in the bank-FinTech environment, this effort necessitates implementing a systematic monitoring and assessment process to evaluate the integration process, facilitate necessary adjustments, and reinforce the new culture through communication, training, and support.

The literature review reveals that cultural integration challenges arising following an M&A operation present a challenge due to the contrasting organisational cultures of traditional banking institutions and FinTech firms. Hierarchical, risk-averse structures characterise traditional banking institutions, whereas FinTech companies are characterised by agility and innovation. Such misalignment may result in operational inefficiencies and conflicts. Furthermore, economic conditions and differing regulatory frameworks serve to compound the difficulties inherent in integration, with banks operating under stricter regulations than FinTech firms. Furthermore, technological integration necessitates a considerable investment in terms of both financial resources and the provision of training. Additionally, the complexity of cross-border M&As is further compounded by the existence of disparate national cultures and business practices, thereby necessitating the implementation of coordinated strategies to harmonies corporate values. As scholars emphasised, the integration process is ongoing, requiring continuous effort to maintain and reinforce the new culture through systematic monitoring, training, and support, especially in a dynamic banking environment.

2.6 Conclusions

This chapter offers a comprehensive and systematic literature review of the interactions between traditional banks and FinTech firms about mergers and acquisitions (M&As). In particular, this chapter focuses on the impact of FinTech M&As on banks' performance metrics, explores the opportunities that benefit new entrants in the financial sector, and discusses the challenges of culture integration processes. The findings highlight the relevance of strategic considerations, regulatory environments, and the importance of effective integration practices in achieving a valuable integration process between banks and FinTech firms.

As outlined in Paragraph 2.1, an examination of M&A trends within the banking sector has revealed a notable decline in global M&A activity. This phenomenon may be attributed to the maturity of the M&A market, where factors such as elevated interest rates, high deal values, and political instability exert a considerable influence. However, sectors such as technology and financial services have witnessed an increase in the frequency of transactions, driven by the prevailing trends of consolidation and streamlining of operations through mergers and acquisitions among banking institutions. This is most evident in regions such as the Americas, where selective high-value products and transactions have flourished despite market turbulence.

Paragraph 2.2 examines the need for banks to invest in FinTech firms and highlights how it has become an imperative triggered by the relentless advancement of financial technologies. Consequently, incumbent banks are now compelled to integrate various forms of digitisation into their operations in order to maintain competitiveness in the face of new entrants in the financial sector, which are categorised as non-banks and neo-banks. Financial technology companies have emerged as valuable partners for banks with their ability to offer customised and cost-effective banking products. The extant literature has identified several strategic options for banks, including the establishment of *alliances*, *joint ventures*, and *full acquisitions*. Each alternative presents a unique set of advantages and disadvantages with regard to the optimisation of banks' performance and operational achievements. As scholars have observed, while *full acquisitions* offer the advantage of control and rapid access to new markets, they also entail a higher risk profile and greater complexity in integration. Conversely, *partial acquisitions* and *strategic partnerships* can facilitate a gradual integration of new technologies without the extensive challenges associated with *full acquisitions*.

In addition to the discussion of FinTech opportunities in the context of bank M&As, as presented in Paragraph 2.3, the potential benefits of FinTech M&As for banking institutions have been outlined in Paragraph 2.4. The empirical evidence suggests that these strategic actions have the potential to enhance traditional banks' operational efficiency, profitability, and risk management capabilities. Scholars have demonstrated that the implementation of FinTech innovations can lead to improvements in the efficiency, profitability, and risk management of banking institutions. However, the literature also presents mixed findings, with some studies in the field reporting negative impacts on long-term performance metrics and increased operational costs. This discrepancy demonstrates the context-specific nature of M&As, whereby the success of integration efforts is contingent upon the distinctive attributes of the involved entities, their strategic alignment, and the broader economic and regulatory environment.

Furthermore, Paragraph 2.5 examines the cultural integration challenges that banks experience after acquiring a FinTech firm. The distinct organisational cultures of traditional banks and FinTech companies present a significant challenge for creating advisable value. The hierarchical structures and risk-averse attitudes that have traditionally characterised banking institutions contrast with the more agile and entrepreneurial nature of FinTech firms. This misalignment can result in operational inefficiencies, conflicts, and resistance to new methods and practices. Effective integration requires addressing these cultural differences through coordinated efforts, including transparent communication, harmonising corporate values, and adaptive leadership. The integration process is further complicated by differing (i) regulatory hurdles, (ii) economic conditions, and (iii) technological disparities. Aligning the different compliance standards and operational practices of banks and

FinTech firms requires significant investment and long-term effort. The paragraph also emphasises the ongoing nature of the cultural integration process. It is insufficient to address integration challenges during the initial phases of mergers and acquisitions; sustained efforts are required to maintain and reinforce the integrated culture over time.

Integrating traditional banking and FinTech cultures through M&A is a multifaceted challenge influenced by organisational, regulatory, technological, and cultural differences. These challenges can only be addressed through a sustained, multifaceted approach, emphasising effective leadership, communication, and adaptive strategies to achieve a harmonious and profitable integration. The findings of this chapter underscore the importance of strategic planning and sustained effort in facing the complex scenario of bank-FinTech M&As, ultimately contributing to enhanced competitiveness and growth in the evolving financial services sector.

References

Akhtar, Q., & Nosheen, S. (2022). The impact of fintech and banks M&A on acquirer's performance: A strategic win or loss? *Borsa Istanbul Review, 22*(6), 1195–1208.

Alaassar, A., Mention, A. L., & Aas, T. H. (2022). Ecosystem dynamics: Exploring the interplay within fintech entrepreneurial ecosystems. *Small Business Economics, 58*(4), 2157–2182.

Alaassar, A., Mention, A. L., & Aas, T. H. (2023). Facilitating innovation in FinTech: A review and research agenda. *Review of Managerial Science, 17*(1), 33–66.

Alt, R., Beck, R., & Smits, M. T. (2018). Fintech and the transformation of the financial industry. *Electronic Markets, 28*(3), 235–243.

Austin, R. E., & Dunham, L. M. (2022). Do fintech acquisitions improve the operating performance or risk profiles of acquiring firms? *Journal of Economics and Business, 121*, 106078.

Ayadi, R., Bongini, P., Casu, B., & Cucinelli, D. (2021). Bank business model migrations in Europe: Determinants and effects. *British Journal of Management, 32*(4), 1007–1026.

Bank for International Settlements (BIS). (2018). Implication of fintech developments for banks and bank supervision.

Bauer, F., & Matzler, K. (2014). Antecedents of M&A success: The role of strategic complementarity, cultural fit, and degree and speed of integration. *Strategic Management Journal., 35*(2), 269–291.

Berger, A. N., Demsetz, R. S., & Strahan, P. E. (1999). The consolidation of the financial services industry: Causes, consequences, and implications for the future. *Journal of Banking and Finance, 23*(2), 135–194.

Bogers, M., Afuah, A., Dahlander, L., Gruber, M., Hilgers, D., Majchrzak, A., & Sims, J. (2017). The open innovation research landscape: Established perspectives and emerging themes across different levels of analysis. *Industry and Innovation, 24*(1), 8–40.

Bömer, M., & Maxin, H. (2018). Why fintechs cooperate with banks—evidence from Germany. *Zeitschrift Für Die Gesamte Versicherungswissenschaft, 107*, 359–386.

Boot, A., Hoffmann, P., Laeven, L., & Ratnovski, L. (2021). Fintech: What's old, what's new? *Journal of Financial Stability, 53*, 100836.

Borello, G., Pampurini, F., & Quaranta, A. G. (2022). Can high-tech investments improve banking efficiency? *Journal of Financial Management, Markets and Institutions, 10*(01), 2250003.

Bussmann, O. (2017). The future of finance: Fintech, tech disruption, and orchestrating innovation. *Equity markets in transition: The value chain, price discovery, regulation, and beyond*, 473–486.

Caiazza, S., Clare, A., & Pozzolo, A. F. (2012). What do bank acquirers want? Evidence from worldwide bank M&A targets. *Journal of Banking & Finance, 36*(9), 2641–2659.

Cappa, F., Collevecchio, F., Oriani, R., & Peruffo, E. (2022). Banks responding to the digital surge through open innovation: Stock market performance effects of M&As with fintech firms. *Journal of Economics and Business, 121*, 106079.

Chatterjee, S., Lubatkin, M. H., Schweiger, D. M., & Weber, Y. (1992). Cultural differences and shareholder value in related mergers: Linking equity and human capital. *Strategic Management Journal, 13*(5), 319–334. https://doi.org/10.1002/smj.4250130502

Chen, Q., & Shen, C. (2024). How fintech affects bank systemic risk: Evidence from China. *Journal of Financial Services Research, 65*(1), 77–101.

Collevecchio, F., Cappa, F., Peruffo, E., & Oriani, R. (2024). When do M&As with fintech firms benefit traditional banks? *British Journal of Management, 35*(1), 192–209.

Dezi, L., Battisti, E., Ferraris, A., & Papa, A. (2018). The link between mergers and acquisitions and innovation: A systematic literature review. *Management Research Review, 41*(6), 716–752.

Dranev, Y., Frolova, K., & Ochirova, E. (2019). The impact of fintech M&A on stock returns. *Research in International Business and Finance, 48*, 353–364.

Elsas, R., Hackethal, A., & Holzhauser, M. (2010). The anatomy of bank diversification. *Journal of Banking and Finance, 34*(6), 1274–1287.

Folta, T. B. (1998). Governance and uncertainty: The trade-off between administrative control and commitment. *Strategic Management Journal, 19*(11), 1007–1028.

Haddad, C., & Hornuf, L. (2023). How do fintech startups affect financial institutions' performance and default risk? *The European Journal of Finance, 29*(15), 1761–1792.

Hankir, Y., Rauch, C., & Umber, M. P. (2011). Bank M&A: A market power story? *Journal of Banking and Finance, 35*(9), 2341–2354.

He, M., Song, G., & Chen, Q. (2023). Fintech adoption, internal control quality and bank risk taking: Evidence from Chinese listed banks. *Finance Research Letters, 57*, 104235.

Hildebrandt, M. (2015). *Smart technologies and the end (s) of law: Novel entanglements of law and technology*. Edward Elgar Publishing.

Hornuf, L., Klus, M. F., Lohwasser, T. S., & Schwienbacher, A. (2021). How do banks interact with fintech startups? *Small Business Economics, 57*, 1505–1526.

International Monetary Fund (IMF). (2023). *Is fintech eating the bank's lunch?* In IMF Working Paper. W.P./23/239.

Katsiampa, P., McGuinness, P. B., Serbera, J. P., & Zhao, K. (2022). The financial and prudential performance of Chinese banks and Fintech lenders in the era of digitalization. *Review of Quantitative Finance and Accounting, 58*(4), 1451–1503. https://doi.org/10.1007/s11156-021-01033-9

Klus, M. F., Lohwasser, T. S., Holotiuk, F., & Moormann, J. (2019). Strategic alliances between banks and fintechs for digital innovation: Motives to collaborate and types of interaction. *The Journal of Entrepreneurial Finance (JEF), 21*(1), 1–23.

Kwon, K. Y., Molyneux, P., Pancotto, L., & Reghezza, A. (2024). Banks and fintech acquisitions. *Journal of Financial Services Research, 65*(1), 41–75. https://doi.org/10.1007/s10693-022-00396-x

Le Floc'h, G., & Scaringella, L. (2017). Another failed M&A: Misaligned business models as culprit. *Journal of Business Strategy, 38*(5), 18–26.

Lee, C. C., Li, X., Yu, C. H., & Zhao, J. (2021). Does fintech innovation improve bank efficiency? Evidence from China's banking industry. *International Review of Economics & Finance, 74*, 468–483.

Lee, G. K., & Lieberman, M. B. (2010). Acquisition vs. internal development as modes of market entry. *Strategic Management Journal, 31*(2), 140–158.

Li, E., Mao, M. Q., Zhang, H. F., & Zheng, H. (2023). Banks' investments in fintech ventures. *Journal of Banking & Finance, 149*, 106754. https://doi.org/10.1016/j.jbankfin.2022.106754

Luo, Y., & Tung, R. L. (2007). International expansion of emerging market enterprises: A springboard perspective. *Journal of International Business Studies, 38*, 481–498.

Marks, M. L., & Mirvis, P. H. (2011). A framework for the human resources role in managing culture in mergers and acquisitions. *Human Resource Management, 50*(6), 859–877.

McKinsey & Company. (2024). Rebound of financial services M&A: Focus on growth and capabilities (by N. Hussein, F. Najjar, M. Van Oostende, and A. Zarrilli).

Nambisan, S., Lyytinen, K., Majchrzak, A., & Song, M. (2017). Digital innovation management: Reinventing innovation management research in a digital world. *MIS Quarterly, 41*(1), 223–238.

Norton Rose Fulbright. (2024). M&A outlook 2024. Green shoots of optimism amid uncertainty. Consolidation and digital transformation to propel global M&A despite rising regulatory burden.

Oliver Wyman. (2024). A comprehensive analysis of bank-fintech M&A. How bank-fintech synergy can drive M&A success.

Panibratov, A. (2017). Cultural and organizational integration in cross-border M&A deals: The comparative study of acquisitions made by EMNEs from China and Russia. *Journal of Organizational Change Management, 30*(7), 1109–1135.

Phan, D. H. B., Narayan, P. K., Rahman, R. E., & Hutabarat, A. R. (2020). Do financial technology firms influence bank performance? *Pacific-Basin Finance Journal, 62*, 101210.

Pinelli, M., Cappa, F., Peruffo, E., & Oriani, R. (2022). Acquisitions of non-controlling equity stakes: Agency conflicts and profitability. *Strategic Organization, 20*(2), 341–367.

Puschmann, T. (2017). Fintech. *Business & Information Systems Engineering, 59*, 69–76.

PWC. (2024). 2024 Mid-year outlook. Global M&A trends in financial services.

Reghezza, A. & Vasilakis, C. (2024). Why do banks acquire fintech? The role of board cultural diversity. *The British Accounting Review*, 101424.

Schein, E. H. (2010). Organizational culture and leadership (Vol. 2). John Wiley & Sons.

Schweiger, D. M., & Goulet, P. K. (2000). Integrating mergers and acquisitions: An international research review. *Advances in Mergers and Acquisitions*, 61–91.

Shahzad, F., Luqman, R. A., Khan, A. R., & Shabbir, L. (2012). Impact of organizational culture on organizational performance: An overview. *Interdisciplinary Journal of Contemporary Research in Business.*

Shin, S. R., Han, J., Marhold, K., & Kang, J. (2017). Reconfiguring the firm's core technological portfolio through open innovation: Focusing on technological M&A. *Journal of Knowledge Management, 21*(3), 571–591.

Stahl, G. K., & Voigt, A. (2008). Do cultural differences matter in mergers and acquisitions? A tentative model and examination. *Organization Science, 19*(1), 160–176.

Stulz, R. M. (2019). Fintech, bigtech, and the future of banks. *Journal of Applied Corporate Finance, 31*(4), 86–97.

Teerikangas, S., & Very, P. (2006). The culture–performance relationship in M&A: From yes/no to how. *British Journal of Management, 17*(S1), S31–S48.

Templeton, W. K., & Severiens, J. T. (1992). The effect of nonbank diversification on bank holding company risk. *Quarterly Journal of Business and Economics, 31*(4), 3.

Turk Ariss, R. (2010). On the implications of market power in banking: Evidence from developing countries. *Journal of Banking and Finance, 34*(4), 765–775.

Vives, X. (2019). Digital disruption in banking. *Annual Review of Financial Economics, 11*(1), 243–272.

Wang, Y., & Larimo, J. (2020). Survival of full versus partial acquisitions: The moderating role of firm's internationalization experience, cultural distance, and host country context characteristics. *International Business Review, 29*(1), Article 101605.

Wang, Y., Hu, J., & Chen, J. (2023). Does fintech facilitate cross-border M&As? Evidence from Chinese A-share listed firms. *International Review of Financial Analysis, 85*, 102435.

Wang, Y., Xiuping, S., & Zhang, Q. (2021). Can fintech improve the efficiency of commercial banks? An analysis based on big data. *Research in International Business and Finance, 55*, 101338.

Zhao, J., Li, X., Yu, C. H., Chen, S., & Lee, C. C. (2022). Riding the fintech innovation wave: FinTech, patents and bank performance. *Journal of International Money and Finance, 122*, 102552.

Zheng, H., & Mao, M. Q. (2024). Fintech mergers and acquisitions. *Journal of International Money and Finance, 143*, 103076.

CHAPTER 3

FinTech Challenges and Opportunities in a Global Perspective

Abstract This chapter examines the evolution of FinTech, with a particular focus on its stages of development, definitions, and regulatory challenges. Specifically, it explores FinTech's evolution process from early digitisation in the mid-twentieth century to the integration of digital platforms in traditional finance, and the current era of decentralised finance driven by blockchain and cryptocurrencies. This chapter critically analyses the definitions and taxonomies provided by international organisations and banking authorities, emphasising the complexity of the FinTech sector. Furthermore, it emphasises the regulatory fragmentation that characterised the FinTech industry, revealing the discrepancies that exist between different jurisdictions and the attempts to achieve a balance between innovation and stability, as well as consumer protection.

Keywords FinTech · Bank · Regulation · Digital transformation · Financial sector

G. B. Ferilli, *Bank-FinTech M&As and Banking Innovation*, Palgrave Macmillan Studies in Banking and Financial Institutions, https://doi.org/10.1007/978-3-031-84445-4_3

3.1 Drivers and Evolution Factors of FinTech

The digitalisation processes have significantly impacted the financial industry, driven by the ***information-based*** nature of financial products and the increasing shift towards ***non-physical*** interactions in financial transactions, such as online payments and stock trading (Murinde et al., 2022). The financial sector has experienced a rise in automation processes, resulting in the restructuring of the value chain of financial services. These drivers have led to the creation of new business models (BMs) and the advent of new financial players in the banking industry (Puschmann, 2017).

The term "*FinTech*", short for "*Financial Technology*", identifies a dynamic and blurred phenomenon (Friedline, 2020). In financial literature, "FinTech" is a broad term covering new financial solutions facilitated by IT and offered by the same FinTech startups and traditional banking services digitised and maintained by established banks. Consequently, the FinTech revolution encompasses and collectively pursues all the previously identified categories of financial innovation objectives (Frame & White, 2014; Haddad & Hornuf, 2019; Tufano, 2003), including (i) products and services; (ii) organisational structures; (iii) processes; (iv) systems; and (v) business models.

However, as Puschmann (2017) asserted, the advent of financial technology has been enabled and accelerated by several factors related to the changes that have characterised the financial ecosystem, the regulatory environment, consumer behaviour, and the prominent role of IT in the financial industry. These factors have contributed to the progressive evolution of FinTech firms within the global financial system, enabling them to offer a broader, efficient, and sophisticated array of financial services.

The evolution of FinTech begins with the *FinTech 1.0* age and culminates with the current *FinTech 3.0* development. Every stage represents a significant change in the delivery and consumption of financial services, technological advancement, and shift in consumer behaviour. These phases are not defined strictly but represent periods of overlapping dominance of trends and innovations (Arner et al., 2015; Ashta, & Biot-Paquerot, 2018).

FinTech 1.0: Digitising Finance (1950s–Early 2000s)

The *"FinTech 1.0"* stage represents this industry's first development step. It involves digitalising financial products and the contextual shift from an analogic-based service supply chain to a digital financial system. This step took place from 1950 to the early 2000s and increased integration across and within the industries, putting the foundations needed for the process of globalisation in place. This evolution has been identified by the introduction of digital transactions following the creation of *Diners Club* credit cards in 1950. Later, in 1959, American Express launched plastic credit cards, setting a standard for extending credit to digital wallets. These advancements led to a move away from using physical money for transactions and raised consumer awareness about the consequences of having electronic debt.

Later advancements involved *Barclays Bank* in London introducing Automated Teller Machines (ATMs) in 1967, revolutionising the banking sector by allowing clients to withdraw funds beyond regular business hours. Following that, the NASDAQ, established in September 1971 as an electronic stock exchange by the National Association of Securities Dealers Automated Quotations, allowed for quicker trading via automation. This new development improved customer service and also promoted the growth of more advanced online financial services.

Financial services permanently incorporated online banking and electronic trading platforms into operational processes in this era. 1982, the year of the *"E*Trade"* foundation, represents a milestone in the evolution of FinTech technology employment in financial services. This institution is one of the first to embrace the online brokerage paradigm, enabling individuals to access securities exchanges through the Internet directly. In the following ten years, the financial industry observed the emergence of Internet banking services provided by reputable incumbent banks. For example, *Wells Fargo's* online checking account platform became popular in the late 1990s. This system allowed clients to supervise their accounts online, quickly becoming a norm in the industry.

One of the significant events that signed the evolution of FinTech in the financial industry was the foundation of *PayPal* and the consequent supply of electronic payments in 1999. *PayPal's* services opened the way for the evolution of the e-commerce market. Meanwhile, the most significant institutions, such as *Bank of America,* were experiencing their digitalisation processes, reaching more than 3 million users by 2001.

FinTech 2.0: Embedded Finance (Late 2000s–2010s)

The decade from the 2000s to 2010s, known as the age of *"FinTech 2.0"* or *"Finance Embedded"*, represents the second phase of financial technology development. In this period, traditional financial institutions have incorporated financial services using digital platforms, observing an increase in their capacity to engage a broader base of customers and exploiting the potentiality of digital platforms. This signifies a shift from offering financial products independently to providing comprehensive financial services integrated into different aspects of daily life through digital devices from the late 1990s to the 2010s. During this time horizon, the rise of online banking, cellular payments, and the merging of financial services with tech platforms represent the significant advancements that shape the digitalisation of the financial industry.

At the beginning of the 2000s, the supply of Internet banking services was widely adopted, and approximately more than 80% of the banks offered online banking services by 2006. Consumers' demand has primarily driven this rapid shift from an analogic to a digital-based financial system. Customers understood the value of accessing banking services without time restrictions, and this innovation was possible due to the rapid advancements in Internet technology and faster communication structures. For example, users could use their personal computers to transfer funds between different accounts, pay bills, or check account balances, among other transactions, through online banking. This made financial institutions increasingly accessible and convenient from any electronic device, accelerating the uptake of digital finance.

The spread and diffusion of smartphones represent a driving factor that has facilitated the adoption of mobile payment services and, more generally, the evolution of mobile banking. Since the 2007 *iPhone* launch by *Apple,* the mobile phone sector has been radically transformed, and this device has become a viable platform exploitable to deliver mobile payment through customers. Firms like *PayPal* and *Square* have quickly become the leaders in this sector, providing valuable solutions to enable small businesses and individuals to receive payments via mobile phones without involving a physical cash transaction. These advanced technologies facilitated seamless integration between people's real-life business dealings offline and online transactions.

Additionally, the "*FinTech 2.0*" age has been characterised by the introduction alternative financial products and services within the financial industry, such as peer-to-peer lending and crowdfunding services. The rise of these new digital platforms has changed the funding channels available to firms. In this way, they facilitate the direct matching between borrowers (retail and business) and lenders (or investors) (Stefanelli et al., 2022). *LendingClub* and *Kickstarter* are two digital platforms offering different financing forms, bypassing normal banking channels altogether. Additionally, a new concept of digital wallets where customers are able to save their details and carry out payments using their mobile devices came into emulation during this period. Therefore, these innovations have made it easier for consumers and businesses across the globe to access related financial services. In addition, they have allowed the customisation of these services depending on someone's need or demand, further cementing their place in a digitally inclined economy.

FinTech 3.0: Decentralising Finance (Late 2010s–Present)

The third and latest phase of FinTech, which has been named *FinTech 3.0*, is about the term 'decentralisation' used to describe financial services. This phase started in 2010 and has seen new trends in financial services delivery, mainly the shift from the centralised mode to the decentralised platform, many of which use blockchain. Introducing cryptocurrencies characterises the third phase, the idea of decentralised finance (DeFi) and blockchain in general. Many of these innovative products have been created by the public in what could be attributed to bitcoins after 2009. *Bitcoin* initially introduced stakeholders to the idea of a barter currency where people can transact with each other directly with the appropriate institution, the central authority handling various transactions. Later, in 2015, *Ethereum* went a step further and expanded blockchain beyond just payment transactions to smart contracts, which are contracts executed by computers, provided that the pre-defined terms and clauses are embedded in the code. Such innovations have created room for another kind of finance, termed decentralised finance or DeFi for short, aiming to mimic all types of financial markets, for instance, lending, borrowing, and trading through decentralised platforms.

A further feature of FinTech 3.0 is the proliferation of DeFi platforms. These platforms operate within blockchain networks, enabling users to engage in financial activities without the intermediary role of traditional institutions such as banks. This leads to the developing of a social ecosystem of platforms in blockchain structure where individuals can perform financial operations using conventional financial institutions. The rationale for this decentralisation is the desire to enhance the level of openness further and, therefore, reduce costs and accessibility of the services of financial institutions for individuals and businesses in places where conventional banking is lacking. This growth has come simultaneously with decentralised exchanges, a platform through which traders can enter the market to either purchase or sell the cryptocurrency without needing the approval of the central authority.

3.2 FinTech Definition and Taxonomy

In the last twenty years, banking supervisory authorities, policymakers, and scholars have tried to offer various definitions of FinTech as a first step to defining the regulatory space of new entrants to the financial sector. However, due to the inherent complexity and the ongoing evolution of the phenomenon, to date, there is no standard definition and classification of FinTech (see, for example, Bank for International Settlements, 2018; European Banking Authority, 2017; Financial Stability Board, 2017; World Economic Forum, 2015).

In this constantly evolving scenario, the World Economic Forum (WEF) has formulated the first integrated reference model of disruptive innovation in the financial industry (WEF, 2015). WEF's report identifies six primary functions of financial services (i.e., Payments, Market Provisioning, Investment Management, Insurance, Deposits and Lending, and Capital Raising) and eleven clusters of innovation that exert pressure on traditional business models (see Fig. 3.1). Specifically, the WEF's taxonomy focuses on the innovation processes that considerably impact the banking sector. The taxonomy identified the scope of innovation (products and services) made available by new players in each core business area of financial intermediaries. Nevertheless, the WEF report does not use *"FinTech"* to identify and categorise new financial activities that new players enabled and provided.

In 2017, the Financial Stability Board (FSB) offered a preliminary definition of "FinTech" as *"technologically enabled innovation in financial services that could result in new business models, applications, processes or products with an associated material effect on financial markets and institutions and the provision of financial services"* (FSB, 2017). This definition emphasises the extensive range of innovation introduced by

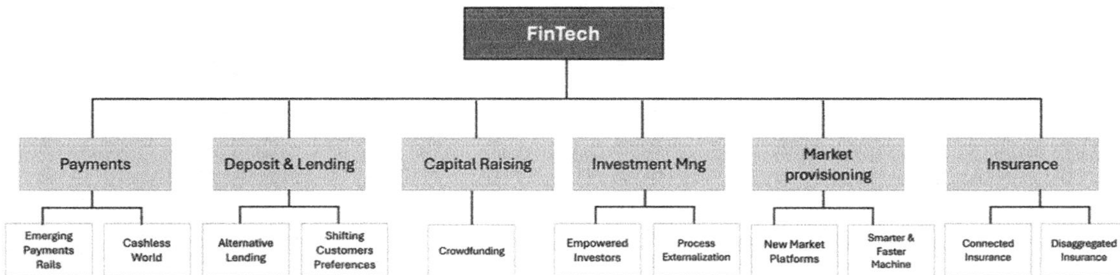

Fig. 3.1 The WEF's taxonomy for disruptive innovation in financial services (*Note* The figure offers a framework identifying six core functions of financial services (Payments, Deposits and Lending Capital Raising, Investment Management, Market Provisioning, and Insurance) and eleven clusters of innovation. These clusters highlight key areas where emerging technologies and business models drive disruption and restructuring of traditional financial services. *Source* Author's elaboration, data from the World Economic Forum-WEF [2015])

FinTech players while also underscoring the considerable implications of this phenomenon on the banking and financial system.

Applying the framework postulated by FSB, the FinTech activities have been divided into five categories from the onset, which relate to the financial service in compliance with WEF's categorisation. These categories are as follows: (i) *Payments, Clearing, and Settlement;* (ii) *Deposits, Lending, and Capital Raising*; (iii) *Insurance*; (iv) *Investment Management*; and (v) *Market Support.* The European Banking Authority has provided a similar classification (EBA, 2017), offering a more detailed framework of FinTech firms' taxonomy, clustering their activity into four main clusters (i.e., Cluster A, B, C, and D). Each cluster is also split into more than ten different subsegments of FinTech activities. On the other hand, the Bank for International Settlements (BIS) was the first to introduce a new categorisation, thus creating a new research direction regarding the FinTech context (BIS, 2020). The BIS' taxonomy emphasises three key areas: (i) *FinTech Activities*, (ii) *Enabling Technologies*, and (iii) *Policy Enablers.*

The initial category comprises the following sub-categories: "*Deposit & Lending*", covering digital banking, balance sheet FinTech lending and loan crowdfunding; "*Capital Raising*", including equity crowdfunding; "*Asset Management*", including robo advice; "*Payment, Clearing and Settlement*", including digital payment services and e-money; "*Insurance*", including Insurtech business models; and finally, "*Crypto Assets*".

The category of Enabling Technologies includes: "*Application Programming Interface*" (API), "*Cloud Computing*", "*Biometrics*", "*Distributed Ledger Technology*" (DLT), "*Artificial Intelligence*" (AI), and "*Machine Learning*" (ML). The third category, which includes "*Policy Enablers*", comprises: "*Digital ID*", "*Data protection*", "*Cyber security*", "*Open banking*", and "*Innovation facilitators*".

In classifying the FinTech firms' areas of expertise, an increasing trend emerged towards a detailed definition of the activities of financial technology players. This trend arises from the exponential growth that the FinTech sector has witnessed globally, the rising sophistication of the technologies deployed by players in this sector, and the growing demand for financial services available through online channels.

One of the most detailed FinTech taxonomies now available is provided by the *Cambridge Centre for Alternative Finance (CCAF).* The CCAF provides a comprehensive classification system for categorising FinTech firms according to their business models in line with the evolving global trends within the FinTech sector. The CCAF's classification encompasses 14 distinct market segments. (i.e., (1) *Digital Lending*, (2) *Digital Capital Raising*, (3) *Digital Banks*, (4) *Digital Savings*, (5) *Digital Payments*, (6) *Crypto Asset Exchange*, (7) *Intermediation & Brokerage*, (8) *Digital Custody*, (9) *InsurTech*, (10) *WealthTech*, (11) *RegTech*, (12) *Digital Identity*, (13) *Tech for Enterprise*, (14) *Consensus Services*) are subdivided into 63 subsegments and 118 categories. The classification system is structured hierarchically, based on an activity-oriented conceptual framework that groups entities according to the services they provide directly to clients or users.

3.3 FinTech Regulatory Challenges and Differences Across Countries

The regulation of FinTech poses a considerable challenge for countries across the globe as regulators and authorities seek to balance the benefits of innovation and the need to ensure financial stability, the protection of consumers, and fairness and transparency in the markets (BIS, 2021). The accelerated growth of the FinTech industry presents a substantial challenge for regulators in formulating suitable regulatory frameworks. These frameworks must balance the need for flexibility to accommodate technological advancements and the robustness required to mitigate potential risks to the financial industry. These challenges are further compounded by significant differences across jurisdictions, which can be attributed to the level of development in each country, legal structures, regulatory barriers, and levels of technology application.

In light of the factors above, this paragraph provides a concise overview of the general regulatory issues and disparities that countries have encountered in regulating FinTech, focusing on the challenges of regulating emerging technologies in the financial market.

The rapid advancement of technologies in the financial industry is emerging as a significant challenge for regulators. The conventional regulatory approaches developed for more traditional financial institutions and products frequently prove inadequate in keeping pace with the rapid evolution of the FinTech sector. This phenomenon has been most evident in sectors such as ***digital payments, peer-to-peer (P2P) lending***, and ***cryptocurrencies***, where the business models have evolved beyond the scope of traditional regulatory frameworks.

As a result of these dynamics, regulators often cannot effectively identify and address emerging issues, leading to regulatory gaps in areas where FinTech activities are concentrated. These gaps pose potential risks to both financial stability and consumer protection. In contrast, some jurisdictions have adopted a *"wait and see"* approach, allowing FinTech innovations to evolve before implementing specific regulations. Although this strategy may be pragmatic in certain contexts, it often leads to regulatory uncertainty or inconsistencies that can hinder innovation and limit market growth (World Bank Group, 2022).

In this regard, the *"Global FinTech-enabling regulations database"*, provided by World Bank Group, offers a comprehensive overview of the number of countries with identified FinTech-specific regulation (Fig. 3.2) and, similarly, the number of countries with identified foundational FinTech regulation (Fig. 3.3). The WBG's database, consisting of nearly 200 countries around the globe, highlights how while there is widespread implementation of regulatory frameworks for established FinTech activities, like digital banking and e-money, as well as foundational areas such as anti-money laundering, cyber security, and data protection, there is a noticeable lag in the regulation of emerging technologies like cryptocurrency, Central Bank Digital Currencies (CBDCs), digital IDs. The data reveals a significant discrepancy, indicating that while many countries have been proactive in regulating established FinTech sectors, there are substantial gaps in the regulatory framework that address the challenges introduced by emerging innovations.

In response to the challenges posed by new-generation technological tools, regulators have also had to address the increasingly complex business models typically adopted by FinTech firms. It is also important to note that most FinTech companies work in various unrelated fields and industries, closely connected to, for example, e-shopping or social networks. This makes it difficult for them to implement traditional legal structures, as industry boundaries have blurred. For instance, the advent of major technology companies (i.e., BigTech firms) that also offer financial services in conjunction with their primary business has prompted concerns regarding market concentration, data protection, and anti-competitive practices. As a result, regulators should assess how these companies may be considered financial operators or treated differently under the framework applicable to technology-based companies. According to Murinde et al. (2022), this challenge is exacerbated by FinTech firms operating in different jurisdictions and thus face different

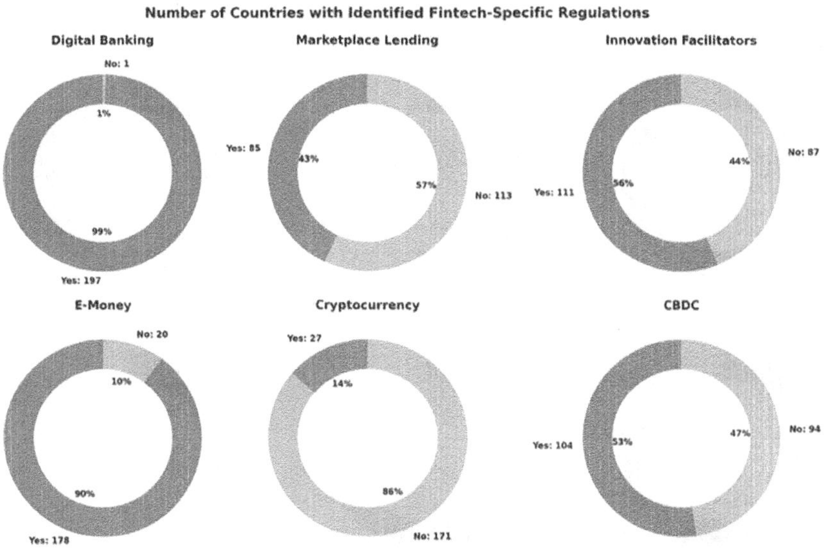

Fig. 3.2 Number of countries with identified FinTech-specific regulations (*Note* The figure shows the number of countries adopting specific regulatory frameworks for FinTech activities, including digital banking, marketplace lending, innovation facilitators, e-money, cryptocurrency, and central bank digital currencies [CBDCs]. The figure provides a brief about the global regulatory framework, indicating that although most countries have implemented specific regulations for digital banking and e-money, a few countries have formulated regulations for relatively new domains like cryptocurrencies and Central Bank Digital Currencies [CBDCs]. *Source* Author's elaboration on data sourced from the World Bank Group [Global FinTech-enabling regulations database])

regulatory requirements. The authors also highlight how consumer protection is critical in a changing financial environment. With new FinTech products and services, consumers may face new risks (e.g., digital, cyber, data protection). New risks have emerged in the use of cryptocurrencies and the activities of algorithmic trading platforms. As a result, regulators have developed new rules and guidelines regarding disclosure requirements, risk management systems, and consumer education at the expense of protecting customer interests rather than promoting innovation in the field.

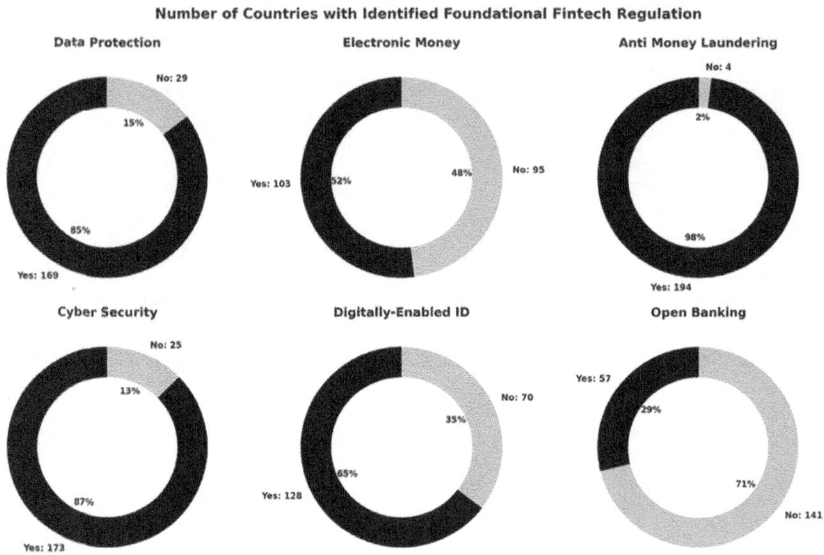

Fig. 3.3 Number of countries with identified foundational FinTech regulations (*Note* The figure shows the number of countries adopting foundational FinTech Regulations like data protection, electronic money, anti-money laundering [AML], cyber security, digitally enabled identification [ID], and open banking. The data demonstrates that many countries have adopted anti-money laundering regulations, cyber security, and data protection; conversely, a relatively smaller proportion of countries have enacted legislation concerning digital IDs and open banking. *Source* Author's elaboration on data sourced from the World Bank Group [Global FinTech-enabling regulations database])

Differences in regulatory approaches across jurisdictions also present challenges for FinTech companies operating globally. In line with the World Bank Group analysis, while some jurisdictions have taken proactive measures to create FinTech-specific regulations, others have relied on existing frameworks or have been slow to develop new rules. For instance, some countries have adopted regulatory sandboxes whereby, through the approval of new regulations, FinTech firms can test their products and services before they are entirely regulated (European Parliament, 2020). These sandboxes are especially common in developing economies to expand the innovative possibilities among the regulators besides controlling risks. However, the success of such undertakings depends on the design and implementation of the sandbox and the general legal environment within sandbox operates (World Bank Group, 2022).

Thirdly, the level of the regulatory approach to certain FinTech activities, including *digital banking*, *E-money*, and *cryptocurrencies*, varies from one jurisdiction to another. In some areas, they are regulated similarly to the *"bricks and mortar"* banks, which is called the approach *"traditional banking license"* used in the United States and some countries of Europe.

Jurisdictions including Chinese Mainland, Hong Kong SAR, Malaysia, the Philippines, Saudi Arabia, Singapore, South Korea, and the United Arab Emirates have created digital-specific licences designed for *digital-only* institutions (McKinsey & Company, 2021). Similarly, the regulation of cryptocurrencies ranges from outright bans in some countries to proactive regulation and integration into the financial system in others, such as the EU countries which have adopted the *Markets in Crypto-assets Act* (MiCa) Regulation or the United Kingdom which in their *Financial Services Markets Act* (FSMA) has introduced a new chapter focalised on crypto-assets regulation. The *MiCa Regulation* is part of the overarching EU *Digital Finance Strategy* comprising a complementary regulation for a DLT pilot regime for market infrastructure, which establishes a scheme to trade and settle transactions involving financial instruments in crypto-asset form.

Therefore, as stated by BIS (2020), the differences in regulation can pose a significant challenge for FinTech companies interested in internationalising their operations. These firms must operate within an unpredictable regulatory framework, often hindering their growth and expansion initiatives.

The international nature of many FinTech activities also raises concerns about regulatory arbitrage, whereby companies seek to operate in jurisdictions with more permissive regulatory environments (IMF, 2023). This could lead to a *"race to the bottom"*, whereby countries compete to attract FinTech companies by offering less stringent regulations. To address this issue, there is a growing recognition of the need for international cooperation and harmonisation of approaches to the regulation of FinTech. Standard-setting bodies, including the *Financial Stability Board* (FSB) and the *Basel Committee on Banking Supervision* (BCBS), have been involved in committing to general standards and guidelines for FinTech activities to achieve a more harmonised regime across borders (BIS, 2024).

Nonetheless, several countries have successfully implemented FinTech regulations to balance innovation and stability and safeguard consumers. To this end, the United Kingdom has devised the New Bank Start-up Unit (NBSU) as a joint initiative set up by financial regulators such as the *Financial Conduct Authority* (FCA) and the *Prudential Regulation Authority* (PRA). The above intervention has fostered an enabling environment for FinTech players' operations while closely regulating those new to the market. Likewise, the *Australian Prudential Regulation Authority* (APRA) has introduced a restricted authorised deposit-taking institution (ADI) licensing framework in Australia.

On the other hand, some emerging markets are struggling to outline and implement sound FinTech regulations due to regulatory capacity and capability constraints. In these countries, there has been a tendency to establish preliminary frameworks to encompass FinTech activities within the regulatory framework. It is anticipated that more comprehensive regulations will be developed over time. For instance, many countries in Sub-Saharan Africa have made laws regarding mobile money services, given their crucial role in advancing financial inclusion in the region. FinTech operators remain largely unregulated in many of these markets regarding *peer-to-peer lending* and *crowdfunding*. The regulatory gap presents a considerable risk to consumers and the broader financial system. Unsupervised or inadequately regulated operations have the potential to destabilise financial markets and facilitate consumer abuse.

The advent of BigTech companies in the financial services sector has introduced new challenges for the regulatory system. By leveraging their customer base, technological expertise, and considerable financial resources, these firms present novel issues for regulators to address. The concentration of power in the BigTech firms may result in excessive control over the financial services market, which could reduce competition and increase systemic risk. In addition, data is again a concern for regulators regarding privacy and the use of BigTech firms' considerable consumer data to tilt the balance of the financial services market in their favour. In some countries, regulators have responded by imposing restrictions on the activities of BigTech firms in the financial sector. In other cases, there have been efforts to integrate these firms into mainstream regulatory systems (Murine et al., 2022).

Finally, the advent of the new generation of digital currencies, including CBDCs (*Central Bank Digital Currencies*) and stablecoins, has also posed severe regulatory questions. While CBDCs may present solutions to limitations in the existing monetary system regarding access to financial services and payment system efficiency, they present concerns about data privacy, competitive risks, and a probable shift in the intermediation mechanism. Similarly, the rapid development of stablecoins—defined by central bank authorities as digital assets backed by real-world assets—has prompted concerns regarding their potential to undermine monetary policy and financial stability. Consequently, it falls upon regulators to devise novel approaches to address these challenges while also contemplating the far-reaching implications of digital currencies for the global economy (World Bank Group, 2022).

3.4 Conclusions

This chapter examines the evolution of the FinTech phenomenon, investigating the main drivers of its expansion and analysing the impact of technological innovation on the financial industry. More in detail, Paragraph 3.1 outlines the evolution of FinTech through three distinct phases. The first phase, *FinTech 1.0*, encompasses the growth of banking from the 1950s to the early 2000s. The second phase, *FinTech 2.0*, is characterised by the emergence of integrated banking services since the late 1990s up to the 2010s. The third and final phase, FinTech *3.0*, represents the advent of decentralised finance using blockchain and cryptocurrencies from the 2010s onwards. This section emphasises the ways in which each phase has contributed to the restructuring of the delivery and consumption of financial services. Paragraph 3.2 offers a critical analysis of the current definition and taxonomy of FinTech as outlined by policymakers, regulators, and practitioners. Several organisations, including the World Economic Forum and the World Bank, have proposed frameworks for the classification of FinTech firms, emphasising the industry's growing breadth and complexity.

Finally, Paragraph 3.3 discusses the FinTech regulatory fragmentation within the countries. As the FinTech sector continues to evolve, regulators should address the challenges associated with integrating new technologies to ensure financial stability and protect banking customers. The regulatory frameworks developed to supervise the financial technology sector differ significantly between countries. Some jurisdictions have implemented proactive measures, such as regulatory sandboxes, to facilitate innovation, while others are struggling to keep pace with the rapid advancements in this field.

Therefore, this chapter provides a detailed examination of the underlying forces, developmental phases, and regulatory concerns that affect the global FinTech industry, offering a perspective for the discussion of the subsequent chapters of this book.

References

Arner, D. W., Barberis, J., & Buckley, R. P. (2015). The evolution of FinTech: A new post-crisis paradigm. *Georgetown Journal of International Law., 47*, 1271.

Ashta, A., & Biot-Paquerot, G. (2018). FinTech evolution: Strategic value management issues in a fast changing industry. *Strategic Change, 27*(4), 301–311.

Bank for International Settlements (BIS). (2018). Sound practices. Implications of FinTech developments for banks and banks supervisors.

Bank for International Settlements (BIS). (2020). FSI insights on policy implementation no 23 policy responses to FinTech: A cross-country overview.

Bank for International Settlements (BIS). (2021). FinTech regulation: How to achieve a level playing field. Occasional Paper (by Fernando Restoy) no 17.

Bank for International Settlements (BIS). (2024). Digitalisation of finance. ISBN 978–92–9259–760–3.

European Banking Authority (EBA). (2017). *Discussion paper on the EBA's approach to financial technology (FinTech)*. EBA/DP/2017/02.

European Parliament. (2020, September). *Regulatory sandboxes and innovation hubs for FinTech. Impact on innovation, financial stability and supervisory convergence*. Policy Department for Economic, Scientific and Quality of Life Policies Directorate-General for Internal Policies. PE 652.752.

Financial Stability Board (FSB). (2017). Financial stability implications from FinTech. Supervisory and regulatory issues that merit authorities' Attention.

Frame, W. S., & White, L. J. (2014). *Technological change, financial innovation, and diffusion in banking*. DIANE Publishing.

Friedline, T. (2020). *Banking on a revolution: Why financial technology won't save a broken system*. Oxford University Press.

Haddad, C., & Hornuf, L. (2019). The emergence of the global FinTech market: Economic and technological determinants. *Small Business Economics, 53*(1), 81–105.

International Monetary Fund (IMF). (2023). *Institutional arrangements for FinTech regulation: Supervisory monitoring*. (by Parma Bains & Caroline Wu), (Vol. 2023: Issue 004, p. 58).

McKinsey & Company. (2021). Lessons from the rapidly evolving regulation of digital banking (by Tarik Alatovic, Luís Cunha, Hernan Gerson, Elias Hajj, Joe Saade, & Giuseppe Siciliani).

Murinde, V., Rizopoulos, E., & Zachariadis, M. (2022). The impact of the FinTech revolution on the future of banking: Opportunities and risks. *International Review of Financial Analysis, 81*, 102103.

Puschmann, T. (2017). FinTech. *Business & Information Systems Engineering, 59*, 69–76.

Stefanelli, V., Ferilli, G. B., & Boscia, V. (2022). Exploring the lending business crowdfunding to support SMEs' financing decisions. *Journal of Innovation & Knowledge, 7*(4), 100278.

Tufano, P. (2003). Financial innovation. In G. M. Constantinides, M. Harris, & R. M. Stulz (Eds.), *Handbook of the economics of finance* (pp. 307–335). Elsevier.

World Bank Group (WBG). (2022). *FinTech and the future of finance overview paper. Finance, competitiveness, and innovation global practice*, World Bank Financial Institutions Group, International Finance Corporation.

World Economic Forum (WEF). (2015). The future of financial services: How disruptive innovations are reshaping the way financial services are structured, provisioned and consumed.

CHAPTER 4

Banking Business Models: Overview, Evolution, and Challenges for Worldwide Banks

Abstract This chapter provides an overview of the definition and classification techniques of banking business models (BBMs), focusing on the evolution processes in response to technological advancements, regulatory changes, and market dynamics that have characterized the banking sector. This chapter, using a sample of worldwide listed banks, identifies three distinct BBMs—retail banks, investment banks, and diversified asset banks—employing a clustering analysis. Additionally, it examines the evolution of BBMs from a traditional intermediary model to a more diversified one, shaped by the advent of FinTech firms and intensified competition in the banking industry, identifying threats and opportunities for enhanced banks' efficiency, innovation, and BBM's sustainability.

Keywords Banking business models · Cluster analysis · Bank · Banking industry · Digital transformation

G. B. Ferilli, *Bank-FinTech M&As and Banking Innovation*, Palgrave Macmillan Studies in Banking and Financial Institutions, https://doi.org/10.1007/978-3-031-84445-4_4

4.1 The Changing Role of Banks in the Financial System

Historically, banks have fulfilled traditional economic roles as liquidity providers, risk managers, and catalysts for financial innovation (Ayadi, 2019). Academic literature has extensively provided evidence of the bank's key role in addressing asymmetric information problems (Aghion & Bolton, 1997; Holmström & Tirole, 1997), mitigating adverse selection, and managing moral hazard issues (Berndt & Gupta, 2009). Banks effectively monitor investment projects that may lack sufficient transparency, offering clients liquidity assurance through deposit-taking activities. The financial intermediation theory emphasises banks' crucial role in directing savings towards borrowers and optimising capital allocation (Gurley & Shaw, 1955). This intermediary role is evidenced by activities such as lot size transformation, maturity adjustment, and risk mitigation, all of which contribute to enhancing the social value of capital within the financial system. The extant literature (Bhimjee et al., 2016) indicates that before the global financial crisis, banks assumed an active role in global financial markets, performing not only the core activities of lending and investment but also effectively participating in the interbank market and assuming short- and long-term liabilities.

Furthermore, banks have acted as insurance contract sellers and buyers for third-party risks and their own via credit derivatives contracts. This period witnessed significant growth and interconnection between banks and markets, redesigning traditional banking roles (Boot & Thakor, 2010). Factors such as increased competition in financial markets, the proliferation of non-bank financial institutions (NBFIs), and a wave of financial innovations have prompted banks to evolve from traditional intermediation approaches to embrace a *one-stop shop* model (Ayadi, 2019). This transaction period has been characterised by the expansion of banks' products and services to meet the challenges and needs of customers in an increasingly dynamic financial environment. Banks evolved to a ***universal banking model*** (Morrison, 2010; Walter, 2012), showing differentiated impacts on their risk-taking, performance, and efficiency metrics. In this regard, extensive literature (Stiroh, 2006; Stiroh & Rumble, 2006) has documented that while diversification can broaden the opportunities available for banks, the associated benefits may be outweighed by the costs resulting from heightened exposure to volatility. In this stream, Focarelli et al. (2011) show that securities underwritten by universal banks are riskier than those underwritten by specialised investment houses, while Baele et al. (2007) and Demirgüç-Kunt and Huizinga (2010) demonstrat how diversification may enhance market valuations, but also expand how banks hold much less capital and engage in riskier activities. Overall, diversification processes may undermine social welfare and financial stability.

In recent years, financial technology (or FinTech) has brought opportunities and risks in the banking industry, giving rise to reconfiguring processes of banks' core activities. According to BIS (2021), FinTech has significantly increased competitive pressure by directly engaging with customers. With their innovative business models, FinTech firms are pushing traditional banks towards digital transformation, altering customer relationships, and introducing user-friendly financial products. FinTech players leverage cutting-edge digital innovations to provide novel solutions that satisfy traditional financial needs, including payment processing, lending, and wealth management (Anagnostopoulos, 2018). Other operators are struggling to compete at scale through re-building processes. These financial technology solutions often offer improved accessibility and reduced fees than traditional banking services. Based on this evidence, starting a process of innovation becomes an essential requirement for banking business models. This process requires a re-definition of the bank's operational framework and investment strategy plan to safeguard competitiveness in the "new" banking environment.

In alignment with this perspective, Drasch et al. (2018) and Hornuf et al. (2021) provide evidence that banks are engaging in collaboration with FinTech entities, forming strategic partnerships (Le et al., 2024), or even pursuing the objective of leveraging the technological expertise and customer-centric approach of FinTech firms (Cappa et al., 2022; Collevecchio et al., 2024; Kwon et al. 2024). In addition to the advantages above, Elia et al. (2023) have indicated that FinTech firms have brought novel risks, prompting regulatory authorities to strike a balance between facilitating innovation facilitation and ensuring the stability and protection of the financial system.

Due to the new dynamics that have characterised the financial environment (i.e., competitive pressure, regulatory changes, and technological advancements), there is the need to periodically assess the adaptability of banking business models (BBMs) to the new market's dynamics. As remarket by literature (Ayadi et al. 2011, 2012; Palmieri et al., 2023), the business models' analysis (BMA) has become a crucial tool for the monitoring of the evolution of banking institutions, as data-driven methods are able to identify emerging risks and assess the impact of technological innovations on the financial industry. This monitoring activity has become particularly important following the FinTech firms' development and the consequently shift towards more diversified and integrated financial services. Thus, the assessment of BBMs facilitates the understanding of how banking institutions respond and adapt to environmental factors, manage and mitigate emerging risks, and pursue objectives of profitability and efficiency.

4.2 Banking Business Models: Definition and Identification

Definitions of Banking Business Model

According to EBA (2022), the term Bank Business Model (BBM) is often utilised in the academic literature and supervisory community; nevertheless, defining what constitutes a model and differentiates it from others can be challenging. As BIS (2014) highlighted, *"Banks choose to be different from one another"* by engaging in strategic intermediation activities and selecting their balance sheet structure to align with business objectives. Consequently, in competitive pursuit of growth opportunities, *"banks choose a business model that capitalises on their organisation's strengths"*. As the integration of this primary definition, scholars such as Martín-Oliver et al. (2017) have defined BBM as *"the result of banks' decisions on the sources and uses of funds, which are reflected in the composition of the assets and liabilities of their respective balance sheets"*.

Beyond this general understanding of the BBM, there is no consensus on the definition of the business model (BM) itself and on which characteristics are most relevant in assigning a bank to a business model. Scholars have also demonstrated how this definition has evolved considerably within economic literature, gaining significant emphasis after the Global Financial Crisis (GFC) (Altunbas et al., 2011; Hryckiewicz & Kozłowski, 2017) and subsequent regulatory changes (Liikanen et al., 2012). Regulators have acknowledged their insufficient and unreliable knowledge of banks' activities, hindering precise assessment of risks and timely response to problems in the banking sector during the crisis. In response to the new regulatory context, banks adapted their business strategies and balance sheet structures to comply with the new rules while focusing on recovering profitability (Ayadi et al., 2011). This awareness and a primary shift from traditional banking activities to more diversified and complex financial strategies have refined the BM concept and analysis. The business model analysis goes beyond the traditional classification of banks based on their ownership structure (e.g., commercial, savings, and cooperatives), including for the European banks, the annual Supervisory Review and Evaluation Process (SREP) as a signal that it is a top supervisory priority.

Banks are initially identified by their role in financial intermediation, mainly focusing on collecting deposits from the public and granting loans (Freixas & Rochet, 1997). The conventional notion has been disputed by the diverse banking activities and funding procedures that emerged during the financial crisis (Ayadi, 2017). Banks expanded beyond their conventional roles, engaging in market and wholesale funding and investing in various financial instruments, including equities and structured financial products. This diversification represented not only a shift in operational activities but was also reflected in banks' sources of income, marking a transition from traditional intermediation to broader financial market activities. Therefore, the complexity and interconnection of banks increased considerably, with banks becoming more closely linked to capital market performance mutually interlinked with one another.

Furthermore, the products offered by banks have become increasingly complex (Boot & Thakor, 2010; Song & Thakor, 2010). In some instances, the size of banks even exceeded the GDP of the countries where they operated (Hryckiewicz & Kozłowski, 2017). Furthermore, there was a lack of clarity regarding the level of risk assumed by the banking institutions. Thus, in response to these challenges, regulators and supervisory authorities started to require more detailed classifications and analyses of bank activities (BIS, 2014; EBA, 2018).

In order to define and differentiate BBMs, academics and banking supervisory authorities have used three main methodological approaches. The first approach involves the application of quantitative techniques based on the implementation of comparative analysis of bank balance sheet data (e.g., Blundell-Wignall et al., 2012; Hryckiewicz & Kozłowski, 2017) or clustering techniques (Ayadi et al., 2014, 2023; Cernov & Urbano, 2018; Farnè and Vouldis, 2017; Lagasio & Quaranta, 2022).

The second approach involves using qualitative methods and has been implemented only by the EBA (2014, 2015, 2016). This method employs a pre-defined business model classification system based on the activities, funding sources, and legal structure of the banks in question. The banks are then allocated to each of these categories based on the informed opinion of a panel of experts.

The third approach is hybrid. It combines both quantitative and qualitative methods to provide a more detailed classification (Cernov & Urbano, 2018). This approach incorporates both quantifiable data, such as financial metrics, and non-quantifiable factors, including legal structure and ownership. This enables the capture of the distinctive characteristics of the banking sector in each country, thus facilitating a more accurate distinction between diversified and specialised business models. Furthermore, this classification method can serve as a standardised framework for analysing institutions, thereby enabling the identification of trends, risks, and regulatory impacts in a broader context.

However, scholars have implemented mainly quantitative methods identifying different business models ranging from traditional retail banking to investment and wholesale banking models (Ayadi et al., 2012; Martín-Oliver et al., 2017; Roengpitya et al., 2017). Researchers have highlighted those banks combining traditional activities with non-interest sources of income, like securities and insurance activities, tend to increase individual and systemic risk (Allen & Jagtiani, 2000). Furthermore, the expansion into trading activities, while profitable in favourable economic conditions, exposes banks to greater risks during downturns (Diamond & Rajan, 2011; Shleifer & Vishny, 2011).

Subsequent research has focused on identifying and assessing bank business models, particularly their contribution to systemic risk and financial stability (Altunbas et al., 2011; Aneta Hryckiewicz & Kozłowski, 2017). This approach has included examining the impact of bank business model choices on their profitability, net interest margin, and default risk (Köhler, 2015; Mergaerts & Vander Vennet, 2016).

In recent years, BBM analysis has become a priority for policymakers and regulators, moving beyond traditional classifications based on ownership structure. This evolution in BBMs reflects the dynamic nature of the banking sector, influenced by regulatory, monetary, and structural reforms. Banks continue to adapt their business models to these changing environments, seeking to balance profitability with risk management (Ayadi et al., 2021).

Identification of Banking Business Model

The existing literature on BBMs is largely based on the assumption that business models are defined in terms of the activities that a firm (or bank) undertakes (Parmigiani & Mitchell, 2009; Saebi & Foss, 2015; Zott et al., 2011). In this broader field of study, as previously mentioned, some scholars and banking supervisory authorities have proposed different approaches to classifying BBM based on their managerial and financial characteristics. These methodologies can be discerned into three primary categories, which utilise quantitative (Ayadi et al., 2014; Farnè & Vouldis, 2017; Lagasio & Quaranta, 2022), qualitative (EBA, 2014, 2015, 2016), or hybrid approaches (EBA, 2018).

Quantitative Methods

Among the categories mentioned above, quantitative methods are the most prevalent. These employ data-driven techniques to identify categories of BMs based on the analysis of the structure of banks' balance sheets. Some scholars utilise balance sheet ratios as indicators of the bank's strategic management choices to perform hierarchical clustering.

In this regard, the literature discloses different quantitative methods used to identify BBMs. For example, Mergaerts and Vennet (2015) used a factor analysis model to identify two distinct BMs (i.e., retail and diversification banks) in a sample of 500 European banks. Consequently, they investigated the impact of these BMs on different banks' performance indicators. Ferstl and Seres (2012) used a k-centroids clustering method based on the "*Mahalanobis distance*" to identify the business models of 234 Australian banks. The method focused on identifying the sources of net income and the structure of loans, following the methodologies developed by Everitt et al. (2011). Besides these approaches, some scholars (Ayadi et al., 2014; Cernov & Urbano, 2018; Farnè & Vouldis, 2021; Lagasio & Quaranta, 2022), following the consolidated data-driven methodologies applied by BIS (2014) and ECB (2016), have implemented clustering algorithmics to classify a sample of banks according to similarity in the structure of bank financial statements.

As evidenced by a review of the literature, these methodologies, which are central to understanding banks' strategic adaptations to market and regulatory changes, have demonstrated a notable progression in their complexity and applicability over time. Ayadi et al., (2011, 2012) made the first effort in the field to explore which variables are relevant to defining a bank's BM. Ayadi offers preliminary evidence on the importance of business model analysis (BMA) for banking regulation and supervision and also highlights the need to monitor BBMs over time. Then, Ayadi and De Groen (2014) introduce the asset-liability approach and use a hierarchical clustering algorithm based on Ward's (1963) method to identify groups of banks with similar balance sheet characteristics. Ward's method is still widely used in recent literature; for example, Palmieri et al. (2024) applied this technique to a sample of 639 European banks to investigate the joint effect of BBMs and banks' ESG pillars performance on credit institutions riskiness profile. At the same time, Ayadi et al. (2023) examine the relationship between BBMs and cooperative banks' cost and profit efficiency from 15 European countries from 2010 to 2020.

As exhibited in Table 4.1, the temporal progression of clustering techniques evinces a growing sophistication in identifying bank BMs. The evolution of clustering techniques in banking has moved from an initial reliance on fundamental financial ratios to a more comprehensive approach that assesses a broader range of financial indicators. This trend reflects the dynamic nature of the banking sector itself. Concerning the table above, scholars have initially focused on a restricted number of large European banks. This approach has gradually expanded, encompassing thousands of banks worldwide. The expansion is evident not only in terms of size but also in terms of geographic scope. This shift emphasises the increasing recognition of the necessity to understand banking business models within a diversified and global context while acknowledging the differing regulatory and market environments under which banks operate. More recent studies have shown a trend towards reducing the number of variables, suggesting a possible refinement of methodologies and a better understanding of the key indicators that define different business models.

Conversely, the complexity and diversity of these models have increased markedly, and business models' categorisation has become more sophisticated. Earlier studies only distinguished fundamental types, such as retail and investment banks. In contrast, subsequent research has introduced more intricate classifications (e.g., *Fee-focused banks* and *International diversified lenders* according to Nucera et al. [2017], *Securities holding banks* and *Complex commercial banks* according to Farnè and Vouldis [2017], and *Real Estate and Mortgage Banking* according to Lagasio and Quaranta [2022]). These findings illustrate an emerging awareness of the specialisation activities within the banking industry.

Table 4.1 Reference literature on bank business model identifications with a clustering methodology

Author(s)	*Sample*	*Period*	*Variables/Indicators*	*Business Models*
Ayadi et al. (2011)	26 large European banks	2006–2009	6 variables/indicators • Customer deposit/Total Assets (TA) • Trading assets/TA • Loans to banks/TA • Total derivative exposures/TA • Tangible common equity/TA • Domestic activity/TA	3 BMs • *Retail banks* • *Investment banks* • *Wholesale banks*
Ayadi and Groen (2014)	147 large banks of the European Economic Area	2006–2013	6 variables/indicators • Loans to banks/TA • Trading assets/TA • Bank liabilities/TA • Customer deposit/TA • Debt liabilities/TA • Derivative exposure/TA	4 BMs • *Investment banks* • *Diversified retail* • *Focused retail banks* • *Wholesale banks*
Ayadi and Groen (2015)	2542 European banks	2005–2014	5 variables/indicators • Loans to banks/TA • Trading assets/TA • Customer deposit/TA • Debt liabilities/TA • Derivative exposure/TA	5 BMs • *Investment banks* • *Wholesale banks* • *Focused retail banks* • *Diversified retail banks—type 1* • *Diversified retail banks—type 2*

(continued)

Table 4.1 (continued)

Author(s)	*Sample*	*Period*	*Variables/Indicators*	*Business Models*
Hryckiewicz and Kozlowski (2017)	458 Large banks from 65 countries	2000–2012	7 variables/indicators • Loans to entities other than banks/Total earning assets (TEA) • Loans and advances to banks/TEA • Securities/TEA • Other earning assets/ TEA • Deposits and short-term funding to sum of interest- and non-interest-bearing liabilities • Other interest-bearing liabilities to sum of interest- and non-interest-bearing liabilities • Non-interest-bearing liabilities to the sum of interest- and non-interest-bearing liabilities	4 BMs • *Investment banks* • *Trader banks* • *Specialised banks* • *Diversified banks*

Author(s)	*Sample*	*Period*	*Variables/Indicators*	*Business Models*
Farnè and Vouldis (2017)	365 SSM Euro Area banks	Last quarter of 2014	1039 variables/indicators	4 BMs • *Wholesale-funded banks* • *Securities holding banks* • *Traditional commercial banks* • *Complex commercial banks*
Nucera et al. (2017)	208 European banks	2012Q2 to 2014Q2	13 variables/indicators • TA • Leverage • Net loans/TA • Risk mix • Assets held for trading; derivatives held for trading • Net interest income • Net fees & commissions income • Trading income • Retail loans on total loans • Domestic loans on total loans • Loans to deposits ratio	6 BMs • *Large universal banks* • *Fee-focused banks* • *Domestic diversified lenders* • *International diversified lenders* • *Domestic retail lenders, Small international banks*

(continued)

Table 4.1 (continued)

Author(s)	*Sample*	*Period*	*Variables/Indicators*	*Business Models*
Roengpitya et al. (2017)	178 European banks	2005–2015	8 variables/indicators • Loans/TA • Trading book/TA • Trading assets/TA • Interbank lending/TA • Interbank borrowing/TA • Deposits/TA • Wholesale f./TA • Stable funding ratio	4 BMs • *Retail-funded banks* • *Wholesale-funded banks* • *Trading-oriented banks*
Martín-Oliver et al. (2017)	Shareholders Banks and Cajas in Spain	1999–2007	6 variables/indicators • Equity/TA • Loans/TA • Loans/Deposits • Net interbank/TA • Bank loans/TA • Securities/TA	4 BMs • *Retail-deposits banks* • *Retail-balanced banks* • *Retail diversified banks* • *Retail-market banks*
Lagasio and Quaranta (2022)	1237 Worldwide banks	2011–2017	7 variables/indicators • Loans to banks/TA • Loans to Customers/TA • Trading assets/TA • Deposit from Customers/TA • Net interest income/Operating income (OI) • Net fee and commission income/OI • Net trading income/OI	5 BMs • *Traditional Banking* • *Financial Banking Oriented* • *Retail Banking* • *Private Banking* • *Real Estate and Mortgage Banking*

Author(s)	*Sample*	*Period*	*Variables/Indicators*	*Business Models*
Palmieri et al. (2023)	60 European banks	2000–2020	5 variables/indicators • Loans to banks • Trading activities • Exposure to derivatives • Customer loans/deposits • Liquidity	4 BMs • *Retail banks* • *Banks with diversified liabilities* • *Banks with diversified assets* • *Investment and wealth management banks*
Ayadi et al. (2023)	3480 of 31 European countries	2010–2020	5 variables/indicators • Loans to customers/ Loans over TA • Loans to banks/TA • Trading assets/TA • Debt liabilities/TA • Derivatives exposure/TA	5 BMs • *Focused retail banks* • *Diversified retail banks—type 1* • *Diversified retail banks—type 2* • *Wholesale banks* • *Investment banks*
Palmieri et al. (2024)	639 European banks	2013–2022	4 variables/indicators • Deposits/TA • Interbank assets/TA • Loans/TA • Derivatives/TA • Trading assets/TA	4 BMs • *Retail banks* • *Diversified assets banks* • *Investments banks* • *Wholesale banks*

Note The table provides a comprehensive overview of the scholars who have employed cluster analysis to identify banking business models. The table lists 12 studies, details on the authors, sample sizes, periods, balance sheet variables/indicators used, and the resulting business models (BMs) identified. *Source* Author's elaboration

Qualitative Methods
The qualitative method enables a more detailed distinction between highly specialised business models. However, it requires expert knowledge, which is mainly applicable to banking supervisory authorities, such as the EBA (2014, 2015, 2016).

The EBA's method primarily focuses on assessing the effects of different liquidity and leverage ratios on banks. Banks are categorised based on supervisors' judgement, who use their extensive expertise and comprehension of each bank's operations and strategies. This method involves collecting data from many banks, with the sample size varying annually, to ensure comprehensive coverage. A qualitative approach, therefore, provides a detailed understanding of specific business models and considers the specificities of national financial sectors.

Hybrid Methods
The third category comprises the hybrid approach, which was initially introduced by banking supervisory authorities (such as the EBA) or international organisations (such as the BIS) and later adopted by scholars such as Cernov and Urbano (2018). This approach uses both qualitative and quantitative methods to classify banks into different BMs. Banks are initially categorised based on qualitative assessments involving expert judgement to recognise the complexities and specificities of different banking models, particularly national financial sectors. This BM categorisation considers various aspects such as funding mix, trading activities, and balance sheet composition. Consequently, these qualitative classifications are rigorously validated against quantitative indicators. This two-step process combines objective data analysis with subjective judgement to provide a more nuanced understanding of each bank's business model, such as retail-focused commercial banks, wholesale-focused banks, commercial banks, and capital market-focused banks, reflecting their key operational characteristics.

Dataset and Sample Selection

This section aims to identify and analyse the types of banking business models (BBMs) that characterised our sample following a data-driven approach. In order to achieve this goal, we employ cluster analysis, recalling many technical aspects of the procedure previously applied by Ayadi and Groen (2015) and the EBA (2018).

Our final sample comprises 170 worldwide listed banks observed during the period ranging from 1997 to 2022. The primary condition for the sample extraction from *BankFocus* is that the bank has performed at least a deal. We include the deals with investment types classified as "*Acquisition*", "*Buyback*", and "*Merger*". The use of listed banks ensures access to standardised and publicly available data, which is critical for the reliability and consistency of the analysis. The extended observation period is particularly significant. The time frame covers critical phases in the evolution of the banking sector, characterised by technological advances (Berger, 2003), evolving regulatory backgrounds, and significant M&A activity (Fiordelisi, 2015). Additionally, adopting a global perspective is essential to build a dataset that is representative of the global banking industry and capture the dynamics that have been affected by BBMs evolution, reflecting the interconnectivity and heterogeneity in the financial industry.

For the sample selection, we apply continuity filters focusing on data availability and consistency throughout the large observation period. Then, we select only banks for which the necessary balance sheet variables are available to run the clustering algorithm. This step is crucial to ensure the integrity of our data, especially given the longitudinal nature of our analysis. Finally, we restrict the initial sample to banks that have performed deals in FinTech firms. In order to establish the nature of the firms involved in the deal operation, the filters "*Target Industry*" and "*Target Short Business Description*" are applied. The focus is on those firms that are coherent with financial technology firms. Finally, we manually check that each "*Target Name*" is a FinTech firm consulting the firm's website. The final sample covers 170 worldwide listed banks. Figure 4.1 exhibits the geographic distribution of the study sample.

The initial dataset extracted from *BankFocus* covers only information about the acquiring banks, including their name, short business description, state, nation, deal number, and announcement date, as well as information about the target firm (i.e., name, short business description, industry, state, and nation). To extend the dataset, we added balance sheet information for each bank using the *Refinitiv Datastream* and *Bloomberg* databases, while macroeconomic variables were collected from the *World Bank* database.

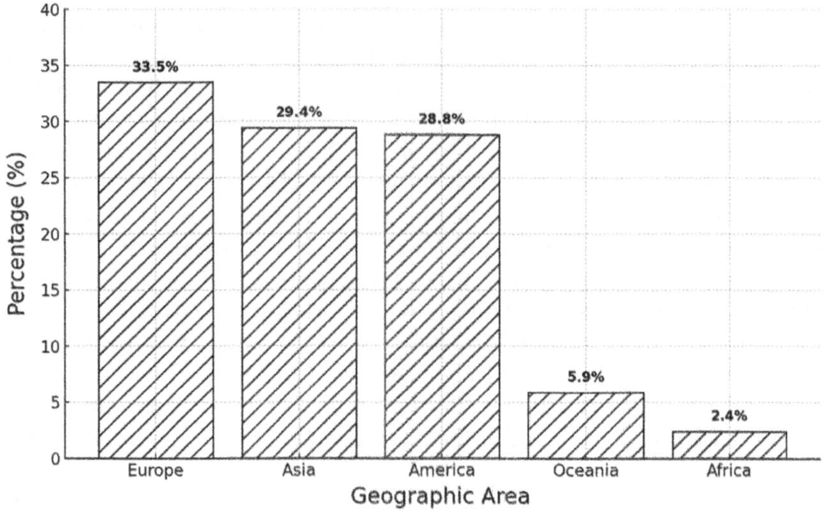

Fig. 4.1 Sample geographical distribution (in percentage values) (*Note* The figure presents the study sample's geographic distribution, detailing each geographic area percentage representation. Europe accounts for 33.5% of the sample, followed by Asia at 29.4%, the Americas with 28.8%, Oceania with 5.9% and Africa with 2.4%. *Source* Author's elaboration)

Clustering Methodology

To identify the BBMs that characterise our sample, we perform a cluster analysis. This is currently one of the most used grouping methods in economic research (Ayadi et al., 2021; Palmieri et al., 2023). Among the different cluster techniques, we adopt the statistical classification algorithm proposed by Ward (1963), which has been demonstrated to perform better than other clustering procedures for variables that involve few outliers and in the presence of overlap (Milligan, 1981).

Ward's algorithm employs a hierarchical classification approach suitable for analysing sets of distinct bank-year observations. Each observation is quantified using a set of metrics, such as balance sheet ratios. The algorithm runs as an agglomerative method, starting with individual observations and gradually creating clusters by combining those with similar metrics. It incrementally creates larger clusters, thereby coarsely partitioning the entire set of observations. The process maximises similarity within each cluster while increasing the disparity between different clusters. The distance between any two observations is quantified by calculating the sum of the squared differences in their metrics, also known as Euclidean distance (Thant et al., 2020). The Euclidean distance is one of the most used metrics for measuring the "straight-line" distance between two points in a multidimensional space. According to our study, each sampled bank can be expressed as a point in the space where each dimension corresponds to one of the balance sheet ratios. Thus, the Euclidean distance between two banks, *i* and *j*, is expressed by the following formula:

$$d(i,j) = \sqrt{\sum_{k=1}^{n} (x_{ik} - x_{kj})^2}$$

where $d(i,j)$ is the Euclidean distance between bank *i* and bank *j*, x_{ik} and x_{kj} are the values of the *k-th* variable for the bank *i* and *j*, respectively, while *n* represents the total number of variables (in our case, the six balance sheet ratios).

In the clustering process, this Euclidean distance serves as the foundation for grouping banks into clusters. Banks with similar financial profiles will have smaller Euclidean distances and are, therefore, grouped by the algorithm. Conversely, banks with more dissimilar profiles will have larger distances and will belong to different clusters. The goal of the clustering algorithm is to minimise the distances within clusters while maximising the distances between clusters, ensuring that each cluster represents a distinct business model (BM).

Based on these assumptions, we perform a cluster analysis, firstly identifying the bank characteristics using some balance sheet ratios that, according to BIS (2014), are indicators of strategic management bank choices. We choose balance sheet ratios as clustering variables, assuming that banks have complete control over these dimensions.

In line with Ayadi and De Groen (2014) and Palmieri et al. (2023), we apply an asset-liability approach, using six (6) different bank ratios which are able to build a valuable dataset for business models' cluster analysis (Table 4.2). Each selected variable reflects a critical aspect of a bank's financial structure and strategy, providing insights into its business model. To ensure the accuracy of the metrics, all variables are expressed as a share of total assets (TA), thus avoiding any distortion due to differences in accounting standards across jurisdictions (BIS, 2014).

The clustering variables used are the following:

a. ***Equity over Total Assets (ETA)*** is a measure of the ability of a banking institution to absorb risk, and it is related to the capital that the institution has at its disposal. This ratio represents the proportion of a bank's assets financed through shareholders' equity instead of debt. The ETA may be utilised to ascertain the bank's methodology for enhancing risk management.
b. ***Loans over Total Assets (LOAN_TA)*** measures a banking institution's lending intensity. This ratio indicates the proportion of a bank's assets that are allocated to loan disbursements, thereby highlighting the bank's focus on traditional banking activities as opposed to other financial operations;
c. ***Trading Activities over Total Assets (TRADE_TA)*** represent the bank's engagement in market-based financial activities. This ratio helps to measure the bank's participation in securities trading and investment activities. These activities are important for banks that aim to diversify their operations beyond conventional retail banking;
d. ***Derivatives over Total Assets (DER_TA),*** which is a measure of a bank's involvement in complex financial instruments. This ratio indicates the bank's exposure to hedging, speculation, and risk management. It is a crucial element in evaluating the bank's risk profile and propensity for innovation;
e. ***Interbank Loans over Total Assets (INTB_TA),*** which is expressed as the bank's lending and borrowing activities with other banks, is an important indicator of the bank's role within a broader financial network and the strategies it employs for liquidity management;
f. ***Deposit over Total Assets (DEP_TA)*** is a proxy for the extent to which a banking institution relies on traditional deposit-taking activities. This ratio indicates the degree to which a bank relies on customer deposits to finance its assets, thereby highlighting its capacity to attract short-term customer funding.

The clustering methodology assumes that banks with similar BM exhibit comparable patterns in the composition of their assets and liabilities as a percentage of total assets (TA). The approach is data-driven and

Table 4.2 Clustering variables used in the reference literature

Reference	*Clustering Variables*					
	Equity (%TA)	*Loans (%TA)*	*Trading activities (%TA)*	*Derivatives (%TA)*	*Interbank loans (%TA)*	*Deposit (%TA)*
Ayadi et al. (2011)	✔	✔	✔	✔		✔
Ayadi and Groen (2014)		✔	✔	✔		✔
Martín-Oliver et al. (2017)	✔	✔			✔	
Roengpitya et al. (2017)		✔			✔	
Palmieri et al. (2023)		✔	✔	✔	✔	✔

Note The table presents the clustering variables most frequently employed in the existing literature. The studies included in this table employ clustering techniques that align with the technical standards outlined in this study
Source Author's elaboration

does not assume the relative significance of specific choice variables in defining BMs. The observations are divided into distinct BM categories through iterative applications of the clustering algorithm. This process identifies a limited number of distinct BM groups without biases.

Clustering Robustness Checks

To ensure that our methodology has identified the correct number of clusters, we have applied the methods of Silhouettes (Rousseeuw, 1987), Gap Statistic (El-Mandouh et al., 2019), and Elbow (Bholowalia & Kumar, 2014) jointly.

These tests serve as robustness checks to identify the optimal number of clusters (k*) for our bank sample (Hardy, 1996). Figure 4.2 displays the graphical results of these techniques, identifying the ideal number of clusters at the first elbow of the split. We have repeated the clustering process and the three tests for each year of observation. This approach allows us to determine that for approximately 96% of the clustering sets, the optimal number of business models (k*) is three.

Clustering Analysis Results: Banking Business Models Identification

The methodology applied and the robustness checks performed document the presence of the following bank business models (BBMs):

- ***Retail banks (BM1)*** are characterised by a predominance of customer loans in their portfolio of activities; in fact, these intermediaries rely primarily on customer deposits for their funding. Retail banks strike a balance between achieving satisfactory performance and minimising risk within the financial system. They are characterised by high levels of loss-absorbing capital, underlining their commitment to safeguard financial stability and improve customer trust.
- ***Investment banks (BM2)*** are characterised by their substantial involvement in securities and derivatives. Their revenue streams are primarily commission-based, deriving from investment activities for clients and their accounts. These banks strongly tend to engage in investment-related activities, with significant trading assets and derivatives activities. In addition, these banks have a lower propensity to engage in interbank lending and tend to be more leveraged.

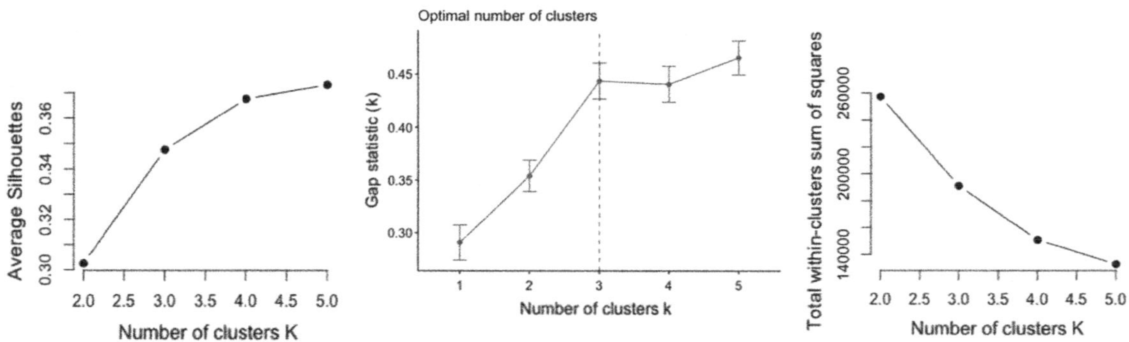

Fig. 4.2 Graphical representation of the techniques used to identify the ideal number (k*) of clusters (*Note* The figure exhibits the results obtained for the robustness checks implemented, respectively, the Silhouettes, the Gap Statistic, and the Elbow methods. *Source* Author's elaboration)

- ***Diversified assets banks (BM3)*** are characterised by a broad asset portfolio that goes beyond traditional banking activities to include a variety of financial instruments such as equities, bonds, liquid assets, and derivatives. Their asset mix avoids heavy concentration in any asset class, providing a balanced approach. Figure 4.3 offers a graphical representation of the three business models identified.

For a more detailed assessment of the BMs identified, Table 4.3 presents a characterisation of the three business models, described in terms of six different selection variables (i.e., rows). For each business model category (i.e., columns), the table shows the average ratio calculated across all banks belonging to a specific business model (i.e., BM1, BM2, and BM3).

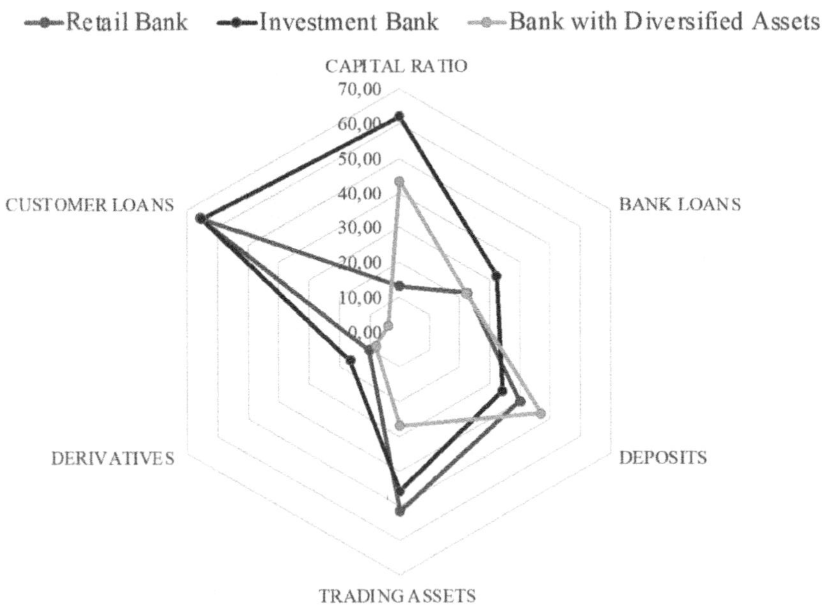

Fig. 4.3 Bank Business Models and Clustering Variables Statistics (*Note* The figure exhibits the indicators employed in cluster analysis to describe bank structure. As illustrated, three distinct business models have been identified: Retail, Investment, and Diversified Assets. *Source* Author's elaboration)

Table 4.3 Business models profiles

Selected Variables	*Retail banks (BM1)*	*Investment banks (BM2)*	*Diversified assets banks (BM3)*
Equity (%TA)	18.22	59.69	38.51
Loans (%TA)	62.88	64.25	18.24
Trading Activities (%TA)	47.61	52.57	27.39
Derivatives (%TA)	10.00	17.75	8.96
Interbank loans (%TA)	22.99	32.26	22.68
Deposit (%TA)	40.17	31.40	42.07

Note The table presents the average values of balance sheet ratios as a percentage of total assets (TA) used for cluster analysis
Source Authors' calculations

The first BM, named *"Retail banks"*, is characterised by a balance sheet ratio profile that reflects a business model focused on traditional banking services. With an *Equity* to TA ratio of 18.22%, these banks have a conservative equity position, typical of institutions that prioritise lower-risk retail banking activities such as deposit taking and personal lending. This is further evidenced by their *Loans* to TA ratio of 62.88%, which indicates that a significant part of the bank assets is dedicated to loan disbursements. Retail banks also engage in trading activities, as evidenced by their *Trading Activities* to TA ratio of 47.61%, although this is not their primary scope. *Derivatives*, often used by these banks for hedging purposes, account for 10.00% of their TA, which aligns with the needs of a typical retail bank. The ratio of *Interbank Loans* to TA, at 22.99%, and the ratio of deposits to TA, at 40.17%, further underline the focus of retail banking on stable deposit collection and interbank borrowing for liquidity management.

The second BM label, *"Investment banks"*, has a significantly different set of balance sheet characteristics, reflecting the high risk and high reward of this business model type. Their equity to TA ratio is significantly higher at 59.69%, reflecting the need for a substantial equity base to buffer the risks associated with investment banking activities, such as securities trading and corporate finance. The ratio of *Loans to TA* characterises this BM as high (64.25%), indicating extensive involvement in large-scale lending activities. A noteworthy aspect of investment banks is their high involvement in trading activities, with a *Trading to TA* ratio of 52.57%, underlining their core focus on securities and financial markets. Their involvement in complex financial instruments is reflected in the derivatives ratio of 17.75%. In addition, the higher *Interbank Loans to TA* ratio of 32.26% indicates a reliance on interbank markets to fund trading activities. The *Deposit-to-TA* ratio of 31.40% is less than that of retail banks, reflecting the lesser significance attributed to deposit collection in this business model. Finally, the third BM identified the *"Diversified assets banks"* as a combination of retail and investment banking characteristics. Their *Equity to TA* ratio of 38.51% strikes a middle ground, reflecting a diversified risk profile. Their *Loans to TA* ratio of 18.24% is relatively lower than that of both Retail and Investment banks, suggesting a more diversified asset portfolio. Their exposure to *Trading Activities*, at 27.39% of TA, is significant but lower than that of pure investment banks, indicating a balanced approach by these credit institutions. *Derivatives* are used at 8.96% of TA, but not as much as investment banks. The ratio of *Interbank loans* to TA, at 22.68%, and *Deposits* to TA, at 42.07%, also reflect this balance, showing mixed funding and deposit-raising strategies typical of banks with a diverse asset base. A graphical representation of the statistical summary of BBM typologies identified is exhibited in Fig. 4.4.

Table 4.4 presents the distribution of our sample across identified business models during the time frame of interest (1997–2022). Each row represents a single year of observation, while the columns denote the three business model categories (i.e., BM1, BM2, and BM3). The table displays the average ratio of banks classified under each BM category, enabling a year-by-year comparison of how banks are distributed across the three business models. This representation highlights trends and shifts in the banking sector's strategic orientations. More in detail, the table shows that in 1997, *Retail banks (BM1)* accounted for 58.82% of the sample. However, over the years, their share declined to 28.82% by 2020, while *Diversified Assets banks (BM3)* saw an increase, reaching 38.82% in the same year. This shift indicates a growing trend towards diversification in banking activities.

Additionally, looking at *Investment banks (BM2),* we observe that this BM reached a peak of 49.41% in 2015. The period from 2015 to 2022 is characterised by a strong transition towards BM2 and BM3 in the banking industry. This outcome reflects changes in the financial market (BIS, 2006), regulatory shifts (BIS, 2015), and several technological progress which have strongly impacted the banking industry (BIS, 2021). Data exhibited in the table indicates a notable shift in the

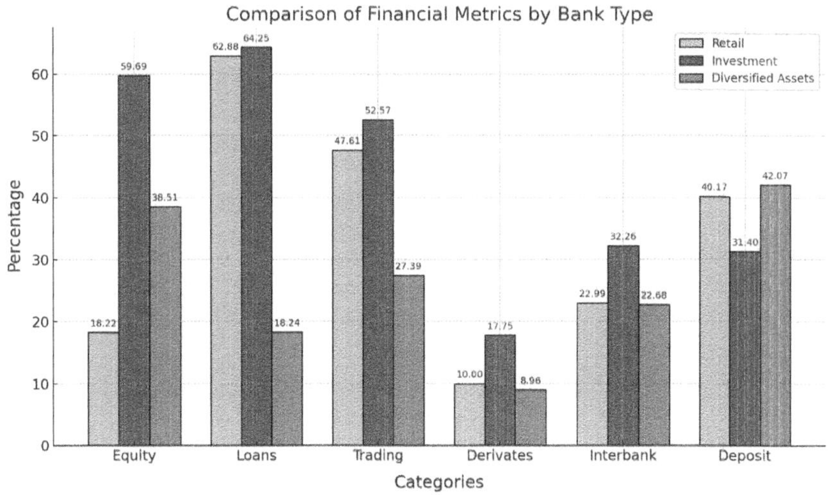

Fig. 4.4 Statistical summary of Business Model (BM) typologies based on the selected clustering variables (*Note* The figure exhibits a statistical distribution of the three BMs identified according to the main clustering selected variables (i.e., Equity (%TA); Loans (%TA); Trading Activities (%TA); Derivatives (%TA); Interbank loans (%TA); Deposit (%TA). *Source* Authors' calculations)

banking industry towards diversified and investment-oriented strategies, which can be interpreted as a strategic response to the evolving financial environment.

Figure 4.5 illustrates the evolution of banking business models over time, employing a stacked area chart. This visual representation emphasises the evolving prevalence of Retail, Investment, and Diversified assets banks, with each model represented by a distinct shade of grey. The chart enables a clear comparison of trends, demonstrating model adoption shifts and each model's relative dominance by year.

4.3 Banking Business Models in the Digital Era

The advent of FinTech and the regulatory push for open banking (OP) practices have emerged as drivers of the *Digital Era*, giving rise to challenges for traditional banking models (Elliehausen & Hannon, 2023).

Table 4.4 Distribution of banks across identified Business Models (BMs)

	Type of Business Model					
	BM1		*BM2*		*BM3*	
Year of Observation	*No*	%	*No*	%	*No*	%
1997	100	*58. 82*	46	*27.06*	24	*14.12*
1998	73	*42.94*	60	*35.29*	37	*21.76*
1999	78	*45.88*	51	*30.00*	41	*24.12*
2000	94	*55.29*	52	*30.59*	24	*14.12*
2001	72	*42.35*	53	*31.18*	45	*26.47*
2002	74	*43.53*	67	*39.41*	29	*17.06*
2003	76	*44.71*	63	*37.06*	31	*18.24*
2004	64	*37.65*	55	*32.35*	51	*30.00*
2005	75	*44.12*	63	*37.06*	32	*18.82*
2006	75	*44.12*	63	*37.06*	32	*18.82*
2007	72	*42.35*	61	*35.88*	37	*21.77*
2008	71	*41.76*	74	*43.53*	25	*14.71*
2009	79	*46.47*	60	*35.29*	31	*18.24*
2010	75	*44.12*	47	*27.65*	48	*28.24*
2011	82	*48.24*	54	*31.76*	34	*20.00*
2012	69	*40.59*	59	*34.71*	42	*24.71*
2013	68	*40.00*	67	*39.41*	35	*20.59*
2014	69	*40.59*	69	*40.59*	32	*18.82*
2015	59	*34.71*	84	*49.41*	27	*15.88*
2016	59	*34.71*	51	*30.00*	60	*35.29*
2017	60	*35.29*	64	*37.65*	46	*27.06*
2018	69	*40.59*	58	*34.12*	43	*25.29*
2019	54	*31.76*	64	*37.65*	52	*30.59*
2020	49	*28.82*	55	*32.35*	66	*38.83*
2021	62	*36.47*	72	*42.35*	36	*21.18*
2022	65	*38.46*	70	*41.42*	35	*20.71*

Note The table provides a distribution of business models (BMs) adopted for the specified years of interest. BM1 refer to a ***Retail bank***, BM2 refer to an ***Investment bank***, and BM3 refer to a ***Diversified Assets bank***. The numbers expressed in italics represent the percentages of each type of bank in the sample per year
Source Authors' calculations

Among the new challenges facing the banking sector, the literature identifies increased competition, changing consumer expectations, heightened security risks, and the complexities of regulatory compliance as the most important threats (Ramdani et al., 2020; Saebi et al., 2017). In order

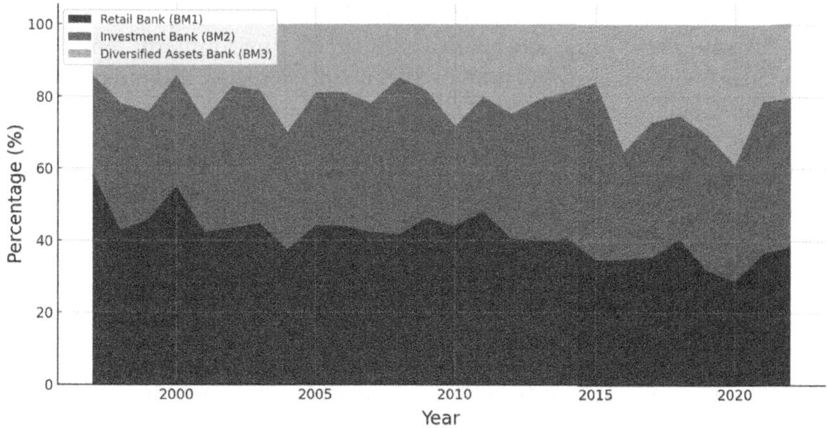

Fig. 4.5 Distribution of Banking Business Model over time (Stacked Area Chart) (*Note* The figure shows the evolution of business model distributions (Retail Bank, Investment Bank, and Diversified Assets Bank) over time, with each model represented by a different shade of grey. The cumulative percentages across years make it easy to see trends in adopting different business models and the dominance of any model in each year. *Source* Author's elaboration)

to maintain competitiveness in this context, traditional banking institutions must overcome these challenges through innovative adaptation and a proactive approach to the digital transformation process.

Threats to the Banking Sector

The advent of new financial players, the use of new technologies, and the development of digital finance have brought several challenges to the banking sector (Tanda & Schena, 2019). These disruptive processes have initiated a shift in consumer expectations and altered market operators' competitive dynamics, compelling incumbent banks to reassess and innovate their operational frameworks in order to remain viable and competitive. Several regulatory challenges and compliance requirements have emerged (Murinde et al., 2022), including the adoption of the Payment Service Providers Directive (PSD) in 2007 and PSD2 in 2015 by the European Parliament, in addition to the introduction of General Data Protection (GDPR) in 2018 and open banking principles by the UK

Competition and Markets Authority (CMA). These developments have significantly altered the competitive financial environment, enhancing competitiveness and innovation in the financial sector (Ramdani et al., 2020; Stefanelli & Manta, 2022).

In this rapidly evolving financial environment, traditional banking institutions face significant threats posed by the spread of FinTech operators (BIS, 2021). These players utilise advanced technology to provide financial services that are more efficient, user-friendly, and cost-effective. Saebi et al. (2017) posit that FinTech companies directly address conventional banks' limitations and inefficiencies to innovate and streamline their service offerings. From this perspective, FinTech companies provide innovative and advanced solutions that traditional banks often find difficult to match and integrate into their business models. This presents a challenge to the retention of bank customers, which may result in revenue loss for traditional financial institutions as customers switch to alternative service providers.

The increasingly sophisticated expectations of consumers represent an additional threat to the banking industry. In the current banking era, customers expect personalised and convenient digital-first services. FinTech companies' technological abilities allow them to meet consumer needs better and more quickly than traditional banks. According to Ramdani et al. (2020), FinTech companies are more capable of fulfilling these needs because of their natural adaptability and digital knowledge. The risks to privacy and security are significant threats, mainly when operating in a context that is "open", which increases the exposure to risks such as data loss and fraud in the banking environment. Compared to FinTech companies, banks are more vulnerable to reputational loss in the event of a breach, primarily owing to the large amounts of information they process. Consequently, investments in cybersecurity are required (Rodrigues et al., 2022).

In response to the need for traditional banking institutions to evolve in digitalisation, existing literature has emphasised the importance of incumbent banks developing adaptation strategies capable of complying with the financial industry's evolving regulatory and competitive environment. In this perspective, scholars have proposed various approaches to innovating business models, including trial-and-error (Morris et al., 2005), learning (Teece, 2010), fine-tuning processes (Demil & Lecocq, 2010), and continuous adjustments (Landau et al., 2016). These approaches have also underscored the banking industry's heightened vulnerability to a new security risk.

Opportunities for the Banking Sector

Focusing on the opportunity side, the existing literature has remarked that digitalisation has emerged as a critical path for traditional banks (or incumbents) to maintain their considerable market power and enhance value creation in a rapidly changing financial sector (Vial, 2019). Assessing the multifaceted impacts on the banking industry arising from the innovation practices and processes, authors such as Grennan and Michaely (2021) have highlighted how financial technology helps banks to mitigate the information asymmetry problems arising from distance barriers and consequently decrease transition costs.

Concurrently, as banking is an *information-intensive* and increasingly *technology-driven* business (Campanella et al., 2023), the FinTech development has provided banks with valuable opportunities to innovate and evolve their business models, thereby improving performance (Cheng & Qu, 2020) and management efficiency (Lee et al., 2021; Zhao et al., 2022). Furthermore, these innovation processes have also reduced the systemic risk exposure of financial institutions (Haddad & Hornuf, 2023).

Indeed, the integration of new technologies and the reengineering activity of some core processes implemented by incumbent banks through established partnerships with FinTech firms has been identified as a strategic effort for financial intermediaries which are oriented to enhance service delivery, increase market share, and improve competitiveness (Murinde et al., 2022; Navaretti et al., 2017). According to Vial (2019), implementing digital technologies allows banks to reassess and modify conventional value-creation methods, requiring structural adjustments that positively impact the organisation's culture, leadership, and skill sets. Furthermore, by operating with FinTech, banks can enhance customer trust in digital financial services by internalising these startups' technological assets and know-how (Birch, 2014).

Furthermore, positive impacts can also be observed in the field of social responsibility and financial inclusion. Indeed, as Demir et al. (2020) demonstrated, incumbent banks have given little attention to providing equal opportunities to access financial services, primarily due to unsustainable business models and low business incentives. Technological advances and FinTech can effectively help overcome these barriers in this context. The implementation of new technologies has the potential to assist financial institutions in reducing the costs associated with sales and customer service. This, in turn, could facilitate the provision of user-friendly, convenient, and flexible banking services to a broader customer base. Due to the growing interconnection between the traditional banking sector and the FinTech ecosystem, according to Murinde et al. (2016), banks will adopt a more socially responsible approach to issues such as diversity, climate change, and work-life balance. Based on these evidence, a relationship emerged between technological innovation of banking business models and gradual sensibility to financial, social, and environmental sustainability issues (Wu et al., 2024).

4.4 Conclusions

This chapter reviews the definitions and identification methods of banking business models (BBMs). It also analyses the challenges and opportunities banks encounter in the digital era. From a theoretical standpoint, the chapter examines the evolution of traditional banking business models in response to shifts in the market, technology, and regulation.

More in detail, Sect. 4.1 examines the changing role of banks within the financial system. The section emphasises how banks, defined initially as financial intermediaries, providers of liquidity, and managers of risks, have transformed their original role mainly after the emergence of NBFI and the growing significance of financial markets. Consequently, banks have also gone beyond the role of providing financial intermediation services, implementing the universal banking model. This shift has introduced both opportunities and risks, particularly in response to banking activities' growing diversification (and *"sophistication"*). Furthermore, the advent of FinTech has brought new competitive challenges and opportunities for collaboration, compelling traditional banks to innovate, adapt to new technologies, and address emerging risks.

Section 4.2 reviews the literature field of interest to properly define a bank's BM, which can be defined as the result of strategic decisions reflected in the financial intermediary's balance sheet structure. Quantitative, qualitative, and hybrid methods have been described as valuable approaches previously used by practitioners, academics, and regulators to identify and define different BBMs. Specifically, this section briefly summarises scholars who have implemented clustering techniques as the quantitative method implemented in our study to identify the three distinct business models (i.e., *Retail banks*—BM1, *Investment banks*—BM2, and *Diversified Assets banks*—BM3) which characterised the sampled banks.

The effects of digitalisation processes on BBMs have been examined in Sect. 4.3. Particularly, threats and opportunities brought by FinTech firms are examined, identifying increased competition, changing consumer expectations, and heightened security risks as threats posed by new financial players. On the other hand, better operational efficiency, a broader and renovated service offering, and a strengthened market position are some of the opportunities that emerged for the incumbent banks. The paragraph also highlights how integrating digital technologies could support traditional banks in better achieving sustainability goals.

As final remarks, this chapter highlights how the banking business models, although a topic extensively investigated in the banking literature, required greater attention by scholars as they evolved in response to multiple endogenous and exogenous forces, such as technological development, regulatory pressure, shift, and financial sophistication of consumer behaviours. Based on these evidence, future research should revise the business model analysis, identifying new crucial financial and non-financial ratios that could be useful to capture the adaptation and resiliency strategy that banks adopt to survive in an increasingly complex financial environment.

References

Aghion, P., & Bolton, P. (1997). A theory of trickle-down growth and development. *Review of Economic Studies, 64*(2), 151–172.

Altunbas, Y., Marqués-Ibáñez, D., & Manganelli, S. (2011). *Bank risk during the financial crisis: Do business models matter?* (ECB Working Paper, No. 1394, European Central Bank (ECB))

Anagnostopoulos, I. (2018). Fintech and regtech: Impact on regulators and banks. *Journal of Economics and Business, 100*, 7–25.

Ayadi, R. (2017). Banks' business models in Europe: Are cooperative banks different? *Institutional Diversity in Banking: Small Country, Small Bank Perspectives*, 51–72.

Ayadi, R. (2019). *Banking business models. Definition, analytical framework and financial stability assessment.* Springer.

Ayadi, R., & Groen, W. (2014). Banking business models monitor 2014—Europe, Centre for European Policy Studies and International Observatory on Financial Services Cooperatives.

Ayadi, R., Arbak, E., & Pieter De Groen, W. (2011). *Business Models in European Banking: A pre-and post-crisis screening*. Center for European Policy Studies.

Ayadi, R., Challita, S., & Cucinelli, D. (2023). Cooperative banks, business models and efficiency: A stochastic frontier approach analysis. *Annals of Operations Research*, 1–43.

Baele, L., De Jonghe, O., & Vander Vennet, R. (2007). Does the stock market value bank diversification? *Journal of Banking and Finance, 31*(7), 1999–2023.

Bank for International Settlements (BIS). (2006, September 26–28). Global banking: Paradigm shift—Towards meeting the emerging challenges (by M.D. Knight). In *BIS speech*.

Bank for International Settlements (BIS). (2014). Bank business models. *BIS Quarterly Review*.

Bank for International Settlements (BIS). (2015). *Regulatory change and monetary policy* (CGFS Papers, No. 54).

Bank for International Settlements (BIS). (2021). *Fintech and the digital transformation of financial services: Implications for market structure and public policy* (by E. Feyen, J. Frost, L. Gambacorta, H. Natarajan and M. Saal) (BIS Paper No. 117).

Berger, A. N. (2003). The economic effects of technological progress: Evidence from the banking industry. *Journal of Money, Credit and Banking*, 141–176.

Berndt, A., & Gupta, A. (2009). Moral hazard and adverse selection in the originate-to-distribute model of bank credit. *Journal of Monetary Economics, 56*(5), 725–743.

Bhimjee, D. C., Ramos, S. B., & Dias, J. G. (2016). Banking industry performance in the wake of the global financial crisis. *International Review of Financial Analysis, 48*, 376–387.

Bholowalia, P., & Kumar, A. (2014). EBK-means: A clustering technique based on elbow method and k-means in WSN. *International Journal of Computer Applications, 105*(9).

Birch, D. (2014). *Identity is the new money*. London Publishing Partnership.

Blundell-Wignall, A., Atkinson, P. E., & Roulet, C. (2012). The business models of large interconnected banks and the lessons of the financial crisis. *National Institute Economic Review, 221*, R31–R43.

Boot, A., & Thakor, A. V. (2010). The accelerating integration of banks and markets and its implications for regulation. In *The Oxford handbook of banking* (pp. 58–90).

Campanella, F., Serino, L., Battisti, E., Giakoumelou, A., & Karasamani, I. (2023). FinTech in the financial system: Towards a capital-intensive and high competence human capital reality? *Journal of Business Research, 155*, 113376.

Cappa, F., Collevecchio, F., Oriani, R., & Peruffo, E. (2022). Banks responding to the digital surge through Open Innovation: Stock market performance effects of M&As with fintech firms. *Journal of Economics and Business, 121*, 106079.

Cernov, M., & Urbano, T. (2018). *Identification of EU bank business models* (European Banking Authority Research Paper 2).

Cheng, M., & Qu, Y. (2020). Does bank FinTech reduce credit risk? Evidence from China. *Pacific-Basin Finance Journal, 63*, 101398.

Collevecchio, F., Cappa, F., Peruffo, E., & Oriani, R. (2024). When do M&as with fintech firms benefit traditional banks? *British Journal of Management, 35*(1), 192–209.

Demil, B., & Lecocq, X. (2010). Business model evolution: In search of dynamic consistency. *Long Range Planning, 43*(2–3), 227–246.

Demir, A., Pesqu´ e-Cela, V., Altunbas, Y., & Murinde, V. (2020). Fintech, financial inclusion and income inequality: A quantile regression approach. *The European Journal of Finance*, 1–22.

Demirgüç-Kunt, A., & Huizinga, H. (2010). Bank activity and funding strategies: The impact on risk and returns. *Journal of Financial Economics, 98*(3), 626–650.

Drasch, B. J., Schweizer, A., & Urbach, N. (2018). Integrating the 'Troublemakers': A taxonomy for cooperation between banks and fintechs. *Journal of Economics and Business, 100*, 26–42.

El-Mandouh, A. M., Abd-Elmegid, L. A., Mahmoud, H. A., & Haggag, M. H. (2019). Optimised K-means clustering model based on gap statistic. *International Journal of Advanced Computer Science and Applications, 10*(1).

Elliehausen, G., & Hannon, S. M. (2023). *FinTech and banks: Strategic partnerships that circumvent state Usury laws* (Finance and Economics Discussion Series 2023056r1). Board of Governors of the Federal Reserve System, https://doi.org/10.17016/FEDS.2023.056r1.

European Banking Authority (EBA). (2014), Second report on impact assessment for liquidity measures under Article 509(1) of the CRR, EBA. https://www.eba.europa.eu/documents/10180/950548/2014+LCR+IA+report.pdf.

European Banking Authority (EBA). (2015), EBA Report on Net Stable Funding Requirements under Article 510 of the CRR EBA/Op/2015/22. https://www.eba.europa.eu/documents/10180/983359/EBA-Op-2015-22+NSFR+Report.pdf.

European Banking Authority (EBA). (2016). EBA Report on the Leverage Ratio Requirements under Article 511 of the CRR, EBA/Op/2016/13.

European Banking Authority (EBA). (2018). Identification of bank business models. A novel approach to classifying banks in the EU Regulatory Framework (by Cernov, M., and Urbano, T.), EBA Staff paper series, N.2 June 2018.

European Banking Authority (EBA). (2022). *Bank, business models and beyond.* Eurofi Event.

European Central Bank (ECB). (2016). Recent trends in euro area banks' business models and implication for banking sector stability. Financial Stability Review. European Central Bank, 1.

Farnè, M., & Vouldis, A. (2017). *Business models of the banks in the euro area* (No. 2070). (ECB Working Paper).

Farnè, M., & Vouldis, A. T. (2021). Banks' business models in the euro area: A cluster analysis in high dimensions. *Annals of Operations Research, 305*, 23–57. https://doi.org/10.1007/s10479-021-04045-9

Ferstl, R., & Seres, D. (2012). Clustering Austrian banks' business models and peer groups in the European Banking Sector. *Financial Stability Report, 24*, 79–95.

Fiordelisi, F. (2015). *Mergers and acquisitions in European banking*. Springer.

Focarelli, D., Marques-Ibanez, D., & Pozzolo, A. F. (2011). *Are universal banks better underwriters? Evidence from the last days of the Glass-Steagall Act* (ECB Working Paper Series, No. 1287, European Central Bank).

Freixas, X., & Rochet, J. C. (1997). *The microeconomics of banking*. MIT Press.

Grennan, J., & Michaely, R. (2021). FinTechs and the market for financial analysis. *J. Financ. Quant. Anal., 56*(6), 1877–1907.

Gurley, J. G., & Shaw, E. S. (1955). Financial aspects of economic development. *The American Economic Review, 45*(4), 515–538.

Haddad, C., & Hornuf, L. (2023). How do fintech start-ups affect financial institutions' performance and default risk? *The European Journal of Finance, 29*(15), 1761–1792.

Holmström, B., & Tirole, J. (1997). Financial intermediation, loanable funds and the real sector. *Quarterly Journal of Economics, 112*(3), 663–691.

Hornuf, L., Klus, M. F., Lohwasser, T. S., & Schwienbacher, A. (2021). How do banks interact with fintech startups? *Small Business Economics, 57*, 1505–1526.

Hryckiewicz, A., & Kozłowski, Ł. (2017). Banking business models and the nature of financial crisis. *Journal of International Money and Finance, 71*, 1–24.

Köhler, M. (2015). Which banks are more risky? The impact of business models on bank stability. *Journal of Financial Stability, 16*, 195–212.

Kwon, K. Y., Molyneux, P., Pancotto, L., & Reghezza, A. (2024). Banks and FinTech acquisitions. *Journal of Financial Services Research, 65*(1), 41–75.

Lagasio, V., & Quaranta, A. G. (2022). Cluster analysis of bank business models: The connection with performance, efficiency and risk. *Finance Research Letters, 47*, 102640.

Landau, C., Karna, A., & Sailer, M. (2016). Business model adaptation for emerging markets: A case study of a German automobile manufacturer in India. *R&D Management, 46*(3), 480–503.

Le, T., Ngo, T., Nguyen, D. T., & Do, T. T. (2024). Fintech and banking: friends or foes? Evidence from bank–fintech cooperation. *International Journal of Bank Marketing*.

Lee, C. C., Li, X., Yu, C. H., & Zhao, J. (2021). Does fintech innovation improve bank efficiency? Evidence from China's banking industry. *International Review of Economics & Finance, 74*, 468–483.

Liikanen, E., Bänziger, H., Campa, J. M., & Gallois, L. (2012). *High-level Expert Group on reforming the structure of the EU banking sector* (p. 2). Final Report.

Martín-Oliver, A., Ruano, S., & Salas-Fumás, V. (2017). The fall of Spanish cajas: Lessons of ownership and governance for banks. *Journal of Financial Stability, 33*, 244–260.

Milligan, G. W. (1981). A review of Monte Carlo tests of cluster analysis. *Multivariate Behavioral Research, 16*(3), 379–407.

Morris, M., Schindehutte, M., & Allen, J. (2005). The entrepreneur's business model: Toward a unified perspective. *Journal of Business Research, 58*(6), 726–735.

Morrison, A. D. (2010). Universal banking. In *The Oxford handbook of banking* (p. 2).

Murinde, V., Rizopoulos, E., & Zachariadis, M. (2022). The impact of the FinTech revolution on the future of banking: Opportunities and risks. *International Review of Financial Analysis, 81*, 102103. https://doi.org/10.1016/j.irfa.2022.102103

Navaretti, G. B., Calzolari, G., & Pozzolo, A. F. (2017). FinTech and banks: Friends or foes. *European Economy, 2*, 9–30.

Palmieri, E., Geretto, E. F., & Polato, M. (2023). European banks' business models as a driver of strategic planning: One size fits all. *Journal of Financial Regulation and Compliance, 31*(1), 16–39.

Palmieri, E., Ferilli, G. B., Altunbas, Y., Stefanelli, V., & Geretto, E. F. (2024). Business model and ESG pillars: The impacts on banking default risk. *International Review of Financial Analysis, 91*, 102978.

Parmigiani, A., & Mitchell, W. (2009). Complementarity, capabilities, and the boundaries of the firm: The impact of within-firm and interfirm expertise on concurrent sourcing of complementary components. *Strategic Management Journal, 30*(10), 1065–1091.

Ramdani, B., Rothwell, B., & Boukrami, E. (2020). Open banking: The emergence of new digital business models. *International Journal of Innovation and Technology Management, 17*(05), 2050033.

Rodrigues, A. R. D., Ferreira, F. A., Teixeira, F. J., & Zopounidis, C. (2022). Artificial intelligence, digital transformation and cybersecurity in the banking sector: A multi-stakeholder cognition-driven framework. *Research in International Business and Finance, 60*, 101616.

Roengpitya, R., Tarashev, N. A., Tsatsaronis, K., & Villegas, A. (2017). Bank business models: popularity and performance. BIS Working Paper. N. 682.

Rousseeuw, P. J. (1987). Silhouettes: A graphical aid to the interpretation and validation of cluster analysis. *Journal of Computational and Applied Mathematics, 20*, 53–65.

Saebi, T., & Foss, N. J. (2015). Business models for open innovation: Matching heterogeneous open innovation strategies with business model dimensions. *European Management Journal, 33*(3), 201–213.

Saebi, T., Lien, L., & Foss, N. J. (2017). What drives business model adaptation? The impact of opportunities, threats and strategic orientation. *Long RangePlanning, 50*(5), 567–581.

Shleifer, A., & Vishny, R. (2011). Fire sales in finance and macroeconomics. *Journal of Economic Perspectives, 25*(1), 29–48.

Song, F., & Thakor, A. V. (2010). Financial system architecture and the co-evolution of banks and capital markets. *The Economic Journal, 120*(547), 1021–1055.

Stefanelli, V., & Manta, F. (2022). Digital financial services and open banking innovation: Are banks becoming 'invisible'?. *Global Business Review*, 09721509231151491.

Stiroh, K. J. (2006). A portfolio view of banking with interest and non-interest activities. *Journal of Money, Credit, and Banking, 38*(5), 1351–1361.

Stiroh, K. J., & Rumble, A. (2006). The dark side of diversification: the case of us financial holding companies. *Journal of Banking and Finance, 30*(8), 2131–2161.

Tanda, A., & Schena, C. M. (2019). *FinTech, BigTech and banks: Digitalisation and its impact on banking business models*. Springer.

Teece, D. J. (2010). Business models, business strategy and innovation. *Long Range Planning, 43*(2–3), 172–194.

Thant, A. A., Aye, S. M., & Mandalay, M. (2020). Euclidean, manhattan and minkowski distance methods for clustering algorithms. *International Journal of Scientific Research in Science, Engineering and Technology, 7*(3), 553–559.

Vial, G. (2019). Understanding digital transformation: A review and a research agenda. *Journal of Strategic Information Systems, 28*(2), 118–144. https://doi.org/10.1016/j.jsis.2019.01.003

Walter, I. (2012). Universal banking and financial architecture. *The Quarterly Review of Economics and Finance, 52*(2), 114–122.

Ward Jr, J. H. (1963). Hierarchical grouping to optimize an objective function. *Journal of the American Statistical Association, 58*(301), 236–244.

Wu, F., Hu, Y., & Shen, M. (2024). The color of FinTech: FinTech and corporate green transformation in China. *International Review of Financial Analysis*, 103254.

Zhao, J., Li, X., Yu, C. H., Chen, S., & Lee, C. C. (2022). Riding the FinTech innovation wave: FinTech, patents and bank performance. *Journal of International Money and Finance, 122*, 102552.

Zott, C., Amit, R., & Massa, L. (2011). The business model: Recent developments and future research. *Journal of Management, 37*(4), 1019–1042.

CHAPTER 5

Empirical Evidence on Banks' Performance Improvements After FinTech M&As

Abstract This chapter analyses the impact of FinTech M&As on acquiring banks' performance, with a particular focus on profitability, efficiency, risk, and ESG metrics. Employed econometric models the analysis shows as the findings differ according to banks' business models—Retail, Investment, and Diversified Assets—and the FinTech category involved in the M&A operation. Findings reveal that while FinTech M&As enhance profitability and ESG performance, they may increase short-term inefficiencies and risk. The study provides empirical evidence of the differential effects of FinTech-Bank M&As, offering understandings on the strategic alignment of banking operations.

Keywords Bank performance · Sustainability · Merger and Acquisition · Bank Business Model · FinTech

G. B. Ferilli, *Bank-FinTech M&As and Banking Innovation*, Palgrave Macmillan Studies in Banking and Financial Institutions, https://doi.org/10.1007/978-3-031-84445-4_5

5.1 FinTech-Bank M&A Operations: An Empirical Approach

Introduction

Financial technology (or FinTech) firms have modernised the financial industry in the past few years, growing the interest of scholars, practitioners, and policymakers. Although technology has been a strategic component of the financial and banking industry since the 1850s (Murinde et al., 2022), only in the last 20 years, through the adoption of open innovation (OI) principles and the rise of FinTech firms, there has been a disruptive transformation of financial services. The financial technology industry has gradually matured, offering a wide range of innovative financial services and products on a global scale. The development of FinTech has also prompted the creation of novel business models, applications, processes, and products (Feyen et al., 2021; Sironi, 2016). This has attracted the attention of incumbent banks, who are seeking to rethink their intermediation processes and business strategies in order to benefit from the opportunities offered by digitalisation (BCBS, 2019; OECD, 2020). Recent studies also show that traditional banks have established partnerships and strategic collaborations with FinTech players (Bellardini et al., 2022; Hornuf et al., 2021; Li et al., 2023a, 2023b). As an alternative to traditional paths of internal and autonomous growth, financial intermediaries have explored external growth solutions, including mergers and acquisitions (M&As) with FinTech firms.

Many FinTech innovations complement the traditional functions of banks, while others serve as alternatives that challenge the established banking sector; consequently, researchers are increasingly focused on examining the effects of these new competitors on the banking industry. This involves thoroughly investigation all potential impacts on banks' performance indicators. An established body of literature has examined the role of banks as equity investors (Jiang et al., 2013) and highlighted how bank's industry knowledge in FinTech firms could help improve their performance (Hornuf et al., 2021; IMF, 2023a; Li et al., 2023a, 2023b).

According to McKinsey & Company report (2023), in 2022, FinTech accounted for 5 per cent (or \$150 billion to \$205 billion) of the global banking sector's net revenue. The forecast data indicate that this share could increase to more than \$400 billion by 2028, representing a 15 per cent annual growth rate of FinTech revenue between 2022 and

2028, three times the overall banking industry's growth rate of roughly 6 per cent. Market data shows that many large and consolidated banks (i.e., JPMorgan Chase & Co, Banking Circle, Barclays, Deutsche Bank) have invested in FinTech firms. Consequently, the booming interest from major banks in investing in FinTech firms encourages a more nuanced understanding of the impact of equity investment impact on the performance of traditional financial institutions.

Literature Gap

This study is the first to analyse FinTech-Bank M&As, providing a comprehensive assessment of incumbents' *financial* and *non-financial* performance metrics after their equity investments, thereby filling a gap in the extant literature.

Prior studies on bank-FinTech M&As have mainly focused on two areas: (i) the *ex-post* valuation of M&As on key financial performance indicators, with a particular emphasis on profitability and efficiency profile (Haddad & Hornuf, 2023; Phan et al., 2019; Wang et al., 2023; Zhao et al., 2022), and (ii) the assessment of *ex-ante* factors that encourage M&As by banks, including governance characteristics, cultural diversity, capital strength, and liquidity (Goddard et al., 2012). Specifically, concerning this second literature stream, scholars have primarily investigated investment drivers in FinTech. This has involved analysing the characteristics of banks' board of directors engaged in strategic operations (Del Gaudio et al., 2024; Kwon et al., 2024; Reghezza & Vasilakis, 2024), assessing how banks finance these startups (Bellardini et al., 2022) and examining how they choose the optimal form of alliance to be established with FinTech (Hornuf et al., 2021), according to a broad taxonomy of banks-FinTech relationships (Drasch et al., 2018). Otherwise, other scholars have empirically analysed the impact of FinTech on banks financial performance, assessing different profitability ratios (IMF, 2023b; Wang et al., 2023; Zhao et al., 2022), income measures (IMF, 2023a) cost efficiency indicators (Lee et al., 2021), systemic risk measures (Li et al., 2022), or the IPO rate (Li et al., 2023a, 2023b).

Other scholars, such as Dranev et al. (2019), have focused on mergers' market perception and financial implications, providing empirical evidence of positive short-term abnormal returns for banks that acquire FinTech firms. These findings indicate that the initial investor confidence in bank-FinTech M&As as a strategic tool for performance enhancement is particularly evident in developed countries where the environment is conducive to implementing acquired technologies. However, existing literature has shown mixed results about the impact of FinTech on bank performance, revealing the controversial effect of financial innovation investments on banks' balance sheet metrics. Additionally, a considerable number of these studies are focused on the Chinese context (see, for instance, Katsiampa et al., 2022; Lee et al., 2021; Wang et al., 2023; Zhao et al., 2022), whereas cross-country analyses appear to be confined mainly to the European context (Carlini et al., 2022; Haddad & Hornuf, 2023).

This study differs from the aforementioned ones in several respects. First, we expand on the existing research in terms of quality, examining a global sample of banks that have engaged in domestic and cross-border M&As with FinTech firms over a long-time horizon (1997–2022). Second, it takes a holistic perspective by examining M&As' effect on several banks' financial and non-financial performance metrics. Third, the study enriches the extant knowledge in the field by discriminating the impact on performance according to the business model (BM) adopted by banks involved in the operations and the specific area of expertise (or BM) of the FinTech firm acquired.

Research Questions Development

We adopt a bottom-up approach to achieve the research scope, outlining four distinct research questions (RQs). Each of these corresponds to a specific level of the empirical analysis performed. The theoretical framework of Synergy Theory (Meckling & Jensen, 1976) and Agency Theory (Ansoff, 1965) provide the foundation for the development of our RQs. Specifically, the Synergy Theory postulates that the combined value of two entities exceeds their individual contributions, making it pertinent to analyse the strategic rationale behind banks' investments in FinTech. The integration of FinTech may enhance banking operations and drive efficiencies that surpass what the separate entities could achieve independently. This theory thus provides a framework for evaluating whether the collaborative effect of these strategic decisions significantly enhances bank performance. Additionally, Agency Theory aids in understanding how internal governance structures shape banks' FinTech investment decisions. This framework is crucial for assessing whether these decisions prioritise shareholder value maximisation or are influenced by managerial self-interest.

Thus, in light of the conflicting findings from previous studies, this research aims to assess the impact of FinTech M&As on the financial and non-financial performances of sampled banks. In order to achieve this objective, we formulate the first RQ:

RQ1: Do FinTech M&As affect bank performance?

Secondly, literature has postulated that past values may explain the current values of the selected banks' performance metrics (Haddad & Hornuf, 2023). Consequently, the study aims to assess the time factor effect. Thus, a second RQ is formulated:

RQ2: Do time factors affect the impact of Fintech M&As on bank performance?

The third research question (RQ3) is designed to identify the differential effects on performance metrics, considering the business adopted by the sampled banks. The study examines whether and how the differing balance sheet compositions of the banks, as reflected in their business models (see Chapter 4), affect the financial and non-financial indicators under consideration. To date, only a study by the IMF (2023b) has examined the differential impact of FinTech on cooperative and commercial banks, revealing that cooperative banks are particularly vulnerable to profit deterioration caused by FinTech transactions. Consequently, we conduct a more detailed analysis, discerning the FinTech M&As effect on *Retail*, *Investment*, and *Diversified Asset* banks, as an output of the clustering analysis performed. The third RQ3 is as follows:

RQ3: Do banks' business model affect the impact of Fintech M&As on bank performance?

The FinTech industry is gradually developing and expanding, offering a wide range of financial services and products on a global scale. Nevertheless, understanding different FinTech business models is an outstanding issue. Although no universal classification system exists, various policy-makers, international organisations as well as banking supervisors have tried to develop different FinTech classifications to outline the boundaries of the FinTech industry (World Economic Forum, 2024[1]; Financial Stability Board, 2017[2]; International Organization of Securities Commissions (IOSCO), 2017[3]; European Banking Authority, 2017[4]; Bank for International Settlements, 2018[5]; and others). Besides these categorisations, some scholars using both qualitative or quantitative approaches have provided additional FinTech taxonomies, emphasising a more remarkable similarity between traditional financial services (i.e., payments, deposits, and investment management) and, differently, a more significant variability about the wide range of financial support services (i.e., analytics, cloud computing, cybersecurity and other). In this stream of studies, Laidroo et al. (2021) identified four clusters of FinTech (i.e., lending community, mixed services, payment service, and payment community) characterised by differences and similarities due to their key activities, key resources, value propositions, customer segments, delivery channels, cost structure, and revenue streams. Differently, Drasch et al. (2018), developing a taxonomy for cooperation between banks and FinTech, tried to categorise financial technology firms based on three main elements such as maturity (i.e., startups, emerging growth stage,

[1] FinTech classifications according to **World Economic Forum** (2015): Payments, Deposits and Lending/Capital Raising, Insurance, Investment Management, Market provisioning (machine learning, big data).

[2] FinTech classifications according to **Financial Stability Board (2017):** Payments, Clearing and settlement, Deposit, Lending and Capital Raising, Insurance, Investment Management, Market support (Cloud computing applications).

[3] FinTech classifications according to **International Organisation of Securities Commission (2017)**: Payments, Lending/Crowdfunding, Insurance, Trading and Investments/Planning (personal finance), Data and Analytics, Security (digital identity, cybersecurity), Blockchain.

[4] FinTech classifications according to **European Banking Authority (2017)**: Credit, deposit, and capital raising services (Cluster A), Payments, clearing and settlement services (Cluster B), Investment services/Investment management services (Cluster C), Other financial-related activities (Cluster D).

[5] FinTech classifications according to **Bank for International Settlements (2018)**: Credit, Deposit and Capital-raising services (Crowdfunding, Lending Marketplace, Mobile banks, Credit Scoring), Payments, Clearing and Settlements services (Mobile wallets, Peer-to-peer transfers, Digital Currencies, Value transfer networks, FX Wholesale, Digital exchange platforms), Investment Management Services (High-frequency trading, Copy trading, E-trading, Robo advice), Market Support Services (Portal and data aggregators, Ecosystem, Data applications, DLT, Security, Cloud computing, IoT, Artificial Intelligence).

mature stage, decline stage), products or services offered (i.e., lending, investing, insurance, payment, current account, cross-product service, and FinTech operators that provide API and infrastructure), and holding (or not) of a full bank licence. These studies were limited to deeply assessing FinTech firms' characteristics developing a more detailed taxonomy for FinTech in line with the growing expansion of the industry. Nevertheless, the several taxonomies that have emerged within the FinTech sector have proved an obstacle to developing a standardised and universally accepted classification framework, thereby indicating the inherent complexity of this rapidly expanding industry.

However, the existing literature lacks empirical studies analysing the impact of FinTech investments on bank performance, considering the business model of each FinTech firm involved in the M&A. Only the IMF (2023b) has measured the differential effect of FinTech on financial institutions' performance, limiting the analysis among FinTech specialising in the credit segment, such as *P2P lending* and *balance sheet lending*. The results confirm a differential impact, indicating that FinTech specialised in *P2P lending* has a slightly greater negative effect on cooperative banks' return on equity (ROE) than *balance sheet lending*. This is primarily due to competitive pressures and technological disadvantages these traditional financial institutions face.

According to our research scope, we aim to perform a more detailed performance assessment that considers the specific expertise of FinTech firms engaged in M&A, as well as the business model of the acquiring bank. Thus, we formulate the latest research question (RQ4):

RQ4: Do FinTech and Bank business models affect the impact of Fintech M&As on bank performance?

5.2 Sample, Data, and Method

Sample and Data

As described in Chapter 4, the final dataset covers 170 worldwide listed banks that have performed at least one deal in FinTech firms from 1997 to 2022. The total number of FinTech deals is 469, which are distributed as shown in Fig. 5.1. We classify a firm as *"FinTech"*, considering the categorisations of the FinTech industry provided by EBA (2017) and BIS (2018). We use a two-step approach to define FinTech in our sample. First, we use the information provided by *"Target Industry"* and *"Target*

Short Business Description" by *Refinitiv DealScan* to confirm the *fin-native* or *tech-native* of each firm involved in a bank's deal. Second, considering the four FinTech categories provided by banking supervisory authorities, we manually check the configuration of each firm in one of the areas of expertise indicated in FinTech's taxonomy.

The *fin-native* firms' category includes three main FinTech areas of expertise, which we have briefly labelled as (i) *FinTech Credit & Capital Raising*, (ii) *FinTech Payments*, and (iii) *FinTech Investment Services*. Differently, the *tech-native* category involves all the firms we have categorised as (iv) *FinTech Market Support*. More specifically, according to BIS and EBA's FinTech taxonomies, the *FinTech Credit & Capital Raising* category includes all activities related to lending and crowdfunding, consumer credit, credit agreements related to immovable property, financial leasing, guarantees and commitments, credit scoring,

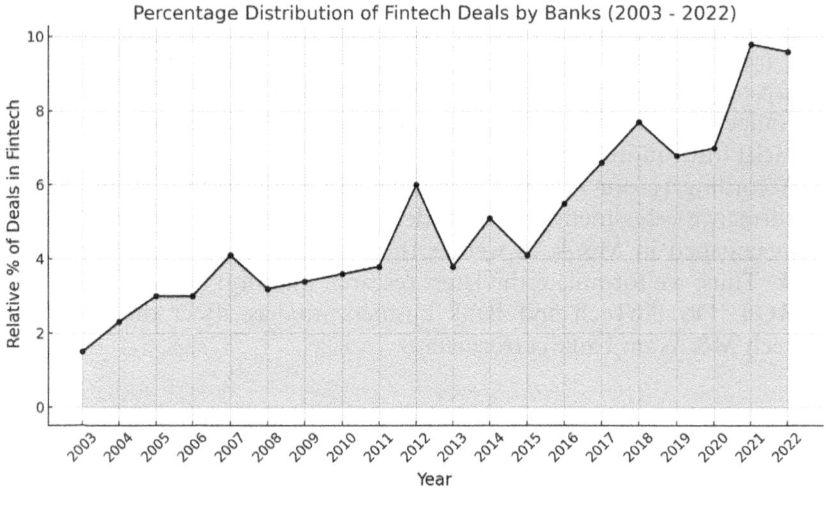

Fig. 5.1 Percentage distribution of FinTech deals by year (*Note* The figure illustrates the relative percentage of total bank-led deals in the fintech sector from 2003 to 2022. The trend demonstrates a steady increase in the banks' involvement in fintech over time, with notable peaks in 2012, 2018, and especially in the early 2020s. This growth highlights banks' strategic shift towards integrating fintech solutions, reflecting the sector's increasing relevance in the digital financial ecosystem. The shaded area emphasises the overall upward trend in banks' fintech engagement. *Source* Author's elaboration)

money broking, and other. The *FinTech Payments* category includes firms that are able to provide services related to mobile wallets, execution of payment transactions, P2P transfers, execution of direct debits including one-off direct debits, execution of payments through a payment card or similar device, digital currencies transactions, digital exchange platforms, and similar one. The third category, *FinTech Investment Services,* includes all activities related to high-frequency trading, copy trading, E-trading, robo-advice operations, portfolio management and advice, participation in securities offerings, and providing services related to such offerings. Lastly, the fourth category, such as *FinTech Market Support,* involves all firms that offer supplementary services related to security (i.e., customer identification and identification), distribution ledger technologies (i.e., blockchain and smart contracts), compliance services, ecosystem services (APIs, open source, infrastructure) and artificial intelligence services (i.e., bots, automation in finance and algorithms).

Dependent Variables

To investigate whether and how FinTech-Bank M&As affect incumbents' financial and non-financial performance metrics, we select seven dependent variables summarised in Table 5.1. The variables identified are classified according to four different analysis profiles:

1. *Bank profitability profile* includes the Return on Equity (ROE), usually used in banking literature as a proxy of bank profitability (Coccorese & Girardone, 2021; Hodula, 2024; Pennacchi & Santos, 2021).
2. *Bank efficiency profile* includes the Cost-to-income ratio (CIR) as a proxy to assess the bank's operational efficiency (Ayadi et al., 2021; Borello et al., 2022; Zhao et al., 2022). The CIR is defined as the operating cost that is necessary to generate one unit of income.
3. *Bank risk profile* includes both balance sheet and market-based riskiness measures. The first category includes the Z-score, a metric that has been extensively used in banking literature to express the *Bank Stability and Financial Soundness* (see Boyd & Graham, 1986; Strobel, 2011; Beck et al., 2013; Schaeck & Cihak, 2014; Chiaramonte et al., 2015; Cuadros-Solas et al., 2024). In line with the

Table 5.1 Variables definitions

Proxy	*Variable name*	*Definition*	*Source*	*Reference*
Dependent Variables				
Bank Profitability	Return on Equity (ROE)	The ROE measures the profitability of a bank in relation to its equity.	Refinitiv EIKON	BIS (2014), Hodula (2024), Katsiampa et al. (2022)
Bank Efficiency	Cost-to-Income (CIR)	The CIR (or efficiency ratio) measures operating costs as a percentage of operating income.	Refinitiv EIKON	Lee et al. (2023), Pennacchi and Santos (2021), Zhao et al. (2022)
Bank Stability	Z-Score (ZSC)	The Z-Score assess the risk of insolvency, the bank. This variable is computed as (ROA + ETA)/ STD (ROA), where ROA is earning before taxes and loan loss provisions, and ETA is Earning/ Total Assets).	Own elaboration	Ayadi et al. (2011), Chiaramonte et al. (2015), Cuadros-Solas et al. (2024), Zhao et al. (2022)
Bank Probability of Default (short term)	Probability of Default within 1 year (PD1)	The PD1 is the likelihood that a bank will default on its obligations within one year.	Bloomberg	Koutsomanoli-Filippaki and Mamatzakis (2009), Milne (2014)
Bank Probability of Default (medium term)	Probability of Default within 3 years (PD3)	The PD3 is the likelihood that a bank will default on its obligations within three years.	Bloomberg	
Bank Probability of Default (long term)	Probability of Default within 5 years (PD5)	The PD5 is the likelihood that a bank will default on its obligations within five years.	Bloomberg	

(continued)

Table 5.1 (continued)

Proxy	*Variable name*	*Definition*	*Source*	*Reference*
Bank ESG Performance	ESG Score	The ESG Score measures the bank's ESG performance based on verifiable reported public data related to 186 subsets of Environmental (E), Social (S), and Governance (G) metrics	Refinitiv EIKON	Palmieri et al. (2023)
Explanatory Variables				
FinTech M&A	FinTech Deals	The FT_DEAL is the number of financial technology-related deals performed by bank.	Refinitiv DealScan	Li et al., (2023a, 2023b)
Control Variables				
Bank Size	Total Assets	The TA is expressed as the natural logarithm of banks' total assets.	Refinitiv EIKON	Zheng and Mao (2024)
Capital Endowment	Capital Ratio	The CAP is calculated as the bank's equity over its total assets.	Refinitiv EIKON	Wu et al. (2024)
Interest income margin	Interest income margin	The interest income margin is the total interest income over total income. It is expressed as a ratio.	Refinitiv EIKON	Mahmud et al. (2023)
Commission Fees	Commission Fees	Commission fees refer to the revenues generated by the bank from service fees.	Refinitiv EIKON	Ayadi and Groen (2015)
Market Capitalisation	Market Capitalisation (MKT_CAP)	The market capitalization expresses the value of the bank equity at market values.	Refinitiv EIKON	Dias (2013)

(continued)

Table 5.1 (continued)

Proxy	*Variable name*	*Definition*	*Source*	*Reference*
Economic Development	Gross Domestic Product Growth (GDP_ GROWTH)	The GDP growth rate measures the increase in economic activity and health of the economy.	World Bank	Lee et al. (2023), Tan et al. (2017)
Inflation	Inflation rate (INF)	The inflation rate reflects that the general level of prices for goods and services is rising.	World Bank	Haddad and Hornuf (2023), Katsiampa et al. (2022)
Bank Concentration	Bank Concentration Index (BNK_CON)	The bank concentration index is calculated as the sum pf assets of three largest commercial banks as a share of total commercial banking assets. Total assets include total earning assets, cash and due from banks, foreclosed real estate, fixed assets, goodwill, other intangibles, current tax assets, deferred tax assets, discontinued operations and other assets (World Bank).	World Bank	Tan et al. (2017), Haddad and Hornuf (2023)

Note The table provides definitions and sources for the variables employed in this study, which have been categorised as dependent, explanatory, and control variables. The dependent variables include measures of profitability (ROE), efficiency (CIR), stability (Z-Score), default probabilities (PD1, PD3, PD5), and ESG performance. The explanatory variable cover FinTech M&A activities, reflecting the bank's engagement in financial technology. Control variables include bank size, capital endowment, income margins, market capitalisation, economic indicators (GDP growth and inflation), and banking concentration. Each variable is sourced from recognised databases and supported by relevant academic references

Source Author's elaboration

methodology applied by Zhao et al. (2022), the Z-score is calculated as the sum of its earnings on total assets (ETA) plus its assets (ROA), divided by the standard deviation of the bank's four-year ROAs before period t. This metric is widely employed in academic papers due to its inverse correlation with the likelihood of bank insolvency, meaning that a higher Z-score indicates a lower probability of bank insolvency (Anginer et al., 2014; Laeven & Levine, 2009). Concerning the market-based riskiness metrics, a series of banks' Probability of Default (PD), ranging from one to five years, is used to assess the likelihood of a bank failing to meet its obligations within these time frames according to market prices (Koutsomanoli-Filippaki & Mamatzakis, 2009; Milne, 2014). In particular, we consider PD within one year (PD1) as a proxy for a *Short-term bank PD*, PD within three years (PD3) as a proxy for a *Medium-term bank PD*, and finally, PD within five years (PD5) as a proxy for a *Long-term bank PD*.

4. *Bank ESG profile* includes the ESG performance score reached by each incumbent (Azmi et al., 2021; Di Tommaso & Thornton, 2020; Palmieri et al., 2024). This composite score provided by *Refinitiv EIKON* captures a balanced view of the bank's performance in the three areas. The Environmental (E), Social (S), and Governance (G) scores are derived through a weighted combination of a series of firm-specific indicators that proxy results towards sustainability practices. According to the *Thomson Reuters ESG method* (Thomson Reuters, 2017), the E score is derived from a weighted average of three constituents: Resource Use, Emissions, and Innovation. The S score aggregates the score of the Workforce, Human Rights, Community, and Product Responsibility dimensions. Differently, the G score combines the scores related to Management, Shareholders, and Corporate Social Responsibility dimensions. All the E, S, and G variables are assigned a score between 0 and 100.

Explanatory Variables

According to our research scope, the main regressor is the variable labelled *"FinTech M&A"*, which expresses the number of deals related to financial technology firms (or FinTech) made by traditional banks. This variable reflects the extent to which a bank is engaged in contemporary financial practices. In the context of FinTech spread, M&As represent a means of achieving the outside-in typology of open innovation (OI), as these innovative financial players tend to favour knowledge inflow from outside organisational boundaries (Bogers et al., 2017; Cammarano et al., 2019). Thus, the M&A operations performed by incumbents with FinTech firms allowed banks to collaborate with external entities or strategically integrate their know-how within the boundaries of the acquirer entities. This strategy enables banks to foster and address pressing innovative challenges that they may be unable to tackle by themselves (Mun et al., 2019).

To enhance the analysis, our model includes several bank-specific and country-specific controls extensively used in the banking literature. The selected variables may affect the banks' performance metrics, enhancing our estimations' accuracy. The first set of bank controls includes *Bank size,* that is the natural logarithm of total assets (Altunbas et al., 2007; Saona, 2016)*; Capital Endowment,* measured by equity on total assets (Rossi et al., 2024). Following Dell'Ariccia et al. (2018), we expect that a larger capital buffer can entail greater bank risk-taking and an increasing propensity to FinTech acquisition, consequently impacting bank performance. Other variables implemented are (iii) *Market Capitalisation* (Daoud & Kammoun, 2020) as an expression of the market value of the bank equity; *Interest Income Margin* and *Commission Fees* (Ayadi & De Groen, 2015), respectively proxies of the bank's profitability regarding their core activities.

The country-specific variables include: (i) *Economic Development,* measured as the GDP growth rate by each country of our sample (Lee et al., 2023; Tan et al., 2017). In line with Rossi and Volpin (2004), we use this variable because the investment decisions made by banks may be affected by overall economic conditions; (ii) *Inflation rate*, as a measure of financial institutions' performance (Trujillo-Ponce, 2013); (iii) *Bank Concentration,* as a proxy to assess the bank market power (Delis & Tsionas, 2009; Maudos & De Guevara, 2007) and their financial constraint (Ratti et al., 2008). In our analysis, we used the Bank Concentration index provided by the World Bank database, which reflects the sum of market share in terms of total assets of the three largest banks in each country (Haddad & Hornuf, 2023).

Regression Models Specification

The method is structured to provide a robust assessment of banks' performance impacts arising from FinTech-Bank M&A operations. Using a pooled panel data model, the research outlines a regression model for each specific level of analysis, ensuring a holistic assessment of banks' performance metrics and robustness in the findings.

To achieve the research goal and reply to *RQ1*, we develop the following baseline regression model (Model 1):

$$BNK_{Performance_{it}} = ß_0 + ß_1 * FINTECH\_M\&A_{it} + \sum_{c=1}^{5} \eta_c * Bank_{ctrl_{cit}} + \sum_{c=1}^{3} \theta_c * Country_{ctrl_{cit}} + \sum_{s=1}^{2} \phi_s * fixed_{effects} + \varepsilon_{it}$$

where $_i$ denotes banks, $_t$ indicates the year, and $_c$ is the country where the bank has its headquarters. Moreover, $\boldsymbol{BNK_{Performance_{it}}}$ represent our dependent variable as a proxy for banks' *profitability, efficiency, riskiness*, and *environmental, social, and governance (ESG)* profile. Thus, the dependent variable is measured alternatively by Return of Equity (ROE), Cost-to-Income (CIR), Z-score (ZSC), Probability of Default within one, three, and five years (PD1, PD3, PD5), and finally by ESG Performance score (ESG Score). ***FINTECH_M&A***$_{it}$ is the primary regressor, expressed by the number of FinTech deals performed by banks, while $\boldsymbol{Bank_{ctrl_{cit}}}$ and $\boldsymbol{Country_{ctrl_{cit}}}$ include all the control variables implemented in the model. Specifically, *Bank Size, Capital Endowment, Interest Income Margin, Commission Fees,* and *Market Capitalisation* represent the bank-specific controls; *Economic Development*, *Inflation*, and *Bank Concentration* represent the country-specific controls. $\boldsymbol{fixed_{effects}}$ includes bank and year fixed effects, while standard errors $\boldsymbol{\varepsilon_{it}}$ were clustered at the bank level.

In order to respond to *RQ2*, Model 2 is implemented:

$$BNK_{Performance_{it}} = ß_0 + \sum_{lag=0}^{3} ß_{lag} * FINTECH\_M\&A_{it-lag} + \sum_{s=1}^{2} \phi_s * fixed_{effects} + \varepsilon_{it}$$

Similar to Model 1, $\boldsymbol{BNK_{Performance_{it}}}$ represent our dependent variable, a proxy for banks' *Profitability, Efficiency, Riskiness*, and *Environmental, Social, and Governance (ESG)* profile. In this case, the main regressor $\boldsymbol{FINTECH\_M\&A_{it-lag}}$ includes variables with lag structure to capture the delayed effects of such M&A activities on different bank performance indicators. $\boldsymbol{fixed_{effects}}$ includes bank and year fixed effects, while standard errors $\boldsymbol{\varepsilon_{it}}$ were clustered at the bank level.

Model 3 responds to RQ3 by performing the same analysis expressed in the baseline model (Model 1) but including the subgroups delineated by the banks' business models (BBMs). These subgroups have been previously identified through a cluster analysis, as detailed in Chapter 4 of this book.

Finally, Model 4 refines the analysis of the bank's performances, considering both banking and FinTech business models. Specifically, Model 4 is designed to assess the impact of diverse banking and FinTech business models on bank performance metrics. In response to *RQ4*, we have developed the following model:

$$BNK_{Performance_{it}} = ß_0 + ß_1 * FINTECH\_M\&A_{it} + ß_2 * BM_{fintech_{it}} + \sum_{f=1}^{4} \delta_f * FINTECH\_M\&A_{it} * BM_{fintech_{fit}} + \sum_{c=1}^{5} \eta_c * Bank_{ctrl_{cit}} + \sum_{c=1}^{3} \theta_c * Country_{ctrl_{cit}} + \sum_{s=1}^{2} \phi_s * fixed_{effects} + \varepsilon_{it}$$

Differently from previous ones, Model 4 incorporates the interaction term $\boldsymbol{FINTECH\_M\&A_{it} * BM_{fintech_{fit}}}$ which captures the effect of bank investment in a specific FinTech category. These FinTech categories have been formalised using categorical variables, thereby enabling an examination of how the specific business model adopted by banks and FinTech firms may affect bank performance metrics differently. Firstly, the analysis was conducted on the entire sample (i.e., General Model), and subsequently, this equation was applied to subgroups distinguished by the bank's business model (i.e., Retail Bank; Investment Bank; Diversified Assets Bank).

Robustness Checks

Several robustness checks are implemented to strengthen the validity of our analyses. Specifically, following Imbens and Wooldridge (2009), we identified the absence of multicollinearity among the regressors implementing a Variance Inflation Factor (VIF). Secondly, we address potential endogeneity concerns by employing a Two-stage Least Squares approach with instrumental variables (2SLS-IV) (Granger, 1969; Wintoki et al., 2012). Our instrument set includes measures such as the depth of financial services supply to customers by country (*Financial_Services_Supply*); the volume of export of technology products and services by country (*Tech_Export*); the weight of the stock market on country GDP (*Stock_Market_GDP*); the level of law enforcement by country (*Law_Enforcement*). In particular, the variable *Financial_Services_Supply* is employed as an indicator of the advancement of the financial market, which in turn exerts an influence on the propensity of banks to engage in mergers and acquisitions (M&As) within the field of financial technology (FinTech).

Consequently, a higher level of this indicator is associated with a more developed financial environment, characterised by an increased demand for financial technologies (Desbordes & Wei, 2017). The export of technology products and services (*Tech_Export*) indicates a country's level of technological advancement and the extent to which its environment is oriented towards innovation. This suggests that banks situated in countries with a high level of technological exports are more likely to engage in M&As within the FinTech sector to integrate advanced technologies and improve their competitiveness (Wang et al., 2013). At the same time, the weight of the stock market on the country's GDP (*Stock_Market_GDP*) could be used as a proxy for the financial market's dynamism and openness to financial innovations. This can encourage banks to seek mergers and acquisitions in financial technology (FinTech) as a strategy to leverage emerging financial technologies (Croci & Petmezas, 2010). Finally, the *Law_Enforcement* is a key instrumental variable that reflects a country's legal and regulatory framework's effectiveness. Efficient law enforcement mechanisms are also crucial in mitigating transaction risks, as legal mechanisms are achieved by enforcing contractual terms, protecting property owners, and ensuring that business activities are legitimate. This is particularly important in FinTech M&As, as it safeguards intellectual property, provides the consistent application of financial regulations, and fosters a competitive market. A stable legal environment also attracts investments by reducing perceived risks, making investors and financial institutions more likely to engage in M&A activities (Glendening et al., 2016).

To ensure the validity of IVs used in our model, a first-stage F-test (Sanderson & Windmeijer, 2016) and a Stock-Yogo test (Stock & Yogo, 2005) have been performed to validate our results. These tests assess the strength of the relationship between our IVs and the main regressor (FinTech M&A). Identifying a strong relationship is important to validate the effectiveness of the 2SLS-IV model.

Additionally, the Cragg-Donald test ensures the absence of endogeneity in the final model (Cragg & Donald, 1993). This test evaluates if our IVs adequately address the endogeneity concern. Additionally, the Hansen J test check for overidentification, and the Sargan-Hansen test ensures that the errors are not correlated with the instrumental variables chosen (Durbin, 1954; Hausman, 1978; Sargan, 1958; Wu, 1973). To solve the heteroskedasticity problems, the Arellano-Bover coefficient estimation has been implemented in the 2SLS-IV final model (Arellano & Bover, 1995).

Table 5.2 provides the summary statistics for the variables used in the analysis. The variable ROE, used as a proxy for bank profitability, ranges from − 37.21 to 38.46. The Cost-to-Income Ratio (CIR), used to assess bank efficiency, ranges from 0.56 to 6.50. Lastly, the median and average values at 1.12 and 1.14 show a low level of dispersion, suggesting that most banks exhibit comparable levels of operational efficiency. The ZSC, which serves as a proxy for bank stability, ranges from 0.00 to 100.00, indicating considerable variability. The first quartile value of 2.98 and the median of 8.29 suggest that many banks demonstrate a stable profile.

Nevertheless, the higher maximum value indicates that some sampled banks have a strong stability profile. The average and median values of the default probabilities (PD1, PD3, and PD5) are low, suggesting that most banks face a low risk of default in all time horizons. Nevertheless, the maximum values (4.79, 10.47, and 11.51) indicate that a few banks face considerable default risk. There is considerable variation in the ESG performance scores, which range from 0.20 to 99.78. The

Table 5.2 Summary statistics

	Minimum	*1st Quart*	*Median*	*Average*	*3rd Quart*	*Maximum*
Dependent variables						
Profitability (ROE)	−37.21	4.22	8.93	10.14	15.17	38.46
Efficiency (CIR)	0.56	1.08	1.12	1.14	1.12	6.50
Stability (ZSC)	0.00	2.98	8.29	18.60	22.78	100.00
Short-term PD (PD1)	0.00	0.15	0.21	0.20	0.25	4.79
Medium-term PD (PD3)	0.03	0.76	0.83	0.82	0.89	10.47
Long-term PD (PD5)	0.12	1.30	1.36	1.36	1.42	11.51
ESG Performance	0.20	18.08	28.42	32.13	42.42	99.78
Explanatory variables						
FinTech M&A (FT_DEAL)	1.00	1.00	2.00	2.76	3.00	21.00
Capital endowment (CAP_END)	0.04	10.28	38.16	37.87	65.00	70.00
Commission fees (FEES)	3.58	15.53	16.43	16.30	17.76	23.66
Interest income margin (IIM)	−0.04	2.35	2.66	2.79	3.21	8.55
Market capitalisation (MKT_CAP)	7.53	17.55	18.70	18.56	19.95	27.34
Economic development (GDP_GROWTH)	−13.13	0.75	2.29	2.52	4.08	24.37
Bank concentration (BNK_CON)	0.00	32.07	43.24	45.05	66.51	100.00
Inflation (INF)	−4.48	0.80	2.09	2.95	3.57	96.09

Note The table reports the summary statistics of the variables used in our empirical analysis. The sample comprises banks worldwide over the period 1997 to 2022. The variable descriptions are provided in Table 5.1
Source Author's elaboration

values of the first quartile, median, and third quartile (18.08, 28.42, and 42.42) demonstrate a skewed distribution, with many banks exhibiting moderately high ESG performance.

The FinTech M&A variable, which is the main regressor between the explanatory variables, indicates that the majority of banks engage in a limited number of deals, with a minimum and first quartile value of 1.

The median value is 2, indicating that at least half of the banks have engaged in up to 2 deals. However, the mean number of deals is 2.76, with a third quartile of 3. This indicates that a less significant proportion of banks participate in more transactions, with a maximum of 21 transactions. Banks' total assets (TA) show significant variability, ranging from 48.00 to around 1.9 trillion. The high median and mean values (14 million and approximately 10.36 billion, respectively) indicate a substantial presence of large banks in the dataset. The CAP_END index, with a range of 0.04 to 70.00, has a median of 38.16 and a mean of 37.87. It should be noted that most banks have proven to have sound capital ratios, which are very important in hedging potential losses by ensuring that the banks are adequately capitalised. Commissions (FEES) range from 3.58 to 23. 6, with median and average values close to 16.43 and 16.30, respectively. The interest income margin (IIM) exhibits a range of −0.04 to 8.55, indicating that most banks exhibit moderate margins, with median and average estimates of 2.66 and 2.79, respectively. The Market Capitalisation (MKT_CAP) ranges from 7.53 to 27.34. The median is equal to 18.70, while the average is 18.56.

Regarding the macroeconomic control variables, the GDP_ GROWTH variable has a relatively wide range, ranging from -13.13 to 24.37, reflecting the different economic characteristics of the countries where sampled banks operate. The variable bank concentration (BNK_CON) value varies from 0.00 to 100.00, with a median value of 43.00, representing the degree of market concentration in the banking industry. In this case, 0 represents perfect competition, and 1 represents monopoly. Furthermore, there was a notable disparity in the inflation rates, which ranged from −4.48 to 96.09, with a median of 2.09 and an average of 2.95. This evidence illustrates the diverse economic conditions that affect the banking sector. Table 5.3 provides the correlation matrix.

5.3 Empirical Results and Discussion

Do FinTech M&As Affect Bank Performance?

Tables 5.4 and 5.5 report the results of baseline regression. Each column of these tables represents one of the seven dependent variables used to assess banks' performance. Specifically, Table 5.4 focuses on balance sheet performance metrics, such as ROE (Bank Profitability), CIR (Bank Efficiency), and Z-Score (Bank Stability). Differently, Table 5.5 exhibits the

Table 5.3 Correlation matrix

	FT_ DEAL	*ROE*	*CIR*	*ZSC*	*PD1*	*PD3*	*PD5*	*ESG*	*TA*	*CAP_ END*	*FEES*	*IIM*	*MRK_ CAP*	*GDP*	*BNK_ CON*	*INF*
FT_ DEAL	**1.00**	0.03	−0.04	0.03	0.00	0.00	0.00	0.00	−0.06	−0.06	−0.03	−0.03	−0.04	0.09	−0.09	0.10
ROE		**1.00**	0.36	−0.11	0.08	−0.09	−0.07	−0.04	0.09	−0.18	0.03	0.44	0.11	0.04	−0.09	0.02
CIR			**1.00**	−0.10	0.01	−0.06	−0.06	−0.06	0.15	0.41	0.24	0.13	0.19	0.01	0.03	−0.01
ZSC				**1.00**	−0.03	0.05	0.03	0.02	−0.05	−0.02	−0.05	−0.05	−0.20	−0.05	0.01	0.00
PD1					**1.00**	−0.09	−0.08	−0.06	0.20	−0.14	−0.06	0.04	−0.01	−0.03	0.09	0.06
PD3						**1.00**	0.89	0.83	−0.04	−0.05	−0.06	0.02	−0.11	0.00	−0.01	−0.01
PD5							**1.00**	0.99	−0.04	−0.09	−0.08	0.03	−0.11	0.01	0.00	−0.01
ESG								**1.00**	−0.04	−0.12	−0.09	0.05	−0.12	0.01	0.00	−0.01
TA									**1.00**	0.15	0.27	0.16	0.24	0.00	0.04	0.00
CAP_ END										**1.00**	0.36	−0.17	0.22	−0.01	0.12	−0.03
FEES											**1.00**	−0.07	0.71	0.01	−0.01	0.00
IIM												**1.00**	0.01	0.07	0.00	0.04
MRK_ CAP													**1.00**	0.01	−0.02	0.00
GDP														**1.00**	−0.02	0.17
BNK_ CON															**1.00**	−0.04
INF																**1.00**

Note The table presents the correlation matrix for the variables used in this study, including dependent, explanatory, and control variables. Dependent variables are profitability (ROE), efficiency (CIR), stability (ZSC), and probability of default for short term (PD1), medium term (PD3), and long term (PD5), as well as ESG performance (ESG). Explanatory variables include FinTech M&A activity (FT_DEAL) and other factors such as capital endowment (CAP_END), commission fees (FEES), interest income margin (IIM), and market capitalisation (MRK_CAP). Control variables include economic development (GDP_GROWTH), bank concentration (BNK_CON), and inflation (INF)

Source Author's elaboration

results related to market-based measures, such as bank Probability of Default (PD) from short-, medium- and long-term perspectives and bank ESG Performance. All the models include bank-specific and country-specific control variables that have an economically meaningful and statistically significant impact on bank performance metrics.

Table 5.4 Bank performance at balance sheet values regression model

	Bank Performance *Bank Profitability*	*Bank Efficiency*	*Bank Stability*
Constant	−8.055***	1.312***	−23.318***
	(0.928)	(0.021)	(2.710)
FinTech M&A	0.341**	0.006*	−0.995**
	(0.141)	(0.003)	(0.435)
Bank Size	0.385***	−0.003***	0.880***
	(0.025)	(0.001)	(0.077)
Capital Endowment	−0.035***	−0.0002*	0.380***
	(0.005)	(0.0001)	(0.014)
Commission Fees	0.127*	0.013***	0.396*
	(0.068)	(0.002)	(0.212)
Interest Income Margin	3.140***	−0.005**	0.051***
	(0.095)	(0.002)	(0.001)
Market Capitalisation	0.161***	−0.017***	0.396**
	(0.054)	(0.001)	(0.166)
Economic Development	0.059*	−0.003***	0.221**
	(0.034)	(0.001)	(0.106)
Bank Concentration	−0.025***	0.0001	−0.023*
	(0.004)	(0.0001)	(0.012)
Inflation	0.006	0.0001	0.055
	(0.024)	(0.001)	(0.076)
Bank fixed effect	*Yes*	*Yes*	*Yes*
Year fixed effect	*Yes*	*Yes*	*Yes*
Observations	4420	4420	4420
R2	0.264	0.064	0.209
Adjusted R2	0.262	0.062	0.208
F Statistic	175.406***	33.714***	145.847***

Note The table reports the baseline results on the effect of FinTech M&A on Bank Profitability (ROE), Efficiency (CIR), and Stability (Z-Score). The sample spans the 1997–2022 period. We estimate the model using a polled panel data model. Standard errors are clustered at the bank level. *t*-statistics are in parentheses. ***, **, and * indicate significance at the 1%, 5%, and 10% levels, respectively

Table 5.5 Bank performance at market-based values regression model

	Bank Performance Short-term Bank PD	*Medium-term Bank PD*	*Long-term Bank PD*	*Bank ESG performance*
Constant	0.391***	1.127***	1.682***	11.066***
	(0.019)	(0.034)	(0.039)	(2.182)
FinTech M&A	−0.006**	−0.012**	−0.014**	1.708***
	(0.003)	(0.005)	(0.006)	(0.331)
Bank Size	−0.008***	−0.012***	−0.011***	1.572***
	(0.001)	(0.001)	(0.001)	(0.059)
Capital Endowment	−0.0005***	−0.001***	−0.001***	−0.061***
	(0.0001)	(0.0002)	(0.0002)	(0.011)
Interest Income Margin	−0.002	−0.0004	0.004	1.070***
	(0.002)	(0.003)	(0.004)	(0.223)
Commission Fees	0.004***	0.005**	0.004	−0.313*
	(0.001)	(0.003)	(0.003)	(0.161)
Market Capitalisation	−0.005***	−0.008***	−0.009***	−0.246*
	(0.001)	(0.002)	(0.002)	(0.127)
Economic Development	−0.001	−0.0002	−0.00004	−0.147*
	(0.001)	(0.001)	(0.001)	(0.080)
Bank Concentration	0.0001	0.0002	0.0002	0.050***
	(0.0001)	(0.0001)	(0.0002)	(0.009)
Inflation	−0.0005	−0.001	−0.001	0.292***
	(0.001)	(0.001)	(0.001)	(0.057)
Bank fixed effect	*Yes*	*Yes*	*Yes*	*Yes*
Year fixed effect	*Yes*	*Yes*	*Yes*	*Yes*
Observations	4420	4420	4420	4420
R2	0.069	0.054	0.049	0.173
Adjusted R2	0.068	0.052	0.047	0.171
F Statistic	121.321***	33.628***	126.812***	75.847***

Note The table reports the baseline results on the effect of FinTech M&A on Short-, Medium-, and Long-term Probability of Default (1-year PD, 3-year PD, and 5-year PD, respectively) and Bank ESG Performance (ESG score). The sample spans the 1997–2022 period. We estimate the model using a polled panel data model. Standard errors are clustered at the bank level. *t*-statistics are in parentheses. ***, **, and * indicate significance at the 1%, 5%, and 10% levels, respectively

The baseline regression model shows the manifold impacts of FinTech investment made by traditional banks on several bank performance metrics widely used in the banking literature. Table 5.4 exhibits how the selected bank *Profitability*, *Efficiency*, and *Stability* metrics have been differently impacted by financial technology investments. These results reflect both the opportunities and challenges related to the integration processes of advanced technological assets within traditional banking structures.

Specifically, our results show that FinTech M&As positively impact *Bank Profitability* (0.341**), suggesting that these strategic activities improve bank ROE through several mechanisms. Firstly, the acquisition of financial technology (FinTech) companies introduces new technologies that have the potential to generate additional revenue streams. This can be achieved by developing innovative financial products or services that attract new customers or enhance the competitive market positioning of incumbent banks. Secondly, according to Bussoli et al. (2023), FinTech firms support banks to make their business models more flexible, efficient, and innovative. This result exacerbates a literature stream showing that banks have historically developed financial innovations to increase profitability (Scott et al., 2017; Spohrer & Maglio, 2010).

When we evaluate the cost-to-income ratio (CIR) as a proxy to assess the *Bank's Efficiency,* the positive coefficient (0.006*) reflects a loss of operational efficiency for the banking industry. This effect, in line with the evidence previously provided by Lee et al. (2023), may arise from the high upfront costs associated with M&A operations, including legal fees, restructuring expenses, and the significant costs involved in integrating technological systems from different entities. Furthermore, cultural and operational discrepancies between traditional banking institutions and FinTech firms often lead to misalignments that can inhibit decision-making processes and affect operational efficiency. This misalignment tends to result in elevated operational costs as efforts are made to harmonise different practices and systems. This discrepancy is typical between incumbents and startup operators. Moreover, FinTech firms initially operate with less developed regulatory and compliance frameworks than established banks, as highlighted by EBA (2020). Thus, substantial investments are frequently required following the acquisition to upgrade FinTech's operations to meet rigorous regulatory standards, further increasing the CIR ratio.

Regarding the FinTech M&A impact on the *Bank Stability* profile, the empirical findings indicate a negative impact on the Z-score variable (−0.995**), suggesting an increase in bank idiosyncratic risk. This may be due to the challenges faced by traditional banks in integrating new digital services and aligning them with existing banking infrastructures (e.g., complex banking legacy systems, Deloitte, 2020) and burdensome banking regulations. Substantially, financial technology investments may bring new intrinsic balance sheet-driven riskiness to the banking sector, which incumbent banks must carefully manage and mitigate. Concurrently, the investment in FinTech results in a reduction of the bank's liquidity. The M&A transactions involve a net outflow of cash flows in exchange for an investment in financial startups that are functional for carrying out activities that may not be core to the incumbent's business model.

Table 5.5 exhibits the impact of bank-FinTech M&As on different market-based metrics. The first three columns of the table examine the effect of a bank's investment in financial innovation on its probabilities of default (PD) over different time horizons (i.e., Short-, Medium-, and Long-term Bank PD). The results indicate that bank equity investments reduce the bank's PD, as measured by Merton's model at market values (Merton, 1974), across all time frames observed. The main regressor (FinTech M&A) shows a coefficient that gradually increases over a long-term perspective: −0.006**, −0.012**, −0.014**, respectively. FinTech investments and the consequent integration of advanced technologies and tools have led to a more diversified range of traditional banking services and products, mainly integrating technology-driven customer services. This diversification contributes to increased revenues and a stabilisation of risk profiles, enhancing risk management capabilities. Specifically, incorporating advanced technologies, such as artificial intelligence (AI) and machine learning (ML), equips banks with the capacity to identify, assess, and manage risks more dynamically. This capability enables real-time decision-making and more personalised risk assessment capabilities, directly improving the bank's risk profile. Furthermore, investment in FinTech can significantly enhance customer experience and retention activity. In particular, introducing digital offerings has increased customer satisfaction and loyalty, which raises revenues and the financial profile of traditional financial institutions.

The last non-financial performance metric assessed in our analysis captures the bank's Environmental, Social, and Governance (ESG) performance score. The integration of *ESG performance* metrics together with more traditional financial performance indicators (ROE, CIR, ZSC; PD) in our analysis arises from the increasing attention of practitioners and scholars on the possible association between ESG and FinTech (Collevecchio et al., 2024; Galeone et al., 2024; Huang et al., 2023; Li et al., 2023a, 2023b; Uddin et al., 2024; Wu et al., 2024). In this perspective, current literature has highlighted the role of FinTech as an accelerator of sustainable economic growth or environmental efficiency (Uddin et al., 2024) and, thus, part of the technological innovations related to sustainable finance (Galeone et al., 2024). Empirical studies have also emphasised how the collaborations with FinTech firms support banks in achieving sustainability objectives more quickly and efficiently (Zhou et al., 2020) and how these new financial entities can assist banks in promoting the corporate green transformation, which could be better achieved by alleviating information asymmetry, relaxing financial constraints and increasing risk-taking (Wu et al., 2024).

In line with previous studies that have found a link between FinTech development and improvements in ESG dimensions in different manners (for example, Dicuonzo et al., 2023), we find a significant and positive relationship (1.708***) between FinTech M&A and bank ESG performance. Specifically, our findings suggest that FinTech equity investments offer a significant opportunity to enhance banks' compliance with ESG criteria, addressing a critical research gap.

This improvement is mainly attributable to FinTech's ability to facilitate more efficient resource management, which can reduce environmental footprint through enhanced operational efficiencies and the promotion of digital over physical processes. Furthermore, FinTech enables better tracking and reporting of ESG metrics, which enhances transparency and accountability. The incorporation of advanced technologies allows banks to address sustainable issues more proactively. For instance, the advent of FinTech has the potential to facilitate the development and implementation of more rigorous ESG policies, thereby encouraging investments in green and sustainable projects. This heightened sensitivity to ESG concerns is not merely a matter of compliance, but it increasingly regards a core component of corporate strategy that aligns with customer and stakeholder expectations in addition to the bank's global sustainability goals.

Our results support the literature field focused on the growing convergence of FinTech and ESG strategies, which represents a relevant alignment with the evolving dynamics of the global financial sector. As policymakers, market operators, supervisory banking authorities, and bank stakeholders (BIS, 2021a) increasingly prioritise sustainability and ethical governance, banks that integrate these sustainable practices into their business models are likely to comply more with current requirements and thus could achieve greater long-term success and business model viability. This strategic alignment emphasises not only profitability but also the role of financial institutions in fostering broader societal well-being.

The results of the baseline regression analysis have been summarised in Table 5.6. It indicates how FinTech M&A positively impacts bank profitability (ROE), as introducing new technologies and innovative financial products increases revenue streams. However, financial technology investments negatively impact bank efficiency (CIR), reflecting higher operating costs due to integration challenges and alignment issues between incumbents and newcomers. FinTech M&A has a negative impact on bank stability (Z-score), suggesting an increased balance sheet riskiness for banks involved in FinTech M&As.

In terms of market-based measures, FinTech M&A reduces the probability of default over short-, medium-, and long-term horizons, improving risk management and diversification. In addition, FinTech M&A significantly improves ESG performance, enabling better resource management, transparency, and compliance with sustainability criteria.

Do Time Factors Affect the Impact of FinTech M&As on Bank Performance?

To address RQ2 and mitigate potential endogeneity concerns, we incorporate the lagged value of the FinTech M&A variable (main regressor), positing that prior FinTech investment may influence current bank performance metrics.

The analysis demonstrates that only the *market-based performance* measures are subject to the temporal factor. Consequently, only the lagged effects of FinTech M&As on PD and ESG performance are reported. Specifically, Table 5.7 illustrates how FinTech M&A activities have a delayed impact on banks' ESG performance. The findings suggest that the magnitude of the influence of FinTech M&A on ESG performance is not immediate, but it evolves gradually, with notable impacts seen in different delayed models.

When the temporal effect is not considered, the results indicate that FinTech M&A transactions significantly and positively impact ESG performance, as evidenced by a coefficient of 4.887***. This evidence suggests a prompt improvement in ESG performance after FinTech acquisitions. Nevertheless, reading the table horizontally as time delays are incorporated into the analysis, the noted impact diminishes, maintaining its statistical significance.

In the *Lag 1 model*, the coefficient of 3.892*** suggests that the influence of FinTech M&A on ESG performance remains significant but with

Table 5.6 Summary of baseline results

	Bank Performance						
	Profitability	*Efficiency*	*Riskiness* (balance sheet)	*Riskiness* (market-based)			*ESG performance*
	ROE	*CIR*	*ZSC*	*PD1*	*PD2*	*PD3*	*ESG score*
Fintech M&As	0.341** Improvement	0.006* Worsening	–0.995** Worsening	–0.006** Improvement	–0.012** Improvement	–0.014** Improvement	1.708*** Improvement

Note The table summarises the baseline results, indicating how the main regressor (FinTech M&As) impacts bank performance metrics. Each arrow indicates an improvement or a worsening for each dependent variable
Source Author's elaboration

Table 5.7 ESG performance and lagged FinTech M&A effects

	Bank ESG Performance			
	No Lag Model	*Lag 1 Year*	*Lag 2 Years*	*Lag 3 Years*
Constant	31.607***	31.464***	31.344***	31.298***
	(0.284)	(0.298)	(0.311)	(0.324)
FinTech M&A	4.887***	3.892***	3.300***	2.651***
	(0.739)	(0.746)	(0.746)	(0.748)
FinTech M&A (Lag 1)		5.064***	4.087***	3.621***
		(0.746)	(0.751)	(0.751)
FinTech M&A (Lag 2)			5.496***	4.600***
			(0.755)	(0.762)
FinTech M&A (Lag 3)				5.152***
				(0.764)
Bank fixed effect	*Yes*	*Yes*	*Yes*	*Yes*
Year fixed effect	*Yes*	*Yes*	*Yes*	*Yes*
Observations	4420	4250	4080	3910
R2	0.010	0.020	0.031	0.041
Adjusted R2	0.010	0.019	0.030	0.040
F Statistic	43.785***	42.914***	43.694***	41.350***

Note The table reports the regression results of the lagged effect of FinTech M&A on Bank ESG Performance (ESG score). The sample spans the 1997–2022 period. We estimate the model using a polled panel data model. Standard errors are clustered at the bank level. *t*-statistics are in parentheses. ***, **, and * indicate significance at the 1%, 5%, and 10% levels, respectively

a slightly diminished effect compared to the model with no lag. This indicates that the beneficial outcomes of FinTech M&A continue in the next period, although with a reduced level of impact. With a growing time delay, the effects of the coefficients on ESG performance in the second (3.300***) and third (2.651***) lagged models persist, progressively diminishing. Even with a decrease, the impact of FinTech M&A on ESG performance is still statistically relevant, showing that this influence persists over time, although it weakens during the time horizon observed. The results also indicate that previous FinTech M&As performed by incumbents significantly impact present banks' ESG score. In the *Lag 1 model,* the coefficient (5.064***) indicates that FinTech M&A activities from the previous period have a greater influence on the current ESG performance than the immediate impact seen in the *no-lag model.* The *Lag 2 model's* coefficient (5.496***) increases, showing that FinTech M&A activities have the strongest impact two periods post-transaction. The *Lag*

3 model shows a slight decrease in the coefficient (5.152***), but the effect is still considered significant.

These outcomes are linked to *post*-M&A integration and the achievement of synergies (Meckling & Jensen, 1976), especially within the FinTech industry. After M&A operations, banks and FinTech firms go through a phase of integration, where the impact on ESG performance could be affected by early restructuring and alignment hurdles. As the partnership between the bank and the acquired FinTech company strengthened and they started to appreciate the benefits of working together, the impact on ESG performance became increasingly noticeable and significant. Nevertheless, once the full benefits of the merger have been realised and the initial advantages have been fully exploited, the subsequent improvements in ESG performance will naturally become less pronounced, resulting in a reduction in the impact size over the longer term.

Table 5.8 exhibits how FinTech M&A activities impact banks' probability of default (PD), assessing both immediate and delayed effects. The findings indicate that the influence of FinTech M&A on default risk is not linear and constant over time. In the overall model with no lag effects, the FinTech M&A coefficient is positive (0.010) but not statistically significant, indicating a small, yet insignificant, rise in default likelihood right after a FinTech M&A. This result suggests that in the short run, the direct effect of these deals on default risk is negligible. Nevertheless, the delayed models offer a more complete understanding of the impact of FinTech M&A on default probability as time progresses. In the *Lag 1 model,* the immediate effect remains unaltered. However, the introduction of a one-period lag results in a positive but statistically insignificant outcome.

In the *Lag 2 model*, the impact of FinTech M&A from two periods earlier suggests a noteworthy decrease in default probability, indicated by a negative coefficient (−0.016**). Similarly, the *Lag 3 model* suggests a reduction in the bank's default risk (−0.015**), even if the coefficient is slightly diminished.

Several factors can be attributed to FinTech M&A's capacity to decrease banks' PD over extended periods. At first, mergers and acquisitions, especially those related to FinTech companies, might bring uncertainty and integration obstacles, resulting in a slight rise in perceived risk. That is why the initial effect on PD is not important or could even indicate a slight rise. Nevertheless, as time progresses and the integration process

Table 5.8 Probability of default and lagged FinTech M&A effects

	Bank Probability of Default			
	No Lag Model	*Lag 1 Year*	*Lag 2 Years*	*Lag 3 Years*
Constant	0.201***	0.200***	0.200***	0.201***
	(0.002)	(0.003)	(0.003)	(0.003)
FinTech M&A	0.010	0.010	0.011*	0.013*
	(0.006)	(0.006)	(0.007)	(0.007)
FinTech M&A (Lag 1)		0.003	0.006	0.007
		(0.006)	(0.007)	(0.007)
FinTech M&A (Lag 2)			−0.016**	−0.013*
			(0.007)	(0.007)
FinTech M&A (Lag 3)				−0.015**
				(0.007)
Bank fixed effect	*Yes*	*Yes*	*Yes*	*Yes*
Year fixed effect	*Yes*	*Yes*	*Yes*	*Yes*
Observations	4420	4250	4080	3910
R2	0.001	0.001	0.002	0.003
Adjusted R2	0.0003	0.0002	0.001	0.002
F Statistic	2.395	1.398	2.873**	3.367***

Note The table reports the regression results of the lagged effect of FinTech M&A on Bank Probability of Default (5-year PD). The sample spans the 1997–2022 period. We estimate the model using a polled panel data model. Standard errors are clustered at the bank level. *t*-statistics are in parentheses. ***, **, and * indicate significance at the 1%, 5%, and 10% levels, respectively

becomes more established, the advantages of these strategic operations become increasingly evident.

This is mainly due to the rationality exercised by banks in balancing the benefits of cooperation between banks and FinTech firms. It also shows how FinTech firms innovate by introducing new technologies, improving efficiency, and expanding access to different customer segments, which is helpful for the financial health of the acquiring bank. These synergies can be somewhat elusive, based on coordinating business activities and applying interfaces and technologies across the bank's functions. Once the integration becomes more established, the bank could see reduced costs, better risk management abilities, and increased revenue streams due to the broader services made possible by acquiring FinTech. The enhancements aid in bolstering the bank's financial standing, subsequently decreasing its overall risk level and likelihood of default. Furthermore, FinTech companies frequently implement quicker and more data-focused decision-making methods, resulting in improved credit risk evaluations and more efficient bank loan portfolio management. Over time, these elements reduce the probability of default, as shown by the notable negative coefficients in the previous models.

The delayed adverse impacts may suggest a market response to perceived risks associated with FinTech M&A. Initially, markets may hesitate due to risks in FinTech-bank integrations; however, if the integration succeeds and anticipated benefits are realised, the market may adjust its view, recognising reduced risk and improved stability.

Do Banks' Business Models Affect the Impact of FinTech M&As on Bank Performance?

In response to RQ3, we perform an additional analysis on all the performance metrics identified, focusing on the business model (BM) adopted by each bank within our sample. As detailed in Chapter 3 of this monograph, a cluster analysis was employed to identify each business model (BM). Three distinct BMs were identified. The first cluster comprises *Retail Banks,* financial institutions that rely predominantly on customer deposits for funding and focus on customer loans within their portfolios. They seek to balance optimal performance and risk minimisation within the financial system. These banks maintain elevated levels of capital endowment capable of absorbing losses, emphasising their commitment to financial stability and enhancing customer trust. The second cluster comprises *Investment Banks*, which are financial institutions that engage in investment activities on behalf of clients and their accounts. These institutions demonstrate a pronounced inclination towards investment-related activities, characterised by substantial trading assets and derivatives operations.

Conversely, they tend to engage in interbank lending to a lesser extent, operating with elevated leverage. These banks are characterised by substantial holdings in securities and active participation in derivatives. Their principal source of income is commissions derived from investment activities conducted on behalf of clients and on their accounts. These banks are inclined to investment-related operations with substantial trading assets and derivatives activities. They typically engage in less interbank lending and operate with elevated leverage. Finally, the third cluster includes *Diversified Assets Banks,* which maintain a diverse asset portfolio encompassing traditional banking products and a range of other financial instruments, including equities, bonds, liquid assets, and derivatives. Their asset allocation strategy is designed to avoid excessive concentration in any asset class, fostering a balanced asset management approach.

The results presented in Table 5.9 exhibit how the intercept coefficient of FinTech M&A on the Bank Profitability metric (i.e., ROE) varies in accordance with the business models adopted by banks. In Table 5.9, the first column, designated "*General*", encompasses analysis results that do not consider the influence of any specific business model (BM). Overall, this indicates that the effect of FinTech M&A on bank ROE varies, suggesting that the operational and funding structure of each type of bank significantly influences the impact of FinTech M&A. Specifically, the subgroup analysis reveals that the effect of FinTech M&A on ROE in the *Retail Bank (BM1)* subgroup is positive and statistically significant, with a coefficient of 0.587***. This result reflects the potential benefits these banks could derive from acquiring FinTech firms, particularly in increasing short-term profitability. The core business of retail banks involves customer deposits and loans, making them more dependent on customer-facing services. Integration of FinTech expertise into these banks significantly improves the customer experience through digital banking platforms, efficient loan processing systems, and personalised financial services and products.

Moreover, FinTech can streamline operations and improve risk management, which is crucial for retail banks, given their focus on retail customers and small businesses. Conversely, *Investment Banks (BM2)* exhibit a negative coefficient for the main regressor (−0–408*), which may be attributed to the nature of investment banks, which are extensively engaged in securities and derivatives trading activities. The integration of FinTech firms in their complex business model may result in operational changes to existing operational workflows or the necessity for substantial adjustments to strategies that are initially expensive, or that can reduce focus on core investment activities. Additionally, an *Investment bank* invests in financial technology assets by adopting a long-term perspective to improve its profitability profile; this can justify the negative impact on the ROE metric in a short-term perspective.

The empirical findings indicate that the investment activity of *Diversified Assets Banks (BM3)* in FinTech players is not expected to significantly impact the profitability profile of the banks in question (−0.379). Following the perspective posited by Ayadi et al. (2021), these banks

Table 5.9 Profitability analysis among Banking Business Models (BBMs) subgroups

	Bank Profitability General	*Retail Bank*	*Investment Bank*	*Diversified Assets Bank*
Constant	2.256**	6.359***	−0.099	−2.862
	(0.878)	(1.573)	(1.429)	(2.091)
FinTech M&A	−0.025	0.587**	−0.408*	−0.379
	(0.156)	(0.258)	(0.225)	(0.366)
Bank Size	0.271***	0.140**	0.348***	0.047
	(0.028)	(0.061)	(0.038)	(0.080)
Capital Endowment	−0.061***	−0.077***	−0.018	−0.049***
	(0.005)	(0.012)	(0.014)	(0.011)
Market Capitalisation	0.336***	0.243***	0.254***	0.816***
	(0.044)	(0.066)	(0.066)	(0.114)
Economic Development	0.124***	0.192***	0.023	0.076
	(0.038)	(0.062)	(0.060)	(0.081)
Bank Concentration	−0.021***	−0.027***	−0.009	−0.023**
	(0.004)	(0.007)	(0.006)	(0.009)
Inflation	0.026	−0.013	0.025	0.099*
	(0.027)	(0.044)	(0.043)	(0.058)
Bank fixed effect	*Yes*	*Yes*	*Yes*	*Yes*
Year fixed effect	*Yes*	*Yes*	*Yes*	*Yes*
Observations	4420	1840	1584	994
R2	0.082	0.049	0.078	0.083
Adjusted R2	0.080	0.045	0.074	0.077
F Statistic	55.933***	13.344***	18.970***	12.812***

Note The table reports the regression results of FinTech M&A on Bank Profitability (ROE), grouping the results according to the identified banking business models (BBMs). The BBMs are Retail Bank (BM1), Investment Bank (BM2), and Diversified Assets Bank (BM3). The sample spans the 1997–2022 period. We estimate the model using a polled panel data model. Standard errors are clustered at the bank level. *t*-statistics are in parentheses. ***, **, and * indicate significance at the 1%, 5%, and 10% levels, respectively

possess a wide-ranging asset portfolio comprising many financial instruments extending beyond traditional banking practices' conventional boundaries. Consequently, although the strategic integration of FinTech may extend the range of products and services, implementing new tools, knowledge, and business processes may also present challenges across all areas of bank activity, particularly regarding the costs and complexities associated with the compliant management of FinTech digital services.

The bank-specific controls that are significant performance predictors in the subgroup models are *Banks Size*, *Capital Endowment,* and

Market Capitalisation. More in detail, the *Bank Size* regressor shows a positive and statistical significance in the models under study, with a coefficient more prominent for the *Investment Bank* cluster (0.348***), which better benefit from economies of scale, particularly when they diversify their investment strategies, looking at new business and market opportunities. Similarly, *Market Capitalisation* positively affects *Bank Profitability*, indicating that banks with higher market valuations are more profitable. The effect is most pronounced in the *Diversified Assets Banks* (0.816***), which may reflect market confidence in this bank's financial stability and asset management strategies. This confidence may attract more investment, enabling more profitable operations. Concerning the *Capital Endowment*, the findings reveal a negative effect on profitability for all bank types, with the strongest effect observed in *Retail Banks* (−0.077***). This indicates that while higher capital reserves may reduce risk, they may also lower profitability and potentially reduce returns on investments (ROI).

Table 5.10 illustrates the impact of FinTech M&As on *Bank Efficiency*, which is measured by the cost-to-income (CIR). In addition to the statistical significance exhibited by the "*General*" model, the "*Retail Bank*" subgroup is the only one to demonstrate, in the short term, a statistically significant loss of efficiency (0.011**). These banks have traditionally focused on deposit-taking and lending activities, resulting in less flexible operating models. These characteristics also make integrating advanced FinTech solutions more challenging and expensive. *Retail banks* are also directly exposed to market competition (such as Challenger banks, Neo Banks, FinTech, TechFin, BigTech, Washington et al., 2022), which can offer more efficient financial services at lower costs. These factors prompt *Retail banks* to invest in innovation to maintain competitiveness, even without an immediate return on investment. Indeed, investment in financial technology may require a substantial change in the business model of a retail bank, which may result in a temporary increase in operating costs (e.g., through the requirement for staff training, process restructuring, etc.), thereby influencing the cost-income ratio.

In contrast, *Investment* and *Diversified Assets banks* operate on a large scale and have a more diversified asset portfolio, which may include trading, equity investments, and derivatives. Diversifying activities may permit greater flexibility in absorbing the costs associated with integrating FinTech technologies without significantly impacting the CIR. Furthermore, *Investment* and *Diversified Assets banks* may possess expertise and

Table 5.10 Efficiency analysis among Banking Business Models (BBMs) subgroups

	Bank Efficiency General	*Retail Bank*	*Investment Bank*	*Diversified Assets Bank*
Constant	1.312***	1.300***	1.309***	1.279***
	(0.021)	(0.030)	(0.059)	(0.024)
FinTech M&A	0.006*	0.011**	0.002	−0.001
	(0.003)	(0.004)	(0.007)	(0.004)
Bank Size	−0.003***	−0.003***	−0.003**	−0.002*
	(0.001)	(0.001)	(0.001)	(0.001)
Capital Endowment	−0.0002*	−0.001***	0.001*	−0.0001
	(0.0001)	(0.0002)	(0.0004)	(0.0001)
Interest Income Margin	−0.005**	−0.007***	−0.009	−0.002
	(0.002)	(0.003)	(0.006)	(0.002)
Commission Fees	0.013***	0.013***	0.017***	0.001
	(0.002)	(0.002)	(0.004)	(0.002)
Market Capitalisation	−0.017***	−0.015***	−0.023***	−0.007***
	(0.001)	(0.002)	(0.002)	(0.002)
Economic Development	−0.003***	−0.002*	−0.008***	−0.001
	(0.001)	(0.001)	(0.002)	(0.001)
Bank Concentration	0.0001	−0.00002	0.0003	−0.00003
	(0.0001)	(0.0001)	(0.0002)	(0.0001)
Inflation	0.0001	−0.0002	0.0002	0.001
	(0.001)	(0.001)	(0.001)	(0.001)
Bank fixed effect	*Yes*	*Yes*	*Yes*	*Yes*
Time fixed effect	*Yes*	*Yes*	*Yes*	*Yes*
Observations	4420	1840	1584	994
R2	0.064	0.070	0.076	0.061
Adjusted R2	0.062	0.065	0.071	0.052
F Statistic	33.714***	15.318***	14.434***	7.096***

Note The table reports the regression results of FinTech M&A on Bank Efficiency (CIR), grouping the results according to the identified banking business models (BBMs). The BBMs are Retail Bank (BM1), Investment Bank (BM2), and Diversified Assets Bank (BM3). The sample spans the 1997–2022 period. We estimate the model using a polled panel data model. Standard errors are clustered at the bank level. *t*-statistics are in parentheses. ***, **, and * indicate significance at the 1%, 5%, and 10% levels, respectively

resources dedicated to technological innovation, which could facilitate the adoption of FinTech solutions. This may result in a reduced impact on the CIR compared to *Retail Banks*, which may lack the in-house expertise in this field.

Looking at the balance sheet riskiness metric in Table 5.11, the subsample analysis confirms the negative impact of FinTech M&As

on ZSC, remarking a worsening in bank stability (−1.062** for the General Model). Nevertheless, our findings indicate that financial technology investments exert a negligible influence when the banking models adopted by banks observed in the study are taken into account. Although the overall stability of the banking system may be negatively impacted, potentially due to heightened competition, technological disruptions, or integration challenges resulting from M&A strategies, the immediate impact on individual banks' balance sheets was not statistically significant.

Tables 5.12, 5.13, and 5.14 show the impact of M&A in FinTech on market risk measures, showing an average decrease in banks' PD in one, three, and five years. In particular, the short-term analysis shows that

Table 5.11 Riskiness analysis at balance sheet values among Banking Business Models (BBMs) subgroups

	Bank Stability General	*Retail Bank*	*Investment Bank*	*Diversified Assets Bank*
Constant	−11.697***	1.375	−8.880**	−18.629***
	(1.574)	(2.014)	(4.000)	(4.349)
FinTech M&A	−1.062**	−0.442	−1.077	−0.980
	(0.436)	(0.466)	(0.856)	−1.088
Bank Size	0.970***	0.098	1.255***	1.165***
	(0.075)	(0.110)	(0.140)	(0.217)
Capital Endowment	0.404***	0.412***	0.307***	0.452***
	(0.013)	(0.022)	(0.053)	(0.031)
Economic Development	0.236**	0.177	0.281	0.340
	(0.106)	(0.112)	(0.230)	(0.242)
Bank Concentration	−0.028**	−0.003	−0.058**	−0.015
	(0.012)	(0.013)	(0.024)	(0.028)
Inflation	0.061	0.127	0.006	0.170
	(0.076)	(0.079)	(0.163)	(0.174)
Bank fixed effect	*Yes*	*Yes*	*Yes*	*Yes*
Time fixed effect	*Yes*	*Yes*	*Yes*	*Yes*
Observations	4420	1840	1584	994
R2	0.204	0.164	0.075	0.265
Adjusted R2	0.203	0.161	0.071	0.260
F Statistic	188.502***	59.901***	21.165***	59.286***

Note The table reports the regression results of FinTech M&A on Bank Stability (Z-Score), grouping the results according to the identified banking business models (BBMs). The BBMs are Retail Bank (BM1), Investment Bank (BM2), and Diversified Assets Bank (BM3). The sample spans the 1997–2022 period. We estimate the model using a polled panel data model. Standard errors are clustered at the bank level. *t*-statistics are in parentheses. ***, **, and * indicate significance at the 1%, 5%, and 10% levels, respectively the market views investments in financial innovation as positive, especially for *Investment Bank* (−0.007**) and *Diversified Assets Bank* (−0.016*) regarding PD. This positive reaction is due to the operational characteristics of these financial intermediaries, which could provide a more efficient risk assessment of the investment. These banks are able to improve their risk management processes and thus increase their attractiveness to investors and other stakeholders.

As illustrated in Table 5.13, only *Investment Banks* are still able to benefit from equity investments over the medium term as their PD decline (−0.012**). This sustained benefit indicates that investment banks have a distinctive capacity to evaluate and oversee the risks of trading assets. Concurrently, the market demonstrates a continued favourable response to their orientation towards financial innovation, which is perceived as a strategic investment which is able to enhance their risk assessment capabilities. Regarding control variables, *Bank size* consistently shows a negative and significant impact across all bank types, suggesting that larger banks tend to have lower default probabilities (Kaufman, 2014). Similarly, *Market Capitalisation* is negatively correlated with our dependent variable, suggesting that banks with higher market capitalisation are generally perceived as less risky. This assumption aligns with the notion that larger, more capitalised banks have greater stability and better risk management capabilities (Anginer & Demirgüç-Kunt, 2014).

A long-run perspective (Table 5.14) reveals that, similarly to the medium-term bank PD results, only *Investment Banks* continue to benefit from a FinTech investment, exhibiting a noteworthy risk mitigation effect of −0.014**. The findings suggest that banks' investments in FinTech firms align with their immediate strategic goals (e.g., innovation strategy, efficiency, new products/services offerings, market expansion) and contribute to long-term risk mitigation and value creation, particularly remarkable for this subgroup of banks.

Table 5.15 illustrates the positive effect of FinTech M&As on the ESG performance of banks across the three business models that have been the subject of our analysis. These findings are consistent with a growing body of literature that identifies FinTech as a catalyst for sustainable economic growth, a key player in advancing sustainable finance and a strategic promoter for a corporate green transformation (Galeone et al., 2024; Li et al., 2023a, 2023b). As highlighted by these recent studies, FinTech collaborations support banks in achieving sustainable goals more efficiently by alleviating information asymmetry, relaxing

Table 5.12 Riskiness analysis at market values among Banking Business Models (BBMs) subgroups (short term)

	Short-term Bank PD General	*Retail Bank*	*Investment Bank*	*Diversified Assets Bank*
Constant	0.391*** (0.019)	0.465*** (0.029)	0.398*** (0.033)	0.339*** (0.056)
FinTech M&A	−0.006** (0.003)	−0.0004 (0.004)	−0.007** (0.004)	−0.016* (0.009)
Bank Size	−0.008*** (0.001)	−0.010*** (0.001)	−0.009*** (0.001)	−0.007*** (0.002)
Capital Endowment	−0.0005*** (0.0001)	−0.0004** (0.0002)	−0.001*** (0.0002)	−0.001* (0.0003)
Interest Income Margin	−0.002 (0.002)	−0.005* (0.003)	−0.0003 (0.004)	0.0001 (0.005)
Commission Fees	0.004*** (0.001)	0.001 (0.002)	0.005** (0.002)	0.012** (0.005)
Market Capitalisation	−0.005*** (0.001)	−0.004*** (0.001)	−0.003** (0.001)	−0.011** (0.005)
Economic Development	−0.001 (0.001)	−0.002** (0.001)	0.0005 (0.001)	0.001 (0.002)
Bank Concentration	0.0001 (0.0001)	−0.0001 (0.0001)	0.0001 (0.0001)	0.0004* (0.0002)
Inflation	−0.0005 (0.001)	−0.001 (0.001)	0.0001 (0.001)	−0.0004 (0.001)
Bank fixed effect	*Yes*	*Yes*	*Yes*	*Yes*
Time fixed effect	*Yes*	*Yes*	*Yes*	*Yes*
Observations	4,42	1,84	1584	994
R2	0.069	0.069	0.149	0.034
Adjusted R2	0.068	0.064	0.145	0.025
F Statistic	36.591***	14.971***	30.719***	3.794***

Note The table reports the regression results of FinTech M&A on Short-term Bank PD (1-Year PD), grouping the results according to the identified banking business models (BBMs). The BBMs are Retail Bank (BM1), Investment Bank (BM2), and Diversified Assets Bank (BM3). The sample spans the 1997–2022 period. We estimate the model using a polled panel data model. Standard errors are clustered at the bank level. *t*-statistics are in parentheses. ***, **, and * indicate significance at the 1%, 5%, and 10% levels, respectively

financial constraints, and enhancing risk-taking (Wu et al., 2024). In alignment with this primary evidence, our analysis demonstrates a positive and statistically significant coefficient in all the models (General, BM1, BM2, BM3) presented in Table 5.15. Specifically, ***Retail banks*** which focus on customer loans and deposit activity (Palmieri et al., 2024)

Table 5.13 Riskiness analysis at market values among Banking Business Models (BBMs) subgroups (medium term)

	Medium-term Bank PD General	*Retail Bank*	*Investment Bank*	*Diversified Assets Bank*
Constant	1.127***	1.248***	1.111***	1.076***
	(0.034)	(0.050)	(0.052)	(0.104)
FinTech M&A	−0.012**	−0.005	−0.012**	−0.025
	(0.005)	(0.007)	(0.006)	(0.017)
Bank Size	−0.012***	−0.015***	−0.013***	−0.011***
	(0.001)	(0.002)	(0.001)	(0.004)
Capital Endowment	−0.001***	−0.001***	−0.002***	−0.001
	(0.0002)	(0.0004)	(0.0004)	(0.001)
Interest Income Margin	−0.0004	−0.002	0.003	−0.001
	(0.003)	(0.005)	(0.006)	(0.009)
Commission Fees	0.005**	0.001	0.005	0.022**
	(0.003)	(0.003)	(0.004)	(0.010)
Market Capitalisation	−0.008***	−0.008***	−0.005**	−0.021**
	(0.002)	(0.003)	(0.002)	(0.009)
Economic Development	−0.0002	−0.002	0.0005	0.003
	(0.001)	(0.002)	(0.002)	(0.004)
Bank Concentration	0.0002	−0.00001	0.0003	0.0004
	(0.0001)	(0.0002)	(0.0002)	(0.0004)
Inflation	−0.001	−0.001	−0.0002	−0.001
	(0.001)	(0.001)	(0.001)	(0.003)
Bank fixed effect	*Yes*	*Yes*	*Yes*	*Yes*
Time fixed effect	*Yes*	*Yes*	*Yes*	*Yes*
Observations	4,42	1,84	1584	994
R2	0.054	0.057	0.120	0.026
Adjusted R2	0.052	0.052	0.115	0.018
F Statistic	28.061***	12.319***	23.822***	2.965***

Note The table reports the regression results of FinTech M&A on Medium-term Bank PD (3-Year PD), grouping the results according to the identified banking business models (BBMs). The BBMs are Retail Bank (BM1), Investment Bank (BM2), and Diversified Assets Bank (BM3). The sample spans the 1997–2022 period. We estimate the model using a polled panel data model. Standard errors are clustered at the bank level. *t*-statistics are in parentheses. ***, **, and * indicate significance at the 1%, 5%, and 10% levels, respectively

exhibit positive coefficient (1.287**), indicating that these financial intermediaries gain from financial technology investment (or FinTech) by developing their digital capabilities (e.g., online banking and mobile applications), optimising their processes, and consequently enhancing both their environmental quality (Yang et al., 2014) and their awareness of

Table 5.14 Riskiness analysis at market values among Banking Business Models (BBMs) subgroups (long term)

	Long-term Bank PD General	*Retail Bank*	*Investment Bank*	*Diversified Assets Bank*
Constant	1.682***	1.824***	1.647***	1.638***
	(0.039)	(0.060)	(0.060)	(0.115)
FinTech M&A	−0.014**	−0.007	−0.014**	−0.025
	(0.006)	(0.008)	(0.007)	(0.019)
Bank Size	−0.011***	−0.015***	−0.011***	−0.012***
	(0.001)	(0.002)	(0.001)	(0.004)
Capital Endowment	−0.001***	−0.001***	−0.002***	−0.001*
	(0.0002)	(0.0004)	(0.0004)	(0.001)
Interest Income Margin	0.004	0.004	0.004	0.0005
	(0.004)	(0.006)	(0.007)	(0.010)
Commission Fees	0.004	0.0005	0.004	0.024**
	(0.003)	(0.004)	(0.004)	(0.011)
Market Capitalisation	−0.009***	−0.009***	−0.005**	−0.024**
	(0.002)	(0.003)	(0.002)	(0.010)
Economic Development	−0.00004	−0.002	0.0001	0.004
	(0.001)	(0.002)	(0.002)	(0.004)
Bank Concentration	0.0002	0.00004	0.0003	0.0004
	(0.0002)	(0.0002)	(0.0002)	(0.0005)
Inflation	−0.001	−0.001	−0.0004	−0.001
	(0.001)	(0.001)	(0.001)	(0.003)
Bank fixed effect	*Yes*	*Yes*	*Yes*	*Yes*
Time fixed effect	*Yes*	*Yes*	*Yes*	*Yes*
Observations	4,42	1,84	1584	994
R2	0.049	0.052	0.080	0.028
Adjusted R2	0.047	0.048	0.074	0.019
F Statistic	25.390***	11.194***	15.123***	3.166***

Note The table reports the regression results of FinTech M&A on Long-term Bank PD (5 Year PD), grouping the results according to the identified banking business models (BBMs). The BBMs are Retail Bank (BM1), Investment Bank (BM2), and Diversified Assets Bank (BM3). The sample spans the 1997–2022 period. We estimate the model using a polled panel data model. Standard errors are clustered at the bank level. *t*-statistics are in parentheses. ***, **, and * indicate significance at the 1%, 5%, and 10% levels, respectively

corporate social responsibility (Zheng et al., 2022). From a long-term perspective, a bank's equity investment in FinTech firms may facilitate the bank's operational efficiency, improve resource allocation, and reduce the environmental impact by minimising the physical branches and paper-based processes. Furthermore, incorporating novel digital technologies may facilitate enhanced data analytics, thus optimising credit risk assessment procedures. This may also facilitate a gradual transition towards more responsible lending practices in alignment with ESG policies and EBA LOM requirements (EBA, 2020).

Similarly, the subgroup of ***Investment Banks*** exhibits a positive coefficient of 0.942***, indicating that this category of banks engaged in

Table 5.15 ESG performance analysis among Banking Business Models (BBMs) subgroup

	Bank ESG Performance General	*Retail Bank*	*Investment Bank*	*Diversified Assets Bank*
Constant	11.066***	26.556***	−0.664	−12.853***
	(2.182)	(3.734)	(4.070)	(4.748)
FinTech M&As	1.708***	1.287**	0.942**	3.484***
	(0.331)	(0.532)	(0.465)	(0.794)
Bank Size	1.572***	1.748***	1.201***	1.973***
	(0.059)	(0.128)	(0.078)	(0.176)
Capital Endowment	−0.061***	−0.073***	−0.138***	−0.086***
	(0.011)	(0.026)	(0.030)	(0.024)
Interest Income Margin	1.070***	−0.985***	3.507***	2.387***
	(0.223)	(0.357)	(0.448)	(0.398)
Commission Fees	−0.313*	−1.131***	0.818***	0.481
	(0.161)	(0.227)	(0.278)	(0.460)
Market Capitalisation	−0.246*	−0.135	−0.344**	−0.473
	(0.127)	(0.195)	(0.170)	(0.397)
Economic Development	−0.147*	−0.188	−0.202	0.046
	(0.080)	(0.128)	(0.125)	(0.174)
Banc Concentration	0.050***	0.031**	0.037***	0.106***
	(0.009)	(0.014)	(0.013)	(0.020)
Inflation	0.292***	0.232***	0.222**	0.500***
	(0.057)	(0.089)	(0.088)	(0.125)
Bank fixed effect	*Yes*	*Yes*	*Yes*	*Yes*
Time fixed effect	*Yes*	*Yes*	*Yes*	*Yes*
Observations	4,42	1,84	1584	994
R2	0.173	0.156	0.201	0.196
Adjusted R2	0.171	0.152	0.196	0.188
F Statistic	102.515***	37.554***	43.993***	26.613***

Note The table reports the regression results of FinTech M&A on Bank ESG Performance (ESG score), grouping the results according to the identified banking business models (BBMs). The BBMs are Retail Bank (BM1), Investment Bank (BM2), and Diversified Assets Bank (BM3). The sample spans the 1997–2022 period. We estimate the model using a polled panel data model. Standard errors are clustered at the bank level. *t*-statistics are in parentheses. ***, **, and * indicate significance at the 1%, 5%, and 10% levels, respectively

FinTech M&As demonstrates enhanced ESG performance. Focusing on the operational peculiarities of an investment bank, the incorporation of FinTech solutions could facilitate enhanced transparency practices, which constitute a critical element of sound governance. FinTech tools facilitate better tracking and reporting of financial activities, ensuring compliance with regulatory requirements and promoting accountability. Advanced technologies, such as blockchain, enable investment banks to create distinctive records of transactions, thereby enhancing trust and reliability among stakeholders. Moreover, FinTech can foster better customer relations by providing more personalised and efficient banking services. Investment banks can employ advanced data analytics and machine learning processes to offer bespoke investment advice and risk management solutions. Overall, enhanced customer satisfaction and engagement are important aspects of the social dimension in the general ESG framework.

Finally, *Diversified Assets Banks*, which oversee a broad portfolio of financial instruments (e.g., equities, bonds, liquid assets, and derivatives), demonstrate the most substantial positive influence from FinTech M&As, with a coefficient of 3.484***. These banks benefit from advanced asset management solutions provided by FinTech, including cutting-edge risk assessment tools and enhanced liquidity management systems. These technologies enable diversified banks to optimise their asset allocation, reduce concentration risks, and improve the sustainability impact of their investments. Additionally, the integration of FinTech solutions also enhances the banks' ability to track and report ESG metrics accurately, ensuring greater transparency and accountability. Through the endorsement of diverse and responsible investment strategies, FinTech firms enable these banks to align their operations with global sustainability goals and customer expectations.

Table 5.16 summarises the subgroup analysis conducted on banking business models, examining the impact of FinTech M&A activity on key performance metrics across three distinct business models. The table includes measures of profitability (ROE), efficiency (CIR), stability (Z-Score), short-, medium-, and long-term probabilities of default (PD1, PD3, PD5), and ESG performance. The "General" column presents the effect of FinTech M&A on these performance metrics without differentiation by business model. The subsequent columns illustrate its impact within each specific model.

Table 5.16 Summary of banking business model subgroups analysis

	Bank Business Model					
	Profile of Analysis	*Metric*	*General*	*Retail*	*Investment*	*Diversified Assets*
Bank Performance	*Profitability*	ROE		0.587**	−0.408*	
	Efficiency	CIR	0.006*	0.011**		
	Stability	ZSC	−1.062**			
	Short-term PD	PD1	−0.006**		−0.007**	−0.016*
	Medium-term PD	PD3	−0.012**		−0.012**	
	Long-term PD	PD5	−0.014**		−0.014**	
	ESG Performance	ESG	1.708***	1.287**	0.942**	3.484***

Note The table summarises the impact of the main regressor, FinTech M&A, on performance metrics across three banking business models: Retail, Investment, and Diversified Assets. The column labelled "General" exhibits the impact of the main regressor on the bank's performance that does not discriminate for banks' BM

Source Author's elaboration

Do FinTech and Bank Business Model Affect the Impact of FinTech M&As on Bank Performance?

The last level of analysis aims to answer the four research questions (RQ4). Thus, we jointly consider the banking business model and the FinTech categories to assess the impact on the bank's performance arising from a FinTech M&A. As stated in Paragraph 5.2.1 (*Sample*), we have manually identified four distinct categories of FinTech. The official EBA (2017) and BIS (2018) taxonomies were employed to cluster the financial technology firms within the dataset. The first cluster is *FinTech Credit & Capital Raising,* which encompasses firms providing credit, deposit, and capital-raising services. The second cluster is labelled as *FinTech Payments* and comprises firms that offer payment, clearing, and settlement services. The third cluster is *FinTech Investment Services,* which includes all the investment-related services and the management of investment activities. Finally, the latest cluster, FinTech *Market Support Services*, encompasses all other financial-related activities.

This section provides the main findings from the interaction between the primary regressor, "*FinTech M&A*", and the FinTech categories (or business models) identified, also considering the BM of banks involved in the strategic operation. The objective is to capture the joint effect of these two dimensions, going beyond the single deal, and consider the type of FinTech firms involved in the banks' investment. Table 5.17 presents the General model results that do not discriminate for banks' BM but consider any potential interaction between the FinTech M&A and each FinTech category identified. We multiply our primary regressor for each FinTech category to assess the banks' performance impact produced by investment in a specific FinTech area.

For the constant, which is an expression of the category labelled as *FinTech Investment Services*, all performance indicators exhibit a statistically significant value, indicating an improvement in profitability (3.109***) and ESG performance (13.888***), and, conversely, a worsening for PD over different time horizons (respectively 0.386***, 1.120***, 1.677***), bank's efficiency (1.302***) and stability (−36.544***) metrics. Thus, each interaction regressor will be interpreted as a shift from the *FinTech Investment Services* as an expression of our baseline level.[6]

Focusing on the interaction terms, we observed that *FinTech M&A* FinTech Credit & Capital Raising* increased profitability (0.305*) more than an investment in the category of *Investment Services FinTech* expressed in the constant term (3.109***). This result implies that bank M&As involving credit and capital-raising activities tend to enhance the ROE of financial intermediaries. M&A activities often lead to economies of scale, where the combined entity can reduce operational costs through shared resources and optimised processes, as highlighted by the theoretical assumption of the Synergy Theory (Meckling & Jensen, 1976). Credit and capital raising are also core banking activities that generate substantial revenue through interest and fees. Consequently, banks may enhance their revenue streams and achieve greater profitability by merging with or acquiring entities specialising in these areas. The investment in this FinTech sector also mitigates the worsening of the risk profile (2.709*)

[6] Assuming that the FinTech business model is a categorical variable in order to avoid multicollinearity issues we have dropped a categorical value that is included in the constant term. Therefore, each interaction regression coefficient represents a positive shift (if the coefficient is positive) or a negative shift (if the coefficient is negative) with respect to the baseline level that in our case is represented by the dependent variable fixed value for (i.e., FinTech Investment Services).

Table 5.17 General model case: FinTech and bank business model interactions

	General Model						
	Profitability	*Efficiency*	*Stability*	*Short-term PD*	*Medium-term PD*	*Long-term PD*	*ESG Performance*
Constant	3.109***	1.302***	−36.544***	0.386***	1.120***	1.677***	13.888***
	(1.000)	(0.021)	(2.851)	(0.020)	(0.035)	(0.040)	(2.217)
FinTech M&A	0.047	0.016***	−1.705***	−0.009**	−0.020***	−0.024***	0.475
	(0.059)	(0.005)	(0.607)	(0.004)	(0.007)	(0.008)	(0.472)
FinTech Credit & Capital Raising	−0.672	0.024*	0.150	0.036***	0.040*	0.032	0.277
	(0.674)	(0.013)	(1.727)	(0.012)	(0.021)	(0.024)	(1.343)
FinTech Market Support Services	−1.830***	0.024***	−4.156***	0.009	0.010	0.003	−5.980***
	(0.431)	(0.008)	(1.074)	(0.007)	(0.013)	(0.015)	(0.835)
FinTech Payments	−0.370	0.016*	−3.178***	0.002	0.010	0.013	−3.369***
	(0.418)	(0.009)	(1.153)	(0.008)	(0.014)	(0.016)	(0.897)
FinTech M&A * FinTech Credit & Capital Raising	0.305*	−0.011	2.709*	−0.009	−0.003	0.003	−0.610
	(0.178)	(0.012)	(1.644)	(0.011)	(0.020)	(0.023)	(1.278)
FinTech M&A * FinTech Market Support Services	0.0004	−0.022***	1.679	−0.004	0.004	0.010	6.026***
	(0.119)	(0.008)	(1.098)	(0.008)	(0.013)	(0.015)	(0.854)
FinTech M&A * FinTech Payments	0.005	−0.023***	3.081***	0.012*	0.022*	0.024	0.696
	(0.086)	(0.008)	(1.058)	(0.007)	(0.013)	(0.015)	(0.822)
Bank-controls	Yes	Yes	Yes	Yes	Yes	Yes	Yes

	General Model						
	Profitability	*Efficiency*	*Stability*	*Short-term PD*	*Medium-term PD*	*Long-term PD*	*ESG Performance*
Macro-controls	Yes	Yes	Yes	Yes	Yes	Yes	Yes
Bank fixed effects	*Yes*	*Yes*	*Yes*	*Yes*	*Yes*	*Yes*	*Yes*
Year fixed effects	*Yes*	*Yes*	*Yes*	*Yes*	*Yes*	*Yes*	*Yes*
Observations	4420	4420	4420	4420	4420	4420	4420
R2	0.091	0.068	0.263	0.073	0.057	0.052	0.187
Adjusted R2	0.088	0.065	0.261	0.070	0.054	0.048	0.185
F Statistic	31.635***	21.501***	104.837***	23.235***	17.734***	15.945***	67.709***

Note The table reports the regression results of FinTech M&A on all bank performance indicators. The interaction terms represent a bank investment (M&A) in a specific FinTech area: Credit & Capital Raising, Market Support Services, and Payments. Differently, the FinTech specialised in Investment Services collapsed in the constant term. The sample spans the 1997–2022 period. We estimate the model using a polled panel data model. Standard errors are clustered at the bank level. *t*-statistics are in parentheses. ***, **, and * indicate significance at the 1%, 5%, and 10% levels, respectively compared to a bank that invests in the category of *Investment Services FinTech* (−36.544***). Furthermore, we observed that the compounded effect of *FinTech Credit & Capital Raising* led to a final decrease of ZSC by - 33.84.

When examining the interaction between *FinTech M&A* and *FinTech Market Support Services*, our findings reveal a statistically significant impact on efficiency and ESG performance metrics. Specifically, investing in financial technology firms that involve ancillary services like market analytics, customer support, and technical infrastructure seems to improve efficiency metric (CIR coefficient of −0.022***, compared to *FinTech Investment Services* (1.302***). The relative improvement of the CIR metric suggests that integrating FinTech, which offers a wide range of market support services, can streamline operations, reduce costs, and enhance revenue generation capabilities. For example, integrating FinTech, which offers highly specialised market analytics services, involves using sophisticated algorithms and data processing techniques to analyse financial markets and predict trends. Such services assist banks in making more informed decisions regarding investment, market trading, and risk management. Conversely, deploying sophisticated customer support technologies, encompassing AI and chatbots and proactive, automated service support, enhances customer satisfaction while concurrently alleviating the burden on human resources.

The analysis demonstrates a positive correlation between this FinTech sector and ESG performance, with a coefficient of 6.026***, compared to the effect produced by FinTech players specialised in *Investment Services* (13.888***) on the same metric. The compounded impact of Market Support Services led to a final increase in bank ESG score by 19.914. As scholars point out, the relevance of ESG factors for investors and stakeholders is increasing, reflecting a growing company's commitment to sustainable and responsible business practices. Financial institutions can enhance their ESG performance by leveraging FinTech services, which, through their technological capabilities, may lead to more responsible investment decisions and better risk management practices, improving the overall sustainability of credit institutions. This will likely result from improved data analytics, better customer engagement, retention, and more efficient technical infrastructure.

Finally, looking at the interaction term between *FinTech M&A* and *FinTech Payments,* we find a statistically significant impact on efficiency (CIR), stability (ZSC), and market-based riskiness metrics (PD).

In particular, the negative coefficient of the CIR (−0.023***) indicates a slight improvement in bank efficiency compared to the effect observed for a bank that invests in the category of *Investment Services FinTech* (1.302***). The observed marginal increase in efficiency can be attributed to the advanced payment processing technologies and automated systems introduced by these FinTech firms. The employment of these technological assets has the effect of reducing transaction times and potential operational bottlenecks.

Secondly, the positive coefficient for ZSC (3.081***), as a measure of a bank's overall stability, suggests an improvement of risk profile and, thus, a lower risk of insolvency. FinTech firms specialised in payments services, as the most consolidated FinTech market segment, is one of the most appetible segments for incumbents as they use payment data provided by FinTech platforms to learn about consumers' credit quality (Parlour et al., 2022). FinTech firms that offer payment services are characterised by the enhanced ability to process transactions quickly and accurately. FinTech payment systems often employ sophisticated algorithms and real-time processing capabilities, which reduce errors and delays. They also used high-level fraud detection procedures and prevention mechanisms to deliver core process activities.

Consequently, banks that are able to integrate these processes through specialised FinTech investments are able to safeguard their assets and preserve a healthy financial viability. These investments may help banks enhance their stability, as the ZSC metric reflects. Furthermore, integrating FinTech payment technologies can facilitate more effective liquidity management. The technologies used in FinTech provide real-time information on the cash flows and possible liquidity positions of the resources the bank can best utilise. There is an increase in the bank's ability to meet its short-term obligations, thereby reducing the frequency of liquidity shocks and thus improving financial stability.

Finally, the interaction term *FinTech M&A* FinTech Payments* has a positive coefficient of 0.012* and 0.022* for short- and medium-term PD, indicating an increase in banks' default probability. This effect is stronger than direct investment in FinTech specialised in investment services, with parameter estimates of 0.386*** and 1.120***, respectively. Thus, an increase or decrease in PD as a market-based measure of risk may reflect the market's reaction to a bank's equity investment in the FinTech sector. The increase in short- and medium-term bank PD confirms shareholder concerns about this type of strategic acquisition.

Nevertheless, the financial technology sector is dynamic, exerting greater pressure on the incumbent organisations' core competencies. This results from banks' adoption of more sophisticated FinTech payment solutions, making constant change inevitable. The necessity to continually identify new prospects and the capacity to adjust to evolving circumstances give rise to strategic and operational risks, heightening the likelihood of an organisation's failure. Moreover, adopting technology heightens exposure to threats, particularly cyber risks, posing potential dangers to the bank. A cybersecurity breach can result in significant financial losses, revenue decline due to system disruptions, reputational damage, and regulatory fines, all of which may elevate default rates (Hasham et al., 2019).

Tables 5.18, 5.19, and 5.20 present the results for the same interaction terms, with the addition of the banking business model (BBM) serving as the discriminating factor.

Firstly, Table 5.18 presents the findings for the *Retail banks,* demonstrating that the impact on banks' performance metrics varies according to the FinTech category involved in the M&A operation. The interaction between *FinTech M&A* and *FinTech Credit & Capital Raising* positively impacts profitability, with a coefficient of 0.731***, contributing to increasing the bank's ROE more than an investment in the category of *Investment Services FinTech* (7.986***). Indeed, the strategic alliances between retail banks and FinTech players, specialised in the credit area, facilitate the capacity of these banks to provide a broad and innovative range of credit products, attract a more extensive customer base, and consequently generate higher revenues. This outcome is consistent with this type of bank, which, according to Ayadi et al. (2011), is kept relatively close to the traditional banking model, as institutions that use customer deposits as the primary funding source and provide predominantly customer loans. Furthermore, capital-raising FinTech firms frequently employ sophisticated risk assessment tools and credit scoring technologies, which enhance the quality of loans and reduce defaults. This, in turn, contributes to improving banks' profitability profiles, especially when we look at the compounded effect (8.717) produced by FinTech on the credit area. Differently, the study demonstrates how the CIR (−0.037**) increases but is less than in the case of an *Investment Services FinTech* acquisition (1.292***). The aggregate coefficient for *Credit & Capital Raising FinTech* on the CIR metric is equal to 1.255, indicating a lower increase in cost-to-income ratio for a retail bank when it decides to invest in this specific FinTech category. The CIR's

Table 5.18 Retail bank: FinTech and bank business model interactions

	Retail Bank						
	Profitability	*Efficiency*	*Stability*	*Short-term PD*	*Medium-term PD*	*Long-term PD*	*ESG Performance*
Constant	7.986***	1.292***	−14.266***	0.447***	1.215***	1.793***	30.120***
	(1.741)	(0.031)	(3.313)	(0.030)	(0.052)	(0.061)	(3.769)
FinTech M&A	0.134	0.031***	−0.121	−0.008	−0.025**	−0.031**	−0.326
	(0.098)	(0.006)	(0.659)	(0.006)	(0.010)	(0.012)	(0.750)
FinTech Credit & Capital Raising	−2.467**	0.007	−2.482	−0.007	−0.004	−0.005	−0.911
	(1.062)	(0.017)	(1.798)	(0.016)	(0.028)	(0.033)	(2.046)
FinTech Market Support Services	−1.584**	0.020*	−2.711**	0.018	0.008	−0.010	−9.929***
	(0.797)	(0.012)	(1.266)	(0.011)	(0.020)	(0.023)	(1.441)
FinTech Payments	−0.828	0.024**	−0.876	0.012	0.028	0.033	1.285
	(0.707)	(0.012)	(1.296)	(0.012)	(0.020)	(0.024)	(1.475)
FinTech M&A * FinTech Credit & Capital Raising	0.731***	−0.037**	3.142*	0.025	0.032	0.028	0.494
	(0.275)	(0.016)	(1.691)	(0.015)	(0.027)	(0.031)	(1.924)
FinTech M&A * FinTech Market Support Services	−0.007	−0.050***	1.024	−0.011	0.012	0.031	12.862***
	(0.236)	(0.012)	(1.262)	(0.011)	(0.020)	(0.023)	(1.436)
FinTech M&A * FinTech Payments	−0.107	−0.030***	−1.082	0.022**	0.045***	0.049**	−2.064
	(0.134)	(0.010)	(1.106)	(0.010)	(0.017)	(0.020)	(1.258)
Bank-controls	Yes	Yes	Yes	Yes	Yes	Yes	Yes

(continued)

Table 5.18 (continued)

	Retail Bank						
	Profitability	*Efficiency*	*Stability*	*Short-term PD*	*Medium-term PD*	*Long-term PD*	*ESG Performance*
Macro-controls	Yes	Yes	Yes	Yes	Yes	Yes	Yes
Bank fixed effect	*Yes*	*Yes*	*Yes*	*Yes*	*Yes*	*Yes*	*Yes*
Time fixed effect	*Yes*	*Yes*	*Yes*	*Yes*	*Yes*	*Yes*	*Yes*
Observations	1840	1840	1840	1840	1840	1840	1840
R2	0.059	0.084	0.212	0.078	0.068	0.062	0.200
Adjusted R2	0.052	0.077	0.206	0.071	0.061	0.055	0.194
F Statistic	8.137***	11.166***	32.799***	10.311***	8.917***	8.101***	30.470***

Note The table reports the regression results of FinTech M&A on all performance indicators for the subgroup of Retail Banks. The interaction terms represent a bank investment (M&A) in a specific FinTech area: Credit & Capital Raising, Market Support Services, and Payments. Differently, the FinTech specialised in Investment Services collapsed in the constant term. The sample spans the 1997–2022 period. We estimate the model using a polled panel data model. Standard errors are clustered at the bank level. *t*-statistics are in parentheses. ***, **, and * indicate significance at the 1%, 5%, and 10% levels, respectively

Table 5.19 Investment bank: FinTech and bank business model interactions

	Investment Bank						
	Profitability	*Efficiency*	*Stability*	*Short-term PD*	*Medium-term PD*	*Long-term PD*	*ESG Performance*
Constant	−1.565	1.287***	−46.344***	0.403***	1.117***	1.655***	2.756
	(1.933)	(0.059)	(7.077)	(0.033)	(0.053)	(0.061)	(4.101)
FinTech M&A	0.065	0.007	−2.839**	−0.007	−0.006	−0.006	−0.051
	(0.089)	(0.010)	(1.197)	(0.006)	(0.009)	(0.010)	(0.694)
FinTech Credit & Capital Raising	2.654**	0.030	1.419	0.061***	0.094***	0.099***	−2.869
	(1.081)	(0.032)	(3.752)	(0.018)	(0.028)	(0.032)	(2.174)
FinTech Market Support Services	−2.136***	0.043***	−5.723***	−0.008	−0.014	−0.018	−3.303***
	(0.588)	(0.016)	(1.947)	(0.009)	(0.014)	(0.017)	(1.128)
FinTech Payments	−0.756	0.023	−4.887**	−0.001	0.002	−0.002	−7.302***
	(0.610)	(0.018)	(2.191)	(0.010)	(0.016)	(0.019)	(1.270)
FinTech M&A * FinTech Credit & Capital Raising	−0.568**	0.017	0.373	−0.030**	−0.053**	−0.059**	0.556
	(0.248)	(0.026)	(3.150)	(0.015)	(0.023)	(0.027)	(1.826)
FinTech M&A * FinTech Market Support Services	0.078	0.005	2.962	0.004	−0.0003	−0.003	0.258
	(0.148)	(0.017)	(1.969)	(0.009)	(0.015)	(0.017)	(1.141)
FinTech M&A * FinTech Payments	0.061	−0.029*	5.552***	−0.003	−0.017	−0.020	4.119***
	(0.138)	(0.018)	(2.102)	(0.010)	(0.016)	(0.018)	(1.218)
Bank-controls	Yes	Yes	Yes	Yes	Yes	Yes	Yes

(continued)

Table 5.19 (continued)

	Investment Bank						
	Profitability	*Efficiency*	*Stability*	*Short-term PD*	*Medium-term PD*	*Long-term PD*	*ESG Performance*
Macro-controls	Yes	Yes	Yes	Yes	Yes	Yes	Yes
Bank fixed effect	*Yes*	*Yes*	*Yes*	*Yes*	*Yes*	*Yes*	*Yes*
Time fixed effect	*Yes*	*Yes*	*Yes*	*Yes*	*Yes*	*Yes*	*Yes*
Observations	1584	1584	1584	1584	1584	1584	1584
R2	0.096	0.089	0.212	0.158	0.129	0.089	0.220
Adjusted R2	0.088	0.080	0.205	0.150	0.121	0.080	0.213
F Statistic	11.853***	10.161***	28.198***	19.560***	15.478***	10.155***	29.490***

Note The table reports the regression results of FinTech M&A on all performance indicators for the subgroup of Investment Banks. The interaction terms represent a bank investment (M&A) in a specific FinTech area: Credit & Capital Raising, Market Support Services, and Payments. Differently, the FinTech specialised in Investment Services collapsed in the constant term. The sample spans the 1997–2022 period. We estimate the model using a polled panel data model. Standard errors are clustered at the bank level. *t*-statistics are in parentheses. ***, **, and * indicate significance at the 1%, 5%, and 10% levels, respectively

Table 5.20 Diversified assets bank: FinTech and Bank Business Model interactions

	Diversified Assets Bank						
	Profitability	*Efficiency*	*Stability*	*Short-term PD*	*Medium-term PD*	*Long-term PD*	*ESG Performance*
Constant	−1.567	1.282***	−47.152***	0.320***	1.050***	1.617***	−8.438*
	(2.178)	(0.024)	(6.526)	(0.057)	(0.107)	(0.118)	(4.800)
FinTech M&A	−0.043	0.005	−1.637	−0.011	−0.025	−0.030	2.839***
	(0.126)	(0.005)	(1.419)	(0.012)	(0.023)	(0.026)	(1.044)
FinTech Credit & Capital Raising	−4.184**	0.052***	−1.810	0.091***	0.050	0.002	3.967
	(1.772)	(0.014)	(3.982)	(0.035)	(0.065)	(0.072)	(2.929)
FinTech Market Support Services	−2.150**	0.003	−1.814	0.040*	0.068	0.062	−5.940***
	(1.004)	(0.010)	(2.621)	(0.023)	(0.043)	(0.047)	(1.928)
FinTech Payments	1.022	0.007	−2.797	−0.010	−0.002	0.004	−4.807**
	(0.905)	(0.010)	(2.700)	(0.024)	(0.044)	(0.049)	(1.986)
FinTech M&A * FinTech Credit & Capital Raising	2.282***	0.012	13.140**	−0.074	−0.023	0.022	1.670
	(0.727)	(0.019)	(5.174)	(0.045)	(0.085)	(0.093)	(3.806)
FinTech M&A * FinTech Market Support Services	−0.173	−0.018*	−0.901	−0.024	−0.027	−0.019	5.489***
	(0.307)	(0.010)	(2.782)	(0.024)	(0.046)	(0.050)	(2.046)
FinTech M&A * FinTech Payments	0.049	−0.017*	5.900**	0.011	0.022	0.023	−1.387
	(0.192)	(0.010)	(2.682)	(0.023)	(0.044)	(0.048)	(1.973)
Observations	994	994	994	994	994	994	994

(continued)

Table 5.20 (continued)

	Diversified Assets Bank						
	Profitability	*Efficiency*	*Stability*	*Short-term PD*	*Medium-term PD*	*Long-term PD*	*ESG Performance*
R2	0.120	0.102	0.320	0.043	0.030	0.031	0.221
Adjusted R2	0.107	0.088	0.310	0.029	0.015	0.016	0.209
F Statistic	9.532***	7.405***	30.740***	2.956***	2.022**	2.062***	18.465***

Note The table reports the regression results of FinTech M&A on all performance indicators for the subgroup of Diversified Assets Banks. The interaction terms represent a bank investment (M&A) in a specific FinTech area: Credit & Capital Raising, Market Support Services, and Payments. Differently, the FinTech specialised in Investment Services collapsed in the constant term. The sample spans the 1997–2022 period. We estimate the model using a polled panel data model. Standard errors are clustered at the bank level. *t*-statistics are in parentheses. ***, **, and * indicate significance at the 1%, 5%, and 10% levels, respectively moderate growth probably arises from integrating advanced credit and capital raising technologies that streamline loan processing and enhance operational workflows. The implementation of such technologies could result in an improvement in the cost-income ratio by reducing the necessity for manual processes and improving the overall efficiency of the bank's operations. In terms of ZSC, our proxy for bank stability, the aggregate coefficient for the *Credit & Capital Raising* category is equal to—11.124, indicating a worsening of the bank profile, which remains lower compared to the impact on the same metric produced by an acquisition of FinTech belonging in the category of *Investment Services FinTech* (−14.266***). The mitigating effect observed in the ZSC, contributed by firms in the Credit & Capital Raising FinTech category, can be attributed to strengthened balance sheets due to more effective capital-raising capabilities and improved credit risk management. In some cases, the implementation of advanced analytics and robust credit evaluation mechanise reduces the probability of bad loans, thereby enhancing the overall financial stability of the bank.

The second term of interaction, namely *FinTech M&A * FinTech Market Support Services*, evidence results only for the efficiency and ESG performance metrics. Specifically, the acquisition of FinTech belonging to the *Market Support Services* category mitigates the CIR (−0.050***) increase compared to the effect observed after an M&A in the category of *Investment Services FinTech* (1.292***). Furthermore, we observed that the compounded effect of the *Market Support Services* category led to a final increase of CIR by 1.242. The marginal improvement in CIR relative to the Investment Services category, consistent with previous findings, indicates that incorporating FinTech firms providing comprehensive support services, such as advanced market analytics and operational infrastructures, can streamline operations, reduce costs, and enhance customer service, ultimately improving efficiency metrics.

Concerning ESG performance, the coefficient is 12.862***, which reflects a positive and more pronounced impact of FinTech belonging to the *Market Support Services* category compared to the category of *Investment Services FinTech* (constant coefficient is equal to 30.120) on the sustainability profile of banks. The compounded effect of *Market Support Services* leads to a final increase of the bank's ESG score by 42.982. In line with an emerging literature stream that emphasises how FinTech firms support banks in achieving sustainability objectives more quickly and efficiently (Zhou et al., 2020), our findings support the evidence that the linkage between complex components, such as technology, and "green" issues, is becoming stronger and tangible. FinTechs in this sub-industry often offer tools to guarantee better reporting and compliance with ESG standards. Enhanced data analytics and reporting capabilities allow banks to monitor and improve their ESG metrics effectively, meeting stakeholder expectations and regulatory requirements, such as the Loan Origination and Monitoring (LOM) guidelines by EBA (2020).

Looking at the third interaction that involves the *Payments FinTech* category, our analysis highlights how FinTech specialised in payments services may increase CIR (compounded effect of 1.262) less than a FinTech belonging to the *Investment Services FinTech* category (1.292***). Moreover, a positive coefficient emerged for the PD over different time horizons (0.022** for 1-year PD, 0.045*** for 3-year PD, and 0.049** for 5-year PD, respectively).

The slight efficiency improvement that emerged, compared to the effect produced by the acquisition of a FinTech specialised in Investment Services, suggests that the collaboration between incumbents and FinTech specialised in payments services allows banks to integrate advanced payment technologies, reducing transaction processing times, enhancing accuracy, and lowering operational costs (McKinsey & Company, 2021). Automated payment systems and real-time processing capabilities streamline bank operations, improving the bank's efficiency profile. Moreover, the interaction term reveals an increase in default probabilities, with a coefficient that grows in magnitude from the short- to long-term PD horizons. Our results indicate a higher likelihood of defaults for retail banks that invest in the *Payments* sub-industry. This effect can be justified by the substantial transitional and integration risks associated with adopting new payment technologies. The initial phase of integrating these technologies can lead to operational disruptions and temporary inefficiencies, thereby increasing the bank's risk exposure. Furthermore, the heightened cybersecurity risks associated with advanced payment systems can contribute to higher default probabilities if not managed effectively.

Table 5.19 presents the findings for *Investment Banks* that are more heavily involved in trading activities, particularly in derivatives transactions. According to Ayadi et al. (2011), these banks are less likely to provide loans, an extension of their strategy to engage in trading activities. Coherently with this perspective, our results demonstrate a decrease in profitability (−0.568**) when an incumbent invests in FinTech, specialising in credit or capital raising services. Regarding the same interaction term (*FinTech M&A * FinTech Credit & Capital Raising*), the findings indicate an increase in short-, medium-, and long-term PD, which is less than the values observed for the constant term (respectively, 0.403***; 1.117***; 1.655***), as explanatory values of Investment Services FinTech impact on bank's PD. In this case, integrating sophisticated credit scoring and risk management tools provided by FinTech platforms specialising in credit and capital raising enables investment banks to make more informed lending decisions and manage risks more effectively. This results in a reduction of PD, thereby enhancing the bank's overall financial health and stability.

Differently, the interaction between *FinTech M&A* and *FinTech Market Support Services* does not exhibit a statistically significant impact on the performance metrics analysed. The latest interaction, *FinTech M&A * FinTech Payments*, presents notable findings. The CIR coefficient of the interaction term (1.258) increases less than the constant one (1.287***), indicating that the acquisition of FinTech specialised in payment services may contribute to a marginal enhancement of a bank's efficiency profile relative to an acquisition of a FinTech specialising in investment services activities. The deployment of sophisticated payment technologies enables financial institutions to automate multiple processes, minimise errors, and guarantee expedited transaction settlements. This enhanced operational efficiency has the dual benefit of reducing costs and accelerating the overall transaction execution speed, which is crucial in high-frequency trading environments and when managing substantial client transaction volumes.

The same interaction mitigates the worsening of the riskiness profile (5.552***) compared to a bank that involved M&A in FinTech belonging to the *Investment Services* sub-industry (−46.344***). Consequently, we observed that the compounded effect of the *FinTech Payments* category resulted in a final reduction of ZSC by −40.792.

The capacity to secure transactions and minimise fraud risk is critical for investment banks that engage in extensive, high-value transactions and manage derivatives. However, the empirical findings indicate a worsening of the risk profile, which may be attributed to the challenges associated with integration. These challenges often require substantial resources and expertise, potentially placing a strain on the bank's existing infrastructure. Consequently, the elevated operational risk and potential for integration failures result in an overall increased risk profile for the bank, leading to a decreased Z-score.

The notable positive coefficient for ESG performance (4.119***) suggests enhancing the bank's sustainability profile. The heightened transparency and adherence to ESG standards are becoming increasingly crucial for investment banks, as they are subjected to intensifying scrutiny from regulators, investors, and stakeholders concerning their environmental, social, and governance practices (Palmieri et al., 2024). Investment banks can employ the technologies provided by payments fintech to gather and analyse substantial amounts of data on their operations, trading activities, and client interactions.

Consequently, investment banks can ensure better reporting and compliance with ESG standards, exhibiting a commitment to responsible and sustainable practices. This overall enhanced transparency can attract more socially conscious investors and clients, potentially leading to increased business opportunities and a stronger reputation in the market.

Finally, Table 5.20 exhibits the results concerning the *Diversified Asset banks*. According to Palmieri et al. (2023), these financial intermediaries aim to balance a universal banking product offering and a set of stock, bonds, liquid assets, and derivatives.

Their strategy is to avoid excessive concentration in any single asset class, promoting a balanced asset management approach. The impact of FinTech categories on diversified asset banks' performance indicators appears to combine the results obtained for the retail and investment bank subgroups. This outcome partially reflects the distinctive managerial and operational characteristics of a *Diversified Assets bank*.

Particularly, when we look at the *Credit and Capital Raising FinTech* sub-category, the findings show a positive and statistically significant ROE coefficient. This empirical evidence suggests that banks may experience an increase in profitability. The enhanced credit assessment and capital management capabilities these FinTech firms provide enable diversified asset banks to improve their loan portfolios and attract more investment, thereby increasing their profitability.

Differently, the ZSC coefficient, used as a proxy for bank stability, exhibits a decrease, albeit to a lesser extent than that observed in the constant term (−47.152***). This suggests a marginal enhancement in the bank's risk profile with diversified activities compared to the impact generated by the bank's acquisition of FinTech companies specialising in investment services. For diversified asset banks, which maintain a diverse portfolio, integrating advanced credit assessment tools and risk management technologies is particularly advantageous for a more accurate evaluation of borrowers' creditworthiness. This results in improved quality of loans because the chance of extending credit to risky borrowers is reduced. These changes are helpful, especially for banks with diversified assets—a significant part of which is credit instruments—because they enable the reduction of non-performing loans and make credit portfolios more stable. Secondly, diversified asset banks are required to manage various financial assets, necessitating an effective risk management system to address the inherent risks associated with each financial asset type. The use of FinTech credit and capital raising firms provides a valuable opportunity for businesses to gain access to analytical tools such as real-time analytics and predictive modelling. These tools enable the identification of potential risks in advance, allowing businesses to implement measures to prevent their occurrence. In addition, the concept of efficiency in this context is not solely concerned with reducing losses; it also encompasses the capacity to guarantee stability and foster confidence among investors and customers. Such capabilities may also enhance the value of the bank by demonstrating a robust capacity for risk management, a robust credit portfolio, and an expanded customer base and investor confidence.

In addition, the interaction term of FinTech M&A and FinTech Market Support Services have a negative impact, reducing the CIR (loss of efficiency) by a smaller extent than that arising from a bank's acquisition of FinTech firms that offer Investment Services. Therefore, a slight enhancement emerged in the efficiency profile of a Diversified Assets bank when a FinTech that belongs to the Market Support Services sub-industry is acquired.

The category of diversified assets banks could benefit from the integration of a FinTech specialised in this field. For instance, using the most sophisticated market analytics helps these banks make better and targeted investment decisions, select the right strategy for the arrangement of assets, and not focus on a particular kind of asset, which is also an important factor in balancing and improving the effectiveness of the banking systems' management of assets. These FinTech services offer operational infrastructure that helps cut back-office work costs related to transactions, compliance, and reportage. Thus, the necessity of stabilising operations is felt most sharply by diversified asset banks that perform many transactions in various types of assets. Lowering operational costs results in a contraction of the cost-to-income ratio (CIR), which means an improvement in efficiency.

Regarding the ESG dimension, the results highlight a strong positive impact of FinTech investment on the environmental, social, and governance profile of diversified asset banks (Galeone et al., 2024; Wang et al., 2022). The implementation of advanced market analytics enables the bank to monitor and manage the environmental impact of their investments more effectively, thereby facilitating the identification of more sustainable investment choices and the tracking of environmental goals. Implementing customer support technologies and enhanced operational infrastructures has the potential to improve customer satisfaction and trust, thereby addressing the social aspect of ESG. Such systems facilitate more transparent and responsive customer interactions. Moreover, the operational efficiencies and advanced reporting tools provided by *FinTech Market Support Services* facilitate the implementation of improved governance practices. The deployment of these technologies enables banks to meet regulatory requirements, maintain high transparency standards, and ensure accountability. These factors are of critical importance for the banking sector's long-term stability and investors' confidence.

Regarding the latest FinTech category, namely the *Payments,* our analysis only evidences a statistically significant effect on CIR and ZSC metrics. Specifically, regarding the efficiency profile, the investment in the FinTech *Payments* sub-industry mitigates the worsening of the efficiency profile (−0.017*) compared to a bank that invests in FinTech in the *Investment Services* category (1.282***). Furthermore, we observe that the compounded effect of the FinTech *Payments* category led to a final increase of CIR by 1.265.

Similarly, the investment in the same FinTech category mitigates the worsening of the riskiness profile (5.900**) compared to a bank that involved M&A in FinTech belonging to the *Investment Services* sub-industry (−47.159***). Consequently, the compounded effect of the *FinTech Payments* category led to a final decrease of the ZSC coefficient of −41.252. This relative improvement of the riskiness profile arises from the capabilities of *FinTech Payments* firms to enhance financial stability by improving transaction security and reducing fraud. For banking institutions with a diversified asset portfolio, these improvements are particularly advantageous as they assist in managing the complexities and risks associated with various financial instruments, thereby contributing to a more balanced and secure approach to asset management.

The following Tables (5.21, 5.22, 5.23, and 5.24) provide a comprehensive overview of the impact of FinTech categories (Credit & Capital

Raising, Market Support Services, and Payments) on key performance indicators across the three business models identified (Retail, Investment, and Diversified Assets), as well as the "General Model" that does not discriminate by banking business model. These tables are a valuable tool for assessing the impact of FinTech investments on performance metrics, including profitability, efficiency, stability, probability of default, and ESG performance.

Robustness Checks

A series of robustness checks were conducted to validate our empirical findings and ensure their reliability. Firstly, to address potential endogeneity concerns in Table 5.25, a Stage Least Squares (2SLS) approach was employed, whereby the following instrumental variables (IV) were utilised: the depth of financial services supply to customers by country (*Financial_Services_Supply*); the volume of export of technology products and services by country (*Tech_Export*); the weight of the stock market on country GDP (*Stock_Market_GDP*); the level of law enforcement by country (*Law_Enforcement*). This method indicates that the statistical significance and sign of all regressor coefficients are confirmed when using predicted values of FinTech M&As, free of endogeneity bias. The same results can be observed in Table 5.26, which exhibits the findings of a 2SLS-IV regression model with Arellano's coefficient estimation. In this model, only the CIR and ZSC variables lose statistical significance, although the sign of the regression coefficients is retained.

Moreover, the variance inflation factor (VIF) test corroborates the absence of multicollinearity among regressors. As demonstrated in Table 5.27, all VIF values are markedly below the threshold of 5, thereby confirming the absence of multicollinearity in our regression model and ensuring the reliability of the coefficient estimates.

We employ the first-stage F-test and the Stock-Yogo test to test the strength of IVs. The results exhibited in Table 5.28 confirm the validity of the instrumental used in the analysis. The first-stage F statistic of 31.64 is considerably higher than the critical value of 19.93, corresponding to a threshold for weak instruments with four instruments and a maximum acceptable bias of 10%. This indicates that the instruments are sufficiently robust and capable of explaining the variation in the endogenous regressor. In conjunction with a highly significant *p*-value ($p < 2.2e-16$), the high F statistic provides compelling evidence that the instruments

Table 5.21 General model summary results

		General Model						
		Profitability	*Efficiency*	*Stability*	*Short-term PD*	*Medium-term PD*	*Long-term PD*	*ESG Performance*
FinTech's Category	Constant	3.109***	1.302***	−36.544***	0.386***	1.120***	1.6777***	13.888***
	Credit & Capital Raising	0.305*		2.709*				
	Market Support Services		−0.022***					6.026***
	Payments		−0.023***	3.081***	0.012*	0.022*		

Note The table presents the summary results of the General Model, showing the impact of different FinTech categories on banks' performance metrics. Significant coefficients highlight areas where FinTech investments contribute to performance enhancements or worsening

Source Author's elaboration

Table 5.22 Retail model summary results

		Retail Bank						
		Profitability	*Efficiency*	*Stability*	*Short-term PD*	*Medium-term PD*	*Long-term PD*	*ESG Performance*
FinTech's Category	Constant	7.986***	1.292***	−14.266***	0.447***	1.215***	1.793***	30.120***
	Credit & Capital Raising	0.731***	−0.037**	3.142*				
	Market Support Services		−0.050***					12.862***
	Payments		−0.030***		0.022**	0.045***	0.049**	

Note The table presents the summary results of the Retail Model, showing the impact of different FinTech categories on banks' performance metrics. Significant coefficients highlight areas where FinTech investments contribute to performance enhancements or worsening

Table 5.23 Investment model summary results

		Investment Bank						
		Profitability	*Efficiency*	*Stability*	*Short-term PD*	*Medium-term PD*	*Long-term PD*	*ESG Performance*
FinTech's Category	Constant		1.287***	−46.344***	0.403***	1.117***	1.655***	
	Credit & Capital Raising	−0.568**			−0.030**	−0.053**	−0.059**	
	Market Support Services							4.119***
	Payments		−0.029*	5.552***				

Note The table presents the summary results of the Investment Model, showing the impact of different FinTech categories on banks' performance metrics. Significant coefficients highlight areas where FinTech investments contribute to performance enhancements or worsening
Source Author's elaboration

Table 5.24 Diversified assets model summary results

		Diversified Assets Bank						
		Profitability	*Efficiency*	*Stability*	*Short-term PD*	*Medium-term PD*	*Long-term PD*	*ESG Performance*
FinTech's Category	Constant		1.282***	−47.152***	0.320***	1.050***	1.617***	−8.438*
	Credit & Capital Raising	2.282***		13.140**				
	Market Support Services		−0.018*					5.489***
	Payments		−0.017*	5.900**				

Note The table presents the summary results of the Diversified Assets Model, showing the impact of different FinTech categories on banks' performance metrics. Significant coefficients highlight areas where FinTech investments contribute to performance enhancements or worsening

Source Author's elaboration

Table 5.25 Robustness test: The 2SLS—IV regression model

	Bank Performance Profitability	*Efficiency*	*Stability*	*Short-term PD*	*Medium-term PD*	*Long-term PD*	*ESG Performance*
Constant	−11.298***	1.312***	−46.200***	0.374***	1.096***	1.637***	16.888***
	(1.031)	(0.023)	(3.111)	(0.022)	(0.038)	(0.043)	(2.430)
FinTech M&A	0.282**	0.006*	−0.551	−0.007**	−0.013**	−0.015***	1.813***
	(0.140)	(0.003)	(0.423)	(0.003)	(0.005)	(0.006)	(0.330)
Bank Size	0.359***	−0.003***	1.003***	−0.009***	−0.012***	−0.011***	1.618***
	(0.025)	(0.001)	(0.076)	(0.001)	(0.001)	(0.001)	(0.059)
Capital Endowment	−0.034***	−0.0002*	0.422***	−0.0005***	−0.001***	−0.001***	−0.063***
	(0.005)	(0.0001)	(0.014)	(0.0001)	(0.0002)	(0.0002)	(0.011)
Commission Fees	0.131*	0.013***	0.628***	0.004***	0.005**	0.004	−0.319**
	(0.068)	(0.002)	(0.205)	(0.001)	(0.003)	(0.003)	(0.160)
Interest Income Margin	3.104***	−0.005**	4.779***	−0.003	−0.001	0.004	1.134***
	(0.095)	(0.002)	(0.286)	(0.002)	(0.004)	(0.004)	(0.223)
Market Capitalisation	0.144***	−0.017***	0.076	−0.005***	−0.008***	−0.009***	−0.217*
	(0.054)	(0.001)	(0.162)	(0.001)	(0.002)	(0.002)	(0.126)
Economic Development	0.032	−0.003***	0.065	−0.001	−0.0004	−0.0004	−0.099
	(0.034)	(0.001)	(0.103)	(0.001)	(0.001)	(0.001)	(0.080)
Bank Concentration	−0.024***	0.0001	−0.028**	0.0001	0.0002	0.0002	0.049***
	(0.004)	(0.0001)	(0.012)	(0.0001)	(0.0001)	(0.0002)	(0.009)
Inflation	0.001	0.0001	0.013	−0.001	−0.001	−0.001	0.302***
	(0.024)	(0.001)	(0.073)	(0.001)	(0.001)	(0.001)	(0.057)
Predicted	1.478***	−0.0001	3.093***	0.008*	0.014*	0.020**	−2.653***
	(0.209)	(0.005)	(0.632)	(0.004)	(0.008)	(0.009)	(0.493)

	Bank Performance Profitability	*Efficiency*	*Stability*	*Short-term PD*	*Medium-term PD*	*Long-term PD*	*ESG Performance*
Observations	4420	4420	4420	4420	4420	4420	4420
R2	0.272	0.064	0.262	0.070	0.055	0.050	0.178
Adjusted R2	0.270	0.062	0.260	0.068	0.053	0.048	0.177
Residual Std. Error	7.033	0.159	21.212	0.147	0.260	0.296	16.568
F Statistic	164.588***	30.336***	156.275***	33.257***	25.609***	23.416***	95.737***

Note The table presents the results of the robustness check using the 2SLS-IV regression model, examining the impact of FinTech M&A on key bank performance indicators: profitability (ROE), efficiency (CIR), stability (Z-Score), short-, medium-, and long-term probabilities of default (PD1, PD3, PD5), and ESG performance. The sample spans the 1997–2022 period. Standard errors are clustered at the bank level. *t*-statistics are in parentheses. ***, **, and * indicate significance at the 1%, 5%, and 10% levels, respectively

Table 5.26 Robustness test: The 2SLS—IV regression model with Arellano's coefficient estimation

Variable	*Bank Performance*						
	Profitability	*Efficiency*	*Stability*	*Short-term PD*	*Medium-term PD*	*Long-term PD*	*ESG Performance*
Constant	−11.298***	1.312***	−46.200***	0.374***	1.096***	1.637***	16.888***
	(1.169)	(0.031)	(3.374)	(0.019)	(0.031)	(0.037)	(2.562)
FinTech M&A	0.282**	0.006	−0.551	−0.007***	−0.013***	−0.015***	1.813***
	(0.142)	(0.005)	(0.421)	(0.002)	(0.004)	(0.005)	(0.321)
Bank Size	0.359***	−0.003***	1.003***	−0.009***	−0.012***	−0.011***	1.618***
	(0.024)	(0.001)	(0.091)	(0.0005)	(0.001)	(0.001)	(0.057)
Capital Endowment	−0.034***	−0.0002*	0.422***	−0.0005***	−0.001***	−0.001***	−0.063***
	(0.005)	(0.0001)	(0.013)	(0.0001)	(0.0002)	(0.0002)	(0.011)
Commission Fees	0.131*	0.013***	0.628***	0.004***	0.005***	0.004*	−0.319*
	(0.073)	(0.003)	(0.180)	(0.001)	(0.002)	(0.002)	(0.169)
Interest Income Margin	3.104***	−0.005***	4.779***	−0.003	−0.001	0.004	1.134***
	(0.134)	(0.001)	(0.343)	(0.002)	(0.005)	(0.005)	(0.231)
Market Capitalisation	0.144**	−0.017***	0.076	−0.005***	−0.008***	−0.009***	−0.217*
	(0.057)	(0.003)	(0.159)	(0.001)	(0.002)	(0.002)	(0.129)
Economic Development	0.032	−0.003***	0.065	−0.001	−0.0004	−0.0004	−0.099
	(0.035)	(0.001)	(0.104)	(0.001)	(0.001)	(0.001)	(0.083)
Bank Concentration	−0.024***	0.0001	−0.028**	0.0001	0.0002	0.0002	0.049***
	(0.004)	(0.0001)	(0.012)	(0.0001)	(0.0001)	(0.0001)	(0.009)
Inflation	0.001	0.0001	0.013	−0.001	−0.001*	−0.001*	0.302***
	(0.024)	(0.0005)	(0.057)	(0.0003)	(0.001)	(0.001)	(0.066)
Predicted	1.478***	−0.0001	3.093***	0.008**	0.014**	0.020***	−2.653***
	(0.203)	(0.003)	(0.639)	(0.003)	(0.006)	(0.007)	(0.468)
Observations	4420	4420	4420	4420	4420	4420	4420

Variable	*Bank Performance*						
	Profitability	*Efficiency*	*Stability*	*Short-term PD*	*Medium-term PD*	*Long-term PD*	*ESG Performance*
R2	0.272	0.064	0.262	0.070	0.055	0.050	0.178
Adjusted R2	0.270	0.062	0.260	0.068	0.053	0.048	0.177
Residual Std. Error	7.033	0.159	21.212	0.147	0.260	0.296	16.568
F Statistic	164.588***	30.336***	156.275***	33.257***	25.609***	23.416***	95.737***

Note The table presents the results of the robustness check using the 2SLS-IV regression model, examining the impact of FinTech M&A on key bank performance indicators: profitability (ROE), efficiency (CIR), stability (Z-Score), short-, medium-, and long-term probabilities of default (PD1, PD3, PD5), and ESG performance. The sample spans the 1997–2022 period. Standard errors are clustered at the bank level. *t*-statistics are in parentheses. ***, **, and * indicate significance at the 1%, 5%, and 10% levels, respectively

Table 5.27 Robustness test: The Variance Inflation Factor (VIF)

FinTech M&A	*Bank Size*	*Capital Endowment*	*Interest Income Margin*	*Commission Fees*
1.0369	1.1001	1.2339	2.2668	1.0685
Market Capitalisation	*Economic Development*	*Bank Concentration*	*Inflation*	
2.1213	1.0414	1.0307	1.0424	

Note The table displays the Variance Inflation Factor (VIF) values for key variables, including *FinTech M&As*, *Bank Size*, *Capital Endowment*, *Interest Income Margin*; *Commission Fees*; *Market Capitalisation*, *Economic Development*, *Bank Concentration*, and *Inflation*. These VIF values are crucial for assessing multicollinearity among the regression models' variables, ensuring the estimated coefficients' reliability and validity

employed in the model are both relevant and valid. Therefore, using these instrumental variables in the regression model is justified, ensuring the reliability and accuracy of the estimated coefficients and the overall integrity of the model.

The values exhibited in Table 5.28 also confirm (i) the absence of endogeneity in the final model with the Cragg-Donald test, (ii) uncorrelation between instrumental variables and the error term with the Sargan-Hansen J-test, and finally, the absence of overidentification problems though the Hansen J Test. Specifically, the Cragg-Donald test (with

Table 5.28 Robustness tests: Endogeneity and overidentification issues

Cragg-Donald Test		*First Stage F-Test*		*Overidentification Test (1)*	
Test	*0.7776165*	F-value	*63.5304*	Hansen J Test	*0.23579*
p-value	0.9998016	*df*	7, 1291	*df*	1
		p-value	1.12e−60	*p-value*	0.6273
	Stock-Yogo Test		*Sargan-Hansen Test*		
	Test	31.641	*Test*		1.3783
	P-value	2.2e−16	*P-value*		0.2404

Note The table summarises the results of robustness tests addressing endogeneity and overidentification issues in the regression models. The Cragg-Donald test (*p*-value: 0.9998) indicates no endogeneity. The first-stage F-test (*F*-value: 31.64) confirms the strength of the instruments. The Hansen *J* test (*p*-value: 0.6273) and the Sargan-Hansen test (*p*-value: 0.2404) validate the exogeneity of the instruments a *p*-value of 0.9998) confirms there is no endogeneity in the final model, reinforcing the reliability of the regression model's estimations. Differently, the latest three tests prove the reliability of the instrumental variables (IVs) used in the analysis. The Hansen J-test (*p*-value of 0.6273) suggests that IVs do not significantly violate the overidentification restrictions at conventional significance levels. Consequently, we can assume that the IVs used in the model are valid and not correlated with the error term in the regression equation.

Sargan-Hansen test also supports this assumption with a *p*-value of 0.2404 as the observed *p*-value is more than the predetermined conventional significance level of 0.05, which means that we could not reject the null hypothesis of instrument exogeneity. Thus, there is no basis for rejecting the null hypothesis, which postulates that the instruments are uncorrelated with the error term.

Cross-Jurisdictional Comparison Analysis

To strengthen our findings, a further robustness analysis was carried out. International organisations have evidence of how the impact of FinTech is growing rapidly worldwide, although this growth is uneven across jurisdictions (IMF, 2021; World Bank, 2020). Divergences across jurisdictions in regulating and supervising FinTech activities are crucial considerations for incumbent banks to identify optimal FinTech firms or FinTech segments to boot a strategic collaboration. Juridical divergences could result in regulatory arbitrage, whereby FinTech firms are attracted by lower regulatory requirements (Anagnostopoulos, 2018). Consequently, in line with the study's aims, we perform a subsample countries analysis to assess any differential impact of bank-FinTech M&As on bank performance indicators arising from differences in the country's juridical framework.

Tables 5.29, 5.30, 5.31, 5.32, and 5.33 illustrate the influence of FinTech M&A on bank performance indicators across the three subgroups of countries that are most representative of the sampled banks. The empirical findings indicate that the sign and magnitude of the main regressor (FinTech M&A) differ significantly across countries. This reflects the influence of the different FinTech regulatory regimes and market dynamics characterising each area. The findings of our study have practical implications for banking authorities, suggesting potential responses to the influence of FinTech. These include monitoring developments without immediate intervention, incorporating new business models into existing regulatory frameworks, creating tailored regulations, and employing adaptive strategies such as innovation hubs and regulatory sandboxes to experiment with and learn from emerging technologies (i.e., the *"text and learn approach")* (IMF, 2023b).

Specifically, Table 5.29 exhibits the impact of FinTech M&As on *Bank Profitability,* revealing geographical differences. More in detail, for the US banks subgroup, the coefficient for FinTech M&A is positive and statistically significant (1.270***), leading to an increase in ROE. The US regulatory approach promotes competition and innovation, adopting a flexible regulatory framework that allows FinTech firms to flourish in the financial environment. Consequently, American banks may advantageously capitalise on the resource savings and operational synergies brought by a partnership with FinTech companies. At the same time, the increased competitiveness of the US financial sector creates further

Table 5.29 Cross-jurisdictional analysis of the impact of FinTech M&As on bank profitability

	Bank Profitability		
	America	*Europe*	*Asia*
Constant	−7.401***	−7.154***	−12.475***
	(1.829)	(2.033)	(1.692)
FinTech M&A	1.270***	−1.132***	0.689***
	(0.260)	(0.303)	(0.232)
Bank-controls	Yes	Yes	Yes
Macro-controls	Yes	Yes	Yes
Bank fixed effect	*Yes*	*Yes*	*Yes*
Time fixed effect	*Yes*	*Yes*	*Yes*
Observations	1118	1274	1404
R2	0.396	0.171	0.319
Adjusted R2	0.391	0.165	0.314
F Statistic	80.757***	28.950***	72.438***

Note The table reports the results of the subsample analysis on the impact of FinTech M&A on Bank Profitability (ROE) across three countries, namely America, Europe, and Asia. The sample spans the 1997–2022 period. We estimate the model using a polled panel data model. Standard errors are clustered at the bank level. *t*-statistics are in parentheses. ***, **, and * indicate significance at the 1%, 5%, and 10% levels, respectively

Table 5.30 Cross-jurisdictional analysis of the impact of FinTech M&As on bank efficiency

	Bank Efficiency		
	America	*Europe*	*Asia*
Constant	1.389***	1.177***	1.352***
	(0.039)	(0.057)	(0.036)
FinTech M&A	0.011**	0.032***	−0.008
	(0.006)	(0.008)	(0.005)
Bank-controls	Yes	Yes	Yes
Macro-controls	Yes	Yes	Yes
Bank fixed effect	*Yes*	*Yes*	*Yes*
Time fixed effect	*Yes*	*Yes*	*Yes*
Observations	1118	1274	1404
R2	0.144	0.035	0.154
Adjusted R2	0.137	0.028	0.148
F Statistic	20.706***	5.143***	28.091***

Note The table reports the results of the subsample analysis on the impact of FinTech M&A on Bank Efficiency (CIR) across three countries, namely America, Europe, and Asia. The sample spans the 1997–2022 period. We estimate the model using a polled panel data model. Standard errors are clustered at the bank level. *t*-statistics are in parentheses. ***, **, and * indicate significance at the 1%, 5%, and 10% levels, respectively

opportunities for economies of scale and scope, thereby enhancing the appeal of Fintech M&A prospects. Differently, the results for Europe present a negative and statistically significant coefficient for FinTech M&A (−1.132***), indicating that these strategic operations could decrease the profitability profile of European banks. These results may be attributed to the European banking and financial system's complex regulatory framework. To achieve a safe and sound financial system (FSB, 2019), the European Union has implemented reforms to enhance the efficacy of financial guidelines, thereby bolstering stability and investor confidence in the financial sector. However, these regulations may also impose additional compliance costs and operational constraints on traditional banks, which could impede their capacity to optimise the benefits of collaboration with FinTech.

Consequently, the high level of prudential requirements and supervision of the European banking system (such as strict legal entity-based regulations that govern capital adequacy, liquidity, and risk management—BIS, 2021b) can create challenges for banks seeking to innovate and integrate new technologies (European Central Bank, 2024a).

Table 5.31 Cross-jurisdictional analysis of the impact of FinTech M&As on bank stability

	Bank Stability *America*	*Europe*	*Asia*
Constant	−31.933***	−43.508***	−33.268***
	(5.189)	(6.480)	(4.754)
FinTech M&A	−0.311	−3.041***	0.831
	(0.736)	(0.967)	(0.653)
Bank-controls	Yes	Yes	Yes
Macro-controls	Yes	Yes	Yes
Bank fixed effect	*Yes*	*Yes*	*Yes*
Time fixed effect	*Yes*	*Yes*	*Yes*
Observations	1118	1274	1404
R2	0.277	0.262	0.244
Adjusted R2	0.271	0.257	0.240
F Statistic	47.092***	49.835***	50.123***

Note The table reports the results of the subsample analysis on the impact of FinTech M&A on Bank Stability (Z-Score) across three countries, namely America, Europe, and Asia. The sample spans the 1997–2022 period. We estimate the model using a polled panel data model. Standard errors are clustered at the bank level. *t*-statistics are in parentheses. ***, **, and * indicate significance at the 1%, 5%, and 10% levels, respectively

Furthermore, these regulatory requirements may hinder the capacity of banking institutions to collaborate effectively with financial technology firms that operate under less onerous regulatory conditions. Consequently, the regulatory discrepancies can place banks at a competitive disadvantage, reducing the potential banks' profitability gains associated with a FinTech M&A. In addition, the cultural difference among the European countries further complicates the integration process for cross-border FinTech M&As, leading to potential inefficiencies and higher operational costs. Regarding the Asian context, our analysis shows the main regressor's positive and significant impact (0.689***) on bank profitability, although it is less pronounced than in the US banks subsample. This result reflects the different levels of regulatory maturity and FinTech market development across the Asian context. As Yong (2021) indicates, the regulatory background in Asian countries differs significantly. Some jurisdictions have proactively fostered a supportive environment for FinTech innovation. At the same time, others have adopted a more cautious and conservative approach (also known as *"wait and see"*) to the

Table 5.32 Cross-jurisdictional analysis of the impact of FinTech M&As on bank probability of default among different time horizons

	Bank Probability of Default								
	America			*Europa*			*Asia*		
	PD1	*PD3*	*PD5*	*PD1*	*PD3*	*PD5*	*PD1*	*PD3*	*PD5*
Constant	0.524***	1.379***	1.987***	0.345***	1.213***	1.864***	0.437***	1.093***	1.572***
	(0.043)	(0.067)	(0.078)	(0.044)	(0.078)	(0.093)	(0.037)	(0.073)	(0.079)
FinTech M&A	−0.010	−0.013	−0.014	−0.014**	−0.023**	−0.022	−0.002	−0.006	−0.009
	(0.006)	(0.010)	(0.011)	(0.007)	(0.012)	(0.014)	(0.005)	(0.010)	(0.011)
Bank-controls	Yes	Yes	Yes	Yes	Yes	Yes	Yes	Yes	Yes
Macro-controls	Yes	Yes	Yes	Yes	Yes	Yes	Yes	Yes	Yes
Bank fixed effect	*Yes*	*Yes*	*Yes*	*Yes*	*Yes*	*Yes*	*Yes*	*Yes*	*Yes*
Time fixed effect	*Yes*	*Yes*	*Yes*	*Yes*	*Yes*	*Yes*	*Yes*	*Yes*	*Yes*
Observations	1118	1118	1118	1274	1274	1274	1404	1404	1404
R2	0.114	0.124	0.118	0.052	0.060	0.062	0.083	0.035	0.028
Adjusted R2	0.107	0.117	0.111	0.045	0.053	0.055	0.077	0.029	0.022
F Statistic	15.801***	17.382***	16.495***	7.638***	8.921***	9.254***	14.033***	5.700***	4.497***

Note The table reports the results of the subsample analysis on the impact of FinTech M&A on Bank Probability of Default (PD1, PD3, PD5) across three countries, namely America, Europe, and Asia. The sample spans the 1997–2022 period. We estimate the model using a polled panel data model. Standard errors are clustered at the bank level. *t*-statistics are in parentheses. ***, **, and * indicate significance at the 1%, 5%, and 10% levels, respectively

Table 5.33 Cross-jurisdictional analysis of bank ESG performance

	Bank ESG Performance		
	America	*Europe*	*Asia*
Constant	5.061	19.886***	14.938***
	(4.069)	(4.984)	(4.212)
FinTech M&A	0.658	5.560***	−0.705
	(0.577)	(0.744)	(0.578)
Bank-controls	Yes	Yes	Yes
Macro-controls	Yes	Yes	Yes
Bank fixed effect	*Yes*	*Yes*	*Yes*
Time fixed effect	*Yes*	*Yes*	*Yes*
Observations	1118	1274	1404
R2	0.267	0.181	0.156
Adjusted R2	0.261	0.175	0.150
F Statistic	44.876***	31.099***	28.540***

Note The table reports the results of the subsample analysis on the impact of FinTech M&A on Bank ESG Performance (ESG score) across three countries, namely America, Europe, and Asia. The sample spans the 1997–2022 period. We estimate the model using a polled panel data model. Standard errors are clustered at the bank level. *t*-statistics are in parentheses. ***, **, and * indicate significance at the 1%, 5%, and 10% levels, respectively

"first generation"[7] FinTech activities and a generally proactive regulatory approach regarding the "second generation"[8] of FinTech activities (World Bank, 2022). Countries like China, Singapore, and South Korea have actively encouraged FinTech innovation through regulatory sandboxes and digital banking licences, facilitating collaboration between traditional banks and FinTech firms. These initiatives have led to operational efficiencies and improved profitability, mainly through adopting digital payment platforms and online lending services (Pažitka et al., 2023). However, as our analysis reveals, the positive impact in Asia is mitigated by an uneven regulatory environment and evolving market structures, which challenge the integration of FinTech across the countries.

Regarding the bank efficiency profile, Table 5.30 exhibits an increase in the CIR (***Bank Efficiency***) metric for US and European banks, suggesting

[7] According to World Bank' report (2022) the *"first generation"* FinTech activities involves mobile payments and e-money.

[8] According to World Bank' report (2022) the *"second generation"* FinTech activities involves digital lending and equity crowdfunding.

a slight loss of efficiency for banks following these strategic operations. In contrast, the coefficient for FinTech M&A in Asia is negative but not statistically significant, indicating no substantial impact on bank efficiency in this geographical context.

The coefficient for the US subsample is 0.011**, indicating a slight decrease in the efficiency of banking institutions. This result can be attributed to the direct costs (i.e., investments in new technologies, the alignment of organisational cultures, and adherence to regulatory standards) incurred when integrating the activities of FinTech companies into conventional banking processes. Despite the favourable regulatory environment for innovation in the United States, incorporating FinTech solutions into traditional and outdated banking systems may initially result in inefficiencies. However, these can be mitigated over time as the integration process develops.

Similarly, the European banks exhibit a decline in efficiency (0.032**) due to the previously mentioned more rigorous EU regulatory framework. The increase in CIR suggests that European banks may face elevated costs when cooperating with FinTech companies. This is due to the need to operate within a complex regulatory framework, manage cultural and operational differences, and meet very strict prudential standards. These challenges are compounded by the regulatory fragmentation across European countries, which can lead to increased integration costs and reduced efficiency.

Table 5.31 presents the findings related to the impact on the Z-Score (*Bank Stability*), which empirically shows differences in how FinTech M&As affect the stability profile of banks. The US subsample analysis reveals a negligible effect on the probability of bank insolvency. This outcome can be attributed to the relatively robust regulatory framework in the United States, which guarantees that banks remain well-capitalised and compliant with rigorous oversight, thereby mitigating potential risks associated with integrating FinTech firms. Conversely, European banks, with a coefficient of −3.041***, exhibit an increase in risk profile following mergers and acquisitions with FinTech firms. This finding highlights the challenges posed by Europe's intricate regulatory framework, characterised by rigorous and fragmented regulations, which amplify the risks associated with integrating FinTech firms due to operational and compliance complexities. In conclusion, the findings indicate that the integration of FinTech has not resulted in a discernible impact on the Z-score of banking institutions in the Asian subsample despite a slight positive coefficient. This result indicates that, on average, the integration of FinTech does not destabilise the banking sector.

The analysis of the impact of the primary regressor (Fintech M&A) on the probability of default (PD) in different geographical regions reveals contrasting outcomes due to the distinctive financial environments and regulatory structures within each area (Table 5.32). The coefficients of *FinTech M&A* activity on bank default probability are presented in the table for three-time horizons (PD1, PD3, and PD5).

In the subset of American banks, the coefficients for *Fintech M&A* on bank default probability demonstrate a negative trend in all time horizons, with values of −0.010, −0.013, and −0.014, respectively. However, these coefficients lack statistical significance. This suggests that while Fintech M&A activity may reduce the probability of default, the impact is not sufficiently significant. The advanced financial markets in the United States, where banking institutions have already embraced digital innovations and the banking industry benefits from a sound digital infrastructure and a strong legal and business environment, might explain the lack of importance (IMF, 2021). FinTech activities may not significantly change current banks' risk profiles in this scenario. Thus, the competitive and financially robust banking industry in the United States is capable of withstanding the impact of FinTech mergers and acquisitions without undergoing significant changes in default probability.

In Europe, the data shows a more substantial impact of *Fintech M&A* on the likelihood of default. The negative coefficients for PD1 (−0.014**) and PD3 (−0.023**) are statistically significant at the 5% level, indicating that FinTech M&A has a more significant effect on decreasing banks' default risk in the short to medium term. Nevertheless, the impact loses statistical significance for PD5 (−0.022), indicating that the effect of FinTech M&A may diminish over an extended period. The more significant influence in Europe may be attributed to the sustained digital transformation of the country's financial sector, which is still evolving compared to the more established market in the United States. Additionally, the European regulatory framework, emphasising consumer protection and financial stability, could enhance the advantages of FinTech M&As by fostering innovative strategies that mitigate risk.

In the case of the Asian banks, the results indicate negative coefficients for all time horizons, with values of −0.002, −0.006, and −0.009, respectively. However, these coefficients are not statistically significant. These findings indicate that FinTech mergers and acquisitions do not significantly influence the probability of banking institutions experiencing a default within this context. The minimal impact may be attributed to the disparate and fluctuating levels of financial growth among Asian nations (Asgari & Izawa, 2023). In specific Asian markets, traditional banks continue to exert considerable influence, and the degree of maturity in FinTech integration may not significantly impact default risk (World Bank, 2020).

The differences in the effect of FinTech M&A on default probability in these countries can be explained by different factors. Firstly, the level of financial market maturity is of paramount importance. In areas such as America, where the financial sector is well-established and digitalisation is advanced, the potential risk reduction from FinTech M&A is likely to be less significant. This is because many banks have already incorporated financial technology advancements, resulting in a situation where further M&A transactions have a relatively limited impact on default risk. Conversely, in Europe, the digital transformation is not yet complete. Thus, FinTech M&A could have a more significant effect as banks adopt new technologies to enhance risk management and operational efficiency. The more negative coefficients observed in Europe, particularly in the short to medium term (e.g., PD1 and PD3), may be attributed to variations in the level of digital adoption.

Furthermore, notable disparities exist in the regulatory environment across these countries, which can influence the efficacy of FinTech M&A transactions (World Bank, 2020). In Europe, regulations are designed to prioritise financial stability and consumer protection (ECB, 2024b), potentially prompting enhanced risk management strategies through FinTech M&A and lowering default risks. Conversely, the regulatory strategy adopted in Asia diverges, exhibiting disparate degrees of support for integrating financial innovation. The discrepancy in regulatory environments could result in a diminished and inconsequential impact of FinTech M&A on default rates, as some markets may not yet have fully capitalised on the benefits of FinTech integration.

Cultural and institutional factors might also exert an influence (Khan et al., 2022). Each country's institutional and cultural environment can impact how new technologies are adopted and how FinTech innovations are integrated. The European focus on regulatory compliance and risk management may enhance the efficacy of FinTech mergers and acquisitions in mitigating default risks. Conversely, the disparate cultural perspectives on technology and innovation in Asia may result in a more gradual or less efficacious integration process.

As exhibited in Table 5.33, the impact of FinTech M&As on the environmental, social, and governance (ESG) scores of banks in the United States is positive but not particularly strong (0.658) and not statistically significant. This suggests that while FinTech M&A transactions enhance ESG performance to a certain extent, this impact is insignificant regarding scores. The relatively high level of FinTech integration and ESG activities within the US finance sector may contribute to the observation that elevated M&A activities in this area do not necessarily result in improved ESG outcomes.

In contrast, within the European context, the influence of FinTech mergers and acquisitions on ESG performance is markedly more pronounced and statistically significant (5.560***). The considerable and growing importance given to ESG factors within the European financial sector, as emphasised by the introduction of the EBA's LOM (EBA, 2020), is reflected in our empirical findings. The robust regulatory framework and prevailing market demands in Europe significantly influence banks, compelling them to demonstrate a high level of commitment to sustainability and social responsibility objectives. Consequently, as some scholars have evidenced, FinTech M&As are expected to be important in helping banks handle data more effectively, increase operational efficiency (Lee et al., 2021), and introduce new solutions that boost ESG performance (Collevecchio et al., 2024). This result demonstrates the crucial role that FinTech M&As play in promoting ESG goals within European banks (Macchiavello & Siri, 2022).

In the context of Asia, the impact of FinTech M&A on ESG performance is found to be negative, with a coefficient of −0.705. However, this result is not deemed to be statistically significant. The evidence indicates that, in contrast to the European context, FinTech M&A in Asia does not improve ESG performance. Furthermore, it suggests the potential for a negative impact, although the findings are not statistically significant. The different stages of financial development and the varying focus on ESG factors in Asian countries may be responsible for this outcome (Gutiérrez-Ponce & Wibowo, 2024).

The differences in the effects of FinTech M&A on banks' ESG performance in these countries analysed can be attributed to many substantial factors. Firstly, the regulatory environment significantly influences how FinTech development and market penetration affect ESG performance.

In Europe, the presence of robust regulatory support for ESG initiatives, along with rigorous requirements for sustainability reporting and performance (La Torre et al., 2021), has contributed to the creation of a conducive environment for bank-FinTech collaboration to exert a substantial beneficial influence on banks' performance. This set of regulations encourages financial institutions to integrate ESG considerations into their operations. Consequently, FinTech M&A contributes to this objective by facilitating the incorporation of technologies that enhance banks' ESG capabilities.

Conversely, significant discrepancies exist between the regulatory frameworks implemented in the United States and Asia. The United States has an emerging emphasis on environmental, social, and governance (ESG) concerns. However, the regulatory response has not been as comprehensive or consistent as in Europe. This may result in a diminished impact of FinTech mergers and acquisitions on ESG performance, as banks may not face significant pressure to enhance their ESG metrics. Moreover, the current level of maturity in the integration of financial technology (FinTech) suggests that additional M&A transactions may not result in notable improvements in ESG performance.

In Asia, the regulatory framework exhibits considerable variation at the intra-regional level, with certain countries accorded greater importance to ESG considerations than others (Ng et al., 2020). This lack of consistency may result in a diminished effect of Fintech mergers and acquisitions on ESG performance throughout the region. In markets where ESG is not a primary focus or regulatory frameworks do not strongly support ESG initiatives, the impact of FinTech M&A on enhancing ESG results may be limited. Furthermore, the subsample of Asian banks demonstrates a non-significant negative coefficient, which may suggest challenges in implementing FinTech solutions that enhance ESG performance. This could be attributed to constraints in infrastructure or varying degrees of technological utilisation.

Finally, market maturity and the level of FinTech adoption are crucial elements. In Europe, where the market increasingly incorporates ESG factors into financial activities, the merging of FinTech companies can significantly enhance ESG outcomes by providing advanced tools and technologies. On the other hand, in markets where FinTech adoption is still developing, or ESG is not yet a top priority in the financial sector, the influence of M&A on ESG performance might be limited. The discrepancies observed in the United States, Europe, and Asia illustrate the crucial role of country-specific elements in influencing the efficacy of FinTech M&A in enhancing the environmental, social, and governance (ESG) performance of banking institutions.

5.4 Conclusions

Chapter 5 examines the impact of financial technology (FinTech) firms on the performance of acquiring banks. A set of performance indicators, validated by the existing banking literature, is employed to evaluate the influence of FinTech M&As on banks' profitability, efficiency, risk, and environmental, social, and governance (ESG) profile. The analysis enriches the knowledge in the bank-FinTech relationship field by investigating the influence of banking and FinTech firms' business models as elements that differentiate performance outcomes.

The novelty of this study arises from the linkage between bank performance and the specific characteristics of FinTech firms involved in M&As. Although previous studies have examined the influence of technology adoption on banking institutions' performance, this study provides a more granular analysis by differentiating the effects based on the type of FinTech firm and bans business model adopted.

The first research question (*RQ1*), as our baseline analysis, investigates the impact of FinTech M&As on bank performance indicators (e.g., ROE, CIR, Z-Score, PD1, PD3, PD5, ESG Performance). The results prove that FinTech M&As positively impact a bank's profitability profile, increasing the return on equity (ROE) ratio. The integration of FinTech firms supports incumbents in adopting new technologies and developing new banking products and services, thereby creating additional revenue streams. The positive impact on the ROE metric emphasised the crucial role played by investments in financial innovation to stimulate revenue growth in the banking sector.

The findings also indicate a negative impact on bank efficiency, as indicated by an increase in the cost-to-income ratio (CIR). The upfront costs associated with M&As, including legal fees, restructuring expenses, and the integration between different technological systems, reduce the bank's efficiency profile, especially in the short term. The operational and cultural differences between traditional banks and FinTech firms further exacerbate these challenges, leading to misalignments that can increase operational costs and hinder decision-making processes.

On the risk profile, findings indicate a reduction in the Z-score, which is used as a proxy of bank stability. This impact suggests an increase in idiosyncratic risk for banks that engage in FinTech M&As. The integration of new digital services or operational frameworks into existing banking infrastructures presents several challenges, particularly in the context of complex legacy systems and strict banking regulations. This contributes to an increase in the risk profile of banks. Furthermore, these transactions adversely impact banks' liquidity, as significant cash outflows are required to invest in financial startups that may not align with the incumbent banks' core business models.

In contrast, the impact of FinTech mergers and acquisitions (M&As) on market-based risk measures is positive, as evidenced by a reduction in the probability of default (PD) over short-, medium-, and long-term horizons. Adopting sophisticated technologies, including artificial intelligence (AI) and machine learning (ML), enables financial institutions to manage and diversify risk profiles more effectively. Using these advanced technologies in core operational activities may facilitate timely risk assessments, real-time decision-making, and personalised risk management services, thereby contributing to a more stable and resilient bank's risk profile. The outcome of the latest non-financial measure shows a significant and positive relationship between Fintech M&A and bank ESG profile. This finding suggests that bank's investments in the financial technology industry present a considerable opportunity to enhance bank's compliance with ESG criteria.

In response to the *RQ2*, the lag effects analysis demonstrates that the impact of FinTech M&A activities on banks' ESG performance and default probability is delayed yet significant. The initial period following a FinTech M&A transaction has a positive impact on banks' ESG performance. Nevertheless, this effect diminishes over time yet remains statistically significant. The impact is most pronounced during the second period following the transaction. Similarly, the initial impact on default probability is negligible; however, a delayed and significant reduction is observed in subsequent periods. These delayed effects reflect the time required for post-merger and acquisition integration and the realisation of synergies between incumbents and newcomers. These processes ultimately enhance operational efficiency, risk management, and financial stability over the long term.

The *RQ3* investigates whether the impact of FinTech M&As on the banks mentioned above performance metrics differs based on the business model (BM) of the acquiring banks, which were previously identified through a cluster analysis. The results suggest that the impact of FinTech M&As differs depending on whether the bank operates as a ***Retail bank***, an ***Investment bank***, or a ***Diversified assets bank***.

Specifically, the findings show that FinTech M&A positively impacts the profitability of ***Retail banks***. These financial intermediaries, primarily focusing on customer deposits and loans, benefit from integrating FinTech solutions that enhance customer experience and streamline operations, leading to improved short-term profitability (ROE). However, this subgroup of financial intermediaries also experiences a short-term decrease in operational efficiency (CIR), presumably attributable to the initial costs and operational complexities associated with integrating novel technologies.

Investment Banks show a different pattern. The impact of FinTech M&As on banks' profitability (ROE) is negative in the short term. This could be attributed to the complexities of integrating FinTech within their investment-focused operations. These banks are involved in securities and derivatives trading, and the adjustments required to incorporate new technologies may temporarily lose continuity in their core activities. Nevertheless, investment banks stand to gain from FinTech M&As regarding risk reduction (bank's PD) over different time horizons and enhanced ESG performance.

Finally, the third subsample of banks englobes the ***Diversified Assets Banks***. For this type of financial intermediaries, which manage a broad portfolio of financial instruments (e.g., equities, bonds, liquid assets, derivatives), the findings do not significantly impact their profitability profile (ROE) after an M&A with a FinTech firm. This may be attributed to the inherent complexities and costs associated with integrating FinTech solutions across a diverse range of activities. Nevertheless, these banks benefit from advanced asset management solutions provided by FinTech and improved liquidity management systems, which can improve their risk profile (1-year PD). In addition, this subsample of banks shows the strongest positive impact on ESG performance, suggesting that FinTech investments facilitate greater alignment with sustainability goals and increase transparency and accountability in their operations.

Based on these evidence, the study enriches the existing literature, providing empirical evidence of how the impact of FinTech mergers and acquisitions (M&As) on bank performance is significantly influenced by the bank's business model. According to the study's findings, following an equity investment in FinTech firms, a ***Retail bank*** typically exhibits enhanced profitability and ESG score, and an ***Investment bank*** experiences an improvement in risk management capabilities, which are reflected in riskiness reduction. In contrast, a ***Diversified asset bank*** shows enhanced ESG performance benefits and a short-term risk reduction. These findings underscore the importance of considering a bank's operational focus (BM) when evaluating the potential advantages or disadvantages of FinTech M&As.

Finally, *RQ4* examines how the impact of FinTech M&As on the same bank performance metrics changes depending on the area of expertise (or BM) of the acquired FinTech firms. For this purpose, four different FinTech sectors were identified according to the available official FinTech taxonomies such as (i) *Credit & Capital Raising,* (ii) *Payments,* (iii) *Investment Services,* and (iv) *Market Support Services.* An additional analysis was performed by dividing the sample of banks into subgroups according to the banks' business models.

The results show that the impact of FinTech mergers and acquisitions is highly variable, depending on the type of FinTech acquired. In particular, equity investments in FinTech companies specialising in *Credit & Capital Raising* are able to increase the profitability (ROE) of banks, especially those with a *Retail* and *Diversified Asset* bank business model. Such technologies serve to enhance loan portfolios and create additional revenue streams. Nevertheless, the impact of this FinTech firm's category on the bank's stability (ZSC) and riskiness (PD) profile is not uniform across BBMs. On the one hand, the enhanced ability to raise capital improves financial positions; on the other hand, heightened involvement in credit markets could also increase risk exposure.

According to the study's findings, FinTech companies specialising in *Payment* activity are able to moderately boost the *Retail* banks', *Investment* banks and *Diversified Assets* banks' efficiency profile (CIR) due to the implementation of advanced payment processing technologies, which help incumbents streamline some of their core operations. Nonetheless, an investment in this FinTech category also increases the likelihood of default (PD) in the short- and mid-term for a *Retail* bank due to operational and cybersecurity risks linked to implementing innovative payment technologies. This FinTech category is also able to improve ESG performance for Investment banks. However, banks continue to benefit from enhanced liquidity management and reduced transaction times, which contribute to the overall stability of their financial position.

The empirical findings also emphasise enhancements in *Diversified Assets* banks' efficiency profile and ESG performance after the acquisition of FinTech companies which are able to provide *Market Support Services*. Investments in this FinTech sub-category boost ESG performance through increased transparency, improvement of banks' energy efficiency, and better data reporting activity. Our cross-country comparison analysis has demonstrated a high level of heterogeneity about the impact of Fintech M&As on the financial institutions' performance metrics. Specifically, in jurisdictions where the regulatory framework for financial innovation and the digitalisation of finance is flexible, such as the United States, incumbents' financial institutions benefit from their investments in the financial technology sector. This outcome reflects the need to design regulatory frameworks that foster fair competition, thereby enabling the proliferation of financial technology firms. Regarding banks' sustainability profile, our findings have exhibited that jurisdictions with stringent ESG regulatory requirements, such as European countries, experience high advantages from strategic collaborations between banks and FinTech players.

In light of the findings offered our analysis is the first to provide empirical evidence that the impact of FinTech M&As on bank performance metrics differs significantly depending on the type of FinTech firm involved in the equity investment.

The results highlight how each type of FinTech category can affect the performance profile of the sampled banks differently. From a managerial standpoint, incumbent banks may utilise these findings to more effectively identify strategic FinTech investment opportunities that align with their operational objectives and market needs.

The study is not without limitations that provide direction for future research in this field. Firstly, despite the extensive observation period (1997–2000) that characterised the analysis, the final sample is limited due to the selection of banks according to the availability of the selected clustering variables. This choice limits our analysis, which future studies of large samples should further validate. Secondly, the analysis includes all bank-FinTech M&As rather than only those that have survived. While this approach avoids the issue of survivorship bias, future research could examine how mergers and acquisitions involving FinTech affect the survival of both FinTech and banking institutions. Additionally, as a proxy of the bank's sustainability performance, we have used the ESG scores provided by Refinitiv Eikon. In this regard, scholars could implement alternative measures to gauge the bank's sustainability and solve the inherent limitations of the metric.

References

Altunbas, Y., Carbo, S., Gardener, E. P., & Molyneux, P. (2007). Examining the relationships between capital, risk and efficiency in European banking. *European Financial Management, 13*(1), 49–70.

Anagnostopoulos, I. (2018). FinTech and regtech: Impact on regulators and banks. *Journal of Economics and Business, 100*, 7–25.

Anginer, D., & Demirgüç-Kunt, A. (2014). *Bank capital and systemic stability* (World Bank Policy research working paper, (6948)).

Anginer, D., Demirguc-Kunt, A., & Zhu, M. (2014). How does competition affect bank systemic risk? *Journal of Financial Intermediation, 23*, 1–26.

Ansoff, H. I. (1965). *The concept of strategy*. Taylor & Francis.

Arellano, M., & Bover, O. (1995). Another look at the instrumental variable estimation of error-components models. *Journal of Econometrics, 68*(1), 29–51.

Asgari, B., & Izawa, H. (2023). Does FinTech penetration drive financial development? Evidence from panel analysis of emerging and developing economies. *Borsa Istanbul Review, 23*(5), 1078–1097.

Ayadi, R., Arbak, E., & Pieter De Groen, W. (2011). Business models in European banking: A pre-and post-crisis screening. *Center for European Policy Studies*.

Ayadi, R., Bongini, P., Casu, B., & Cucinelli, D. (2021). Bank business model migrations in Europe: Determinants and effects. *British Journal of Management, 32*(4), 1007–1026.

Ayadi, R., & De Groen, W. (2015). State aid to banks and credit for SMEs: Is there a need for conditionality? Available at SSRN 2784300.

Azmi, W., Hassan, M. K., Houston, R., & Karim, M. S. (2021). ESG activities and banking performance: International evidence from emerging economies. *Journal of International Financial Markets, Institutions and Money, 70*, 101277.

Bank for International Settlements (BIS). (2018). Sound practices. Implications of FinTech developments for banks and banks supervisors.

Bank for International Settlements (BIS). (2021a). Achievements and challenges in ESG markets (M. Scatigna, D. Xia, A. Zabai, O. Zulaica, Eds.). in BIS Quarterly Review.

Bank for International Settlements (BIS). (2021b). FinTech regulation: How to achieve a level playing field.

Basel Committee on Banking Supervision (BCBS). (2019). Report on open banking and application programming interfaces.

Beck, T., De Jonghe, O., & Schepens, G. (2013). Bank competition and stability: Cross-country heterogeneity. *Journal of Financial Intermediation, 22*(2), 218–244.

Bellardini, L., Del Gaudio, B. L., Previtali, D., & Verdoliva, V. (2022). How do banks invest in FinTechs? Evidence from advanced economies. *Journal of International Financial Markets, Institutions and Money, 77*, 101498.

Bogers, M., Zobel, A. K., Afuah, A., Almirall, E., Brunswicker, S., Dahlander, L., ... & Ter Wal, A. L. (2017). The open innovation research landscape: Established perspectives and emerging themes across different levels of analysis. *Industry and Innovation, 24*(1), 8–40.

Borello, G., Pampurini, F., & Quaranta, A. G. (2022). Can High-tech investments improve banking efficiency? *Journal of Financial Management, Markets and Institutions, 10*(01), 2250003.

Boyd, J. H., & Graham, S. L. (1986). Risk, regulation, and bank holding company expansion into nonbanking. *Quarterly Review, 10*(2).

Cammarano, A., Michelino, F., & Caputo, M. (2019). Open innovation practices for knowledge acquisition and their effects on innovation output. *Technology Analysis & Strategic Management, 31*(11), 1297–1313.

Carlini, F., Del Gaudio, B. L., Porzio, C., & Previtali, D. (2022). Banks, FinTech and stock returns. *Finance Research Letters, 45*, 102252.

Chiaramonte, L., Croci, E., & Poli, F. (2015). Should we trust the Z-score? Evidence from the European banking industry. *Global Finance Journal, 28*, 111–131. https://doi.org/10.1016/j.gfj.2015.02.002

Coccorese, P., & Girardone, C. (2021). Bank capital and profitability: Evidence from a global sample. *The European Journal of Finance, 27*(9), 827–856.

Collevecchio, F., Cappa, F., Peruffo, E., & Oriani, R. (2024). When do M&As with fintech firms benefit traditional banks? *British Journal of Management, 35*(1), 192–209. https://doi.org/10.1111/1467-8551.12701

Cragg, J. G., & Donald, S. G. (1993). Testing identifiability and specification in instrumental variable models. *Econometric Theory, 9*(2), 222–240.

Croci, E., & Petmezas, D. (2010). Minority shareholders' wealth effects and stock market development: Evidence from increase-in-ownership M&As. *Journal of Banking & Finance, 34*(3), 681–694.

Cuadros-Solas, P. J., Cubillas, E., Salvador, C., & Suárez, N. (2024). Digital disruptors at the gate. Does FinTech lending affect bank market power and stability? *Journal of International Financial Markets, Institutions and Money, 92*, 101964.

Daoud, Y., & Kammoun, A. (2020). Financial stability and bank capital: The case of Islamic banks. *International Journal of Economics and Financial Issues, 10*(5), 361.

Dell'Ariccia, M. G., Ferreira, C., Jenkinson, N., Laeven, M. L., Martin, A., Minoiu, M. C., & Popov, A. (2018). Managing the sovereign-bank nexus.

Del Gaudio, B. L., Gallo, S., & Previtali, D. (2024). Exploring the drivers of investment in FinTech: Board composition and home bias in banking. *Global Finance Journal, 60*, 100944.

Delis, M. D., & Tsionas, E. G. (2009). The joint estimation of bank-level market power and efficiency. *Journal of Banking & Finance, 33*(10), 1842–1850.

Deloitte. (2020). Modernizing legacy banking systems. Practical advice to help banks succeed at core and application modernization.

Desbordes, R., & Wei, S. J. (2017). The effects of financial development on foreign direct investment. *Journal of Development Economics, 127*, 153–168.

Di Tommaso, C., & Thornton, J. (2020). Do ESG scores effect bank risk taking and value? Evidence from European banks. *Corporate Social Responsibility and Environmental Management, 27*(5), 2286–2298.

Dias, A. (2013). Market capitalization and value-at-risk. *Journal of Banking & Finance, 37*(12), 5248–5260.

Dicuonzo, G., Palmaccio, M., & Shini, M. (2023). ESG, governance variables and FinTech: An empirical analysis. *Research in International Business and Finance, 69*, 102205.

Dranev, Y., Frolova, K., & Ochirova, E. (2019). The impact of FinTech M&A on stock returns. *Research in International Business and Finance, 48*, 353–364.

Drasch, B. J., Schweizer, A., & Urbach, N. (2018). Integrating the 'Trouble-makers': A taxonomy for cooperation between banks and FinTechs. *Journal of Economics and Business, 100*, 26–42.

Durbin, J. (1954). Errors in variables. *Revue de l'institut International de Statistique*, 23–32.

European Banking Authority (EBA). (2017). *Discussion Paper on the EBA's approach to financial technology (FinTech).* (EBA/DP/2017/02).

European Banking Authority (EBA). (2020). *Final report—Guidelines on loan origination and monitoring* (EBA/GL/2020/06).

European Central Bank (2024a). *Digital innovation and banking regulation* (Occasional paper series (By Chryssa Papathanassiou). No 351).

European Central Bank (2024b). Financial stability review. May 2024.

Feyen, E., Frost, J., Gambacorta, L., Natarajan, H., & Saal, M. (2021). *FinTech and the digital transformation of financial services: implications for market structure and public policy* (BIS papers).

Financial Stability Board (FSB). (2017). Financial stability implications from FinTech. Supervisory and regulatory issues that merit authorities' attention.

Financial Stability Board (FSB). (2019). FinTech and market structure in financial services: Market developments and potential financial stability implications.

Galeone, G., Ranaldo, S., & Fusco, A. (2024). ESG and FinTech: Are they connected? *Research in International Business and Finance, 69*, 102225.

Glendening, M., Khurana, I. K., & Wang, W. (2016). The market for corporate control and dividend policies: Cross-country evidence from M&A laws. *Journal of International Business Studies, 47*, 1106–1134.

Goddard, J., Molyneux, P., & Zhou, T. (2012). Bank mergers and acquisitions in emerging markets: Evidence from Asia and Latin America. *The European Journal of Finance, 18*(5), 419–438.

Granger, C. W. (1969). Investigating causal relations by econometric models and cross-spectral methods. *Econometrica: Journal of the Econometric Society*, 424–438.

Gutiérrez-Ponce, H., & Wibowo, S. A. (2024). Do sustainability practices contribute to the financial performance of banks? An analysis of banks in Southeast Asia. *Corporate Social Responsibility and Environmental Management, 31*(2), 1418–1432.

Haddad, C., & Hornuf, L. (2023). How do FinTech startups affect financial institutions' performance and default risk? *The European Journal of Finance, 29*(15), 1761–1792.

Hasham, S., Joshi, S., & Mikkelsen, D. (2019). *Financial crime and fraud in the age of cybersecurity*. McKinsey & Company.

Hausman, J. A. (1978). Specification tests in econometrics. *Econometrica: Journal of the Econometric Society*, 1251–1271.

Hodula, M. (2024). Beyond innovation: FinTech credit and its ripple effects on traditional banking profitability. *Finance Research Letters, 63*, 105307.

Hornuf, L., Klus, M. F., Lohwasser, T. S., & Schwienbacher, A. (2021). How do banks interact with FinTech startups? *Small Business Economics, 57*, 1505–1526.

Huang, Q., Fang, J., Xue, X., & Gao, H. (2023). Does digital innovation cause better ESG performance? an empirical test of a-listed firms in China. *Research in International Business and Finance, 66*, 102049.

Imbens, G. W., & Wooldridge, J. M. (2009). Recent developments in the econometrics of program evaluation. *Journal of Economic Literature, 47*(1), 5–86.

International Monetary Fund (IMF). (2023a). *Institutional arrangements for FinTech regulation: Supervisory monitoring* (P. Bains & C. Wu, Eds.).

International Monetary Fund (IMF). (2023b). *Is FinTech eating the bank's lunch?* (IMF Working Paper. WP/23/239).

IOSCO (International Organization of Securities Commissions). (2017). Research report on financial technologies (Fintech), Report of the board of IOSCO, February 2017.

Jiang, C., Yao, S., & Feng, G. (2013). Bank ownership, privatization, and performance: Evidence from a transition country. *Journal of banking & finance, 37*(9), 3364–3372.

Katsiampa, P., McGuinness, P. B., Serbera, J. P., & Zhao, K. (2022). The financial and prudential performance of Chinese banks and FinTech lenders in the era of digitalization. *Review of Quantitative Finance and Accounting, 58*(4), 1451–1503.

Kaufman, G. G. (2014). Too big to fail in banking: What does it mean? *Journal of Financial Stability, 13*, 214–223.

Khan, M. A., Gu, L., Khan, M. A., & Meyer, N. (2022). The effects of national culture on financial sector development: Evidence from emerging and developing economies. *Borsa Istanbul Review, 22*(1), 103–112.

Koutsomanoli-Filippaki, A., & Mamatzakis, E. (2009). Performance and Merton-type default risk of listed banks in the EU: A panel VAR approach. *Journal of Banking & Finance, 33*(11), 2050–2061.

Kwon, K. Y., Molyneux, P., Pancotto, L., & Reghezza, A. (2024). Banks and FinTech acquisitions. *Journal of Financial Services Research, 65*(1), 41–75.

La Torre, M., Leo, S., & Panetta, I. C. (2021). Banks and environmental, social and governance drivers: Follow the market or the authorities? *Corporate Social Responsibility and Environmental Management, 28*(6), 1620–1634.

Laeven, L., & Levine, R. (2009). Bank governance, regulation and risk taking. *Journal of Financial Economics, 93*, 259–275.

Laidroo, L., Koroleva, E., Kliber, A., Rupeika-Apoga, R., & Grigaliuniene, Z. (2021). Business models of FinTechs–Difference in similarity? *Electronic Commerce Research and Applications, 46*, 101034.

Lee, C. C., Li, X., Yu, C. H., & Zhao, J. (2021). Does FinTech innovation improve bank efficiency? Evidence from China's banking industry. *International Review of Economics & Finance, 74*, 468–483.

Lee, C. C., Ni, W., & Zhang, X. (2023). FinTech development and commercial bank efficiency in China. *Global Finance Journal, 57*, 100850.

Li, C., He, S., Tian, Y., Sun, S., & Ning, L. (2022). Does the bank's FinTech innovation reduce its risk-taking? Evidence from China's banking industry. *Journal of Innovation & Knowledge, 7*(3), 100219. https://doi.org/10.1016/j.jik.2022.100219

Li, B., Du, J., Yao, T., & Wang, Q. (2023a). FinTech and corporate green innovation: An external attention perspective. *Finance Research Letters, 58*, 104661.

Li, E., Mao, M. Q., Zhang, H. F., & Zheng, H. (2023b). Banks' investments in FinTech ventures. *Journal of Banking & Finance, 149*, 106754.

Macchiavello, E., & Siri, M. (2022). Sustainable finance and FinTech: Can technology contribute to achieving environmental goals? A preliminary assessment of 'green FinTech'and 'sustainable digital finance.' *European Company and Financial Law Review, 19*(1), 128–174.

Mahmud, K., Joarder, M. M. A., & Sakib, K. (2023). FinTech ecosystem across developing countries: Cross-country exploratory comparison. *Journal of Business Administration, 43*(2), 103–130.

Maudos, J., & De Guevara, J. F. (2007). The cost of market power in banking: Social welfare loss vs. cost inefficiency. *Journal of Banking & Finance, 31*(7), 2103–2125.

McKinsey & Company. (2021, March). Global banking practice—McKinsey on Payments. 13, 31.

McKinsey & Company (2023). FinTech: A new paradigm of growth. https://shorturl.at/mL45X

Meckling, W. H., & Jensen, M. C. (1976). Theory of the Firm. *Managerial Behavior, Agency Costs and Ownership Structure, 3*(4), 305–360.

Merton, R. C. (1974). On the pricing of corporate debt: The risk structure of interest rates. *The Journal of Finance, 29*(2), 449–470.

Milne, A. (2014). Distance to default and the financial crisis. *Journal of Financial Stability, 12*, 26–36.

Mun, C., Kim, Y., Yoo, D., Yoon, S., Hyun, H., Raghavan, N., & Park, H. (2019). Discovering business diversification opportunities using patent information and open innovation cases. *Technological Forecasting and Social Change, 139*, 144–154.

Murinde, V., Rizopoulos, E., & Zachariadis, M. (2022). The impact of the FinTech revolution on the future of banking: Opportunities and risks. *International review of financial analysis, 81*, 102103. https://doi.org/10.1016/j.irfa.2022.102103

Ng, T. H., Lye, C. T., Chan, K. H., Lim, Y. Z., & Lim, Y. S. (2020). Sustainability in Asia: The roles of financial development in environmental, social and governance (ESG) performance. *Social Indicators Research, 150*, 17–44.

OECD. (2020). Digital disruption in banking and its impact on competition.

Palmieri, E., Ferilli, G. B., Stefanelli, V., Geretto, E. F., & Polato, M. (2023). Assessing the influence of ESG score, industry, and stock index on firm default risk: A sustainable bank lending perspective. *Finance Research Letters, 57*, 104274.

Palmieri, E., Ferilli, G. B., Altunbas, Y., Stefanelli, V., & Geretto, E. F. (2024). Business model and ESG pillars: The impacts on banking default risk. *International Review of Financial Analysis, 91*, 102978.

Parlour, C. A., Rajan, U., & Zhu, H. (2022). When fintech competes for payment flows. *The Review of Financial Studies, 35*(11), 4985–5024.

Pažitka, V., Wójcik, D., & Wu, W. (2023). Cultivating China's FinTech ecosystem: The visible hand of the state. *Regional Studies, 58*(5), 1111–1123.

Pennacchi, G. G., & Santos, J. A. (2021). Why do banks target ROE? *Journal of Financial Stability, 54*, 100856.

Ratti, R. A., Lee, S., & Seol, Y. (2008). Bank concentration and financial constraints on firm-level investment in Europe. *Journal of Banking & Finance, 32*(12), 2684–2694.

Reghezza, A., & Vasilakis, C. (2024). Why do Banks acquire FinTech? The role of board cultural diversity. *The British Accounting Review*, 101424.

Rossi, S., & Volpin, P. F. (2004). Cross-country determinants of mergers and acquisitions. *Journal of Financial Economics, 74*(2), 277–304.

Rossi, S., Barbieri, L., & Lippi, A. (2024). Determinants of the profitability and stability of euro area banks during the ice age of interest rates. *Review of European Studies, 16*(1), N-A.

Sanderson, E., & Windmeijer, F. (2016). A weak instrument F-test in linear IV models with multiple endogenous variables. *Journal of Econometrics, 190*(2), 212–221.

Saona, P. (2016). Intra-and extra-bank determinants of Latin American Banks' profitability. *International Review of Economics & Finance, 45*, 197–214.

Sargan, J. D. (1958). The estimation of economic relationships using instrumental variables. *Econometrica: Journal of the econometric society, 26*, 393–415.

Schaeck, K., & Cihak, M. (2014). Competition, efficiency, and stability. *Financial Management, 43*. 215–241.

Scott, S. V., Van Reenen, J., & Zachariadis, M. (2017). The long-term effect of digital innovation on bank performance: An empirical study of SWIFT adoption in financial services. *Research Policy, 46*(5), 984–1004.

Sironi, P. (2016). *FinTech innovation: From robo-advisors to goal based investing and gamification*. John Wiley & Sons.

Spohrer, J. C., & Maglio, P. P. (2010). Toward a science of service systems: Value and symbols. *Handbook of service science*, 157–194.

Stock, J., & Yogo, M. (2005). Asymptotic distributions of instrumental variables statistics with many instruments. *Identification and Inference for Econometric Models: Essays in Honor of Thomas Rothenberg, 6*, 109–120.

Strobel, F. (2011). Bank insolvency risk and Z -score measures with unimodal returns. *Applied Economics Letters, 18*(17), 1683–1685.

Tan, Y. et al. (2017). The impacts of risk and competition on bank profitability in China. *Journal of International Financial Markets, Institutions and Money, 40*, 85–110. https://doi.org/10.1016/j.intfin.2015.09.003

Thomson Reuters. (2017). *Thomson reuters ESG scores*. Thomson Reuters.

Trujillo-Ponce, A. (2013). What determines the profitability of banks? Evidence from Spain. *Accounting & Finance, 53*(2), 561–586.

Uddin, M., Siddik, A. B., Yuhuan, Z., Naeem, M. A. (2024). FinTech and environmental efficiency: The dual role of foreign direct investment in G20 nations. *Journal of Environmental Management, 360*, 121211.

Wang, D., Peng, K., Tang, K., & Wu, Y. (2022). Does FinTech development enhance corporate ESG performance? *Evidence from an Emerging Market. Sustainability, 14*(24), 16597.

Wang, Y., Cao, W., Zhou, Z., & Ning, L. (2013). Does external technology acquisition determine export performance? Evidence from Chinese manufacturing firms. *International Business Review, 22*(6), 1079–1091.

Wang, Y., Hu, J., & Chen, J. (2023). Does FinTech facilitate cross-border M&As? Evidence from Chinese A-share listed firms. *International Review of Financial Analysis, 85*, 102435.

Washington, P. B., Rehman, S. U., & Lee, E. (2022). Nexus between regulatory sandbox and performance of digital banks—A study on UK digital banks. *Journal of Risk and Financial Management, 15*(12), 610.

Wintoki, M. B., Linck, J. S., & Netter, J. M. (2012). Endogeneity and the dynamics of internal corporate governance. *Journal of Financial Economics, 105*(3), 581–606.

World Bank (2020). FinTech in Europe and central Asia: Maximizing benefits and managing risks. FinTech Note. No. 4.

World Bank. (2022). Regulation and supervision of FinTech: Considerations for EMDE Policymakers.

World Economic Forum (WEF). (2015). The future of financial services how disruptive innovations are reshaping the way financial services are structured, provisioned and consumed.

World Economic Forum. (2024, January). *The future of global FinTech: Towards resilient and inclusive growth* (Insight Report).

Wu, D. M. (1973). Alternative tests of independence between stochastic regressors and disturbances. *Econometrica: Journal of the Econometric Society*, 733–750.

Wu, F., Hu, Y., & Shen, M. (2024). The color of FinTech: FinTech and corporate green transformation in China. *International Review of Financial Analysis, 94*, 103254. https://doi.org/10.1016/j.irfa.2024.103254

Yang, Y., Cai, W., & Wang, C. (2014). Industrial CO2 intensity, indigenous innovation and RandD spillovers in China's provinces. *Applied Energy, 131*, 117–127.

Yong, L. (2021). On the development of FinTech in Asia. *In International Forum on Financial Mathematics and Financial Technology, Singapore: Springer Nature Singapore*, 1–30.

Zhao, J., Li, X., Yu, C. H., Chen, S., & Lee, C. C. (2022). Riding the FinTech innovation wave: FinTech, patents and bank performance. *Journal of International Money and Finance, 122*, 102552.

Zheng, J., Khurram, M. U., & Chen, L. (2022). Can green innovation affect ESG ratings and financial performance? Evidence from Chinese GEM listed companies. *Sustainability, 14*, 8677.

Zheng, H., & Mao, M. Q. (2024). FinTech mergers and acquisitions. *Journal of International Money and Finance, 143*, 103076.

Zhou, X., Tang, X., & Zhang, R., 2020. Impact of green finance on economic development and environmental quality: A study based on provincial panel data from China. *Environmental Science and Pollution Research, 27*, 19915–19932.

CHAPTER 6

Conclusions and Implications

Abstract This chapter summarises the book's aims, findings, and implications, focusing on the impact of FinTech M&As on banks' performance. It highlights how FinTech investments enhance profitability, ESG performance, and risk management but may introduce short-term inefficiencies and increased risk. The study emphasises the influence of bank and FinTech business models on performance outcomes, offering a detailed examination of the dynamics of bank-FinTech collaborations. It emphasises the necessity of flexible regulatory frameworks to facilitate innovation while ensuring financial stability. Practical implications for banks, FinTech firms, and policymakers highlight strategies to optimise M&A synergies and align with digital and sustainability goals.

Keywords Bank Performance · Profitability · Risk · Efficiency · ESG

6.1 Research Objectives and Key Findings Recap

The mistrust of financial intermediaries and the proven inefficiency of long-established methods of delivering financial services, which are unable to meet the technological demands of consumers, have led to the advent

G. B. Ferilli, *Bank-FinTech M&As and Banking Innovation*, Palgrave Macmillan Studies in Banking and Financial Institutions, https://doi.org/10.1007/978-3-031-84445-4_6

of specialised FinTech firms to fill this gap. Based on these assumptions, the book examines one of the banking innovation strategies which *incumbent* institutions adopt to ensure their survival and facilitate their evolution within a dynamic financial environment. Specifically, the book analyses the impact of FinTech innovation on the banking industry, focusing on the relationship between traditional financial intermediaries (*banks*) and newcomers (*FinTech firms*). The relationship is formalised through merger and acquisition (M&A) operations, which represents a topic of consolidated interest in the banking literature. In the present case, the entity designated as the *"acquirer"* is a listed bank, and the entity designated as the *"acquired"* is a financial technology (FinTech) firm.

The main objective of this book is to empirically assess the impact of banks' equity investments in FinTech firms on *incumbent* banks' performance, identifying opportunities and threats inherent in these relationships. According to the study's perspective, the FinTech-Bank M&As also support the evolution processes affecting the banking business models. In order to maintain the market's competitiveness, traditional banking institutions must overcome financial innovation challenges through adaptation and a proactive approach towards new financial players.

Several *financial* and *non-financial* performance metrics have been identified to perform a holistic assessment of banks' performance after an equity investment in FinTech. The first category includes variables proxies of a bank's *profitability, efficiency*, and *stability*. The second category involves variables that express the bank's *default probability* over different time-horizons and its *environmental, social,* and *governance (ESG) scores.*

The analysis is applied to a global sample of listed banks engaged in domestic and cross-border M&As with FinTech firms over a long-time horizon (1997–2022). As an element of novelty, the study enriches the knowledge in the reference field of literature considering the heterogeneity of banks and FinTech firms (in terms of the business model adopted) to assess different impacts on bank performance.

A bottom-up approach has been applied to achieve the research scope. Thus, the study explores the following research questions (RQs):

RQ1: Do Fintech M&As affect bank performance?
RQ2: Do time factors affect the impact of Fintech M&As on bank performance?
RQ3: Do banks' business models affect the impact of Fintech M&As on bank performance?

RQ4: Do FinTech and bank business models affect the impact of Fintech M&As on bank performance?

The findings of the study are relevant and multifaceted. Overall, the study provides empirical evidence on the different impacts of FinTech M&As on bank performance, depending on critical factors such as the bank's business models (BMs) and the area of expertise of the acquired FinTech firms.

The baseline analysis replies to the first research question (*RQ1*), showing that FinTech M&As positively affect banks' profitability, as indicated by a boost in return on equity (ROE). This is primarily the result of the technological innovations that FinTech firms bring into the banking industry, which allow traditional banks to develop new products and services, thus creating additional revenue streams. Investments in FinTech also lead to a short-term decrease in operational efficiency, as reflected in the cost-to-income ratio (CIR), mainly due to integration costs and misalignments between traditional banking infrastructures and FinTech activities. Moreover, the increase in idiosyncratic risk, evidenced by a reduction in the Z-score, indicates an increase in the bank's vulnerability to new emerging and digital risks. The same investments, over long-time horizons, aid banks in reducing their default probability (PD) by adopting advanced risk management technologies such as artificial intelligence (AI) tools and machine learning (ML).

The results obtained in response to *RQ2* highlight that FinTech M&As exert a positive influence on banks' environmental, social, and governance (ESG) and probability of default (PD) over time, although these effects are delayed. This lag effect reflects the time needed for post-investment integration and the realisation of synergies between banks and FinTech firms. Although the short-term impact may be limited, long-term improvements in risk management and ESG performance are significant.

The study's novelty primarily lies in the results obtained from addressing *RQ3* and *RQ4*. In answering the third research question (*RQ3*), the study demonstrates how the impact of FinTech M&As differs depending on the business model (BM) of the acquiring banks. Specifically, *Retail Banks (BM1)* benefit from improved profitability (ROE) but face short-term declines in efficiency (CIR) due to several integration challenges. *Investment Banks (BM2)* experience short-term profitability challenges, but they gain improvements in risk management and ESG performance. *Diversified Assets Banks (BM3)* do not significantly impact the profitability metric, but they may benefit from improvements in risk management and ESG performance. These empirical findings highlight the importance of targeting FinTech investments with the specific core activities and business models that characterised the bank involved in the M&A.

The results related to the fourth research question (*RQ4*) demonstrate how the impact of FinTech M&As on a bank's performance indicators differs depending on the sector of expertise of the acquired FinTech firm. In this perspective, when analysing the effects of different FinTech models on various types of financial institutions, the findings indicate that investments in FinTech specialising in *Credit & Capital Raising* activities are able to improve a bank's profitability, particularly for a *Retail* and *Diversified Assets* bank. However, these operations can also increase the risk exposure of these intermediaries coherently with the risk-return profile paradigm. Investments in FinTech specialised in *Payment* services can slightly improve a retail bank's efficiency profile. However, they may expose the credit institution to cybersecurity risks, raising their short- to medium-term default probability. Investments in the *Market Support Services* category have been found to enhance both efficiency and ESG performance. This reflects the benefits arising from implementing advanced data management processes and energy-efficient technologies, particularly for *Diversified Assets* banks.

Furthermore, the analysis reveals discrepancies in the impact of FinTech M&As on the performance of traditional financial institutions, contingent on different country contexts (such as the United States, Europe, and Asia) and regulatory frameworks. The findings highlight how incumbents in countries characterised by adopting more flexible regulatory standards reap the benefits of bank-FinTech M&As and advantageously capitalise on the resource savings and operational synergies brought by an equity investment in FinTech operators. This indicates that well-designed regulations can foster a level playing field, enabling financial technology players to grow while safeguarding incumbent banks from uneven competitive practices. Regarding the bank's sustainability outcomes, the study shows that countries, such as Europe, with stronger regulatory standards and pressures about environmental, social, and governance (ESG) issues reap the advantages that arise from this strategic relationship. Thus, in line with the evidence provided by Macchiavello and Siri (2022), these findings reinforce the relevance of the link between sustainability, finance, and technology, which has also emerged during the Covid-19 pandemic crisis.

Overall, the findings underscore the need for ongoing monitoring of FinTech-Bank M&As and their impact on all segments of the financial system. The aim is to balance bank and FinTech in the new banking industry, broadening the regulatory scope and creating a favourable environment for FinTech-Bank relationships. The study's findings, supported by extensive robustness checks, offer empirical evidence of the multifaceted impact of FinTech mergers and acquisitions (M&As) on banks' *financial* and *non-financial* performance indicators. In particular, the findings demonstrate that the impact of FinTech M&As on bank's performance differs according to the bank and FinTech business model. Consequently, the analysis emphasises the central role of the business model (BM) in fostering financial innovation and ensuring the success of banks' performance optimisation strategies.

6.2 Contribution to the Reference Literature Field

The book provides several contributions to the emerging literature on the bank-FinTech relationship (Li et al., 2023; Wang et al., 2023; Zheng & Mao, 2024), showing that financial technology investments are valuable strategies to gain competitive advantage in the financial industry. Specifically, the book offers new and multifaceted evidence of the impact of FinTech M&As on the performance metrics of established financial institutions. Firstly, the study advances knowledge about the impact of technology adoption on banks' performance by focusing only on equity investment in FinTech firms, namely M&A operations. In the study, M&As are a strategic tool for improving banks' performance. Secondly, the book assesses bank's performance metrics using a worldwide sample of listed banks, differing from previous country-specific studies (Haddad & Hornuf, 2023; Katsiampa et al., 2022; Lee et al., 2021; Wang et al., 2023). Thirdly, the bank's performance has been declined into two main spheres: (i) *financial* performance, which involves metrics used as proxies to assess the bank's profitability, efficiency, and stability, and (ii) *non-financial* performance, which involves metrics used to evaluate bank's probability of default and ESG score.

This book offers a significant contribution to the existing financial economics literature by focusing on the role played by business models

(BMs) in shaping the impacts of the FinTech M&A operations. Previous studies have overlooked to consider the operational characteristics of banks when evaluating the impact of technology investments (Li et al., 2023; Wang et al., 2023; Zhao et al., 2022). This book addresses the gap that emerged by assessing the impact of the business model of the acquiring bank—classified as either *Retail (BM1), Investment (BM2),* or *Diversified Asset (BM3)*—on post-FinTech M&A performance outcomes. This differentiation offers a comprehensive understanding of how different types of banks benefit from or are challenged by FinTech M&As.

Furthermore, the book introduces a new dimension by analysing the business models (BM) of the financial technology firms involved in these transactions. By categorising FinTech firms according to areas of specialisation, including *Credit & Capital Raising, Payments, Investment Services*, and *Market Support Services*, the research identifies the impact of these FinTech categories on the banks' performance metrics. This approach, introducing an additional level of analysis, is able to capture all the impact on performance arising from all the possible interactions between the bank's business models and FinTech business models.

Furthermore, the book enriches the understanding of the effects of time lags the integration of FinTech into banking operations. The empirical findings demonstrate that while certain benefits, such as profitability (ROE), may be realised in the short term, other outcomes, such as improvements in risk management (PD) and ESG performance, may require a longer timeframe to materialise. This delayed effect has been insufficiently explored in previous studies, making the findings relevant for academic researchers and practitioners seeking a comprehensive understanding of the post-M&A integration outcomes.

In alignment with the growing literature field that merges technology (or FinTech) with environmental goals (or ESG), the findings of the book coherently found that banks' investments in financial technology are able to enhance the established banks' environmental, social, and governance (ESG) practices. As an element of novelty, the study strictly identifies which type of FinTech model that can optimise a bank's investment in financial technology. Consequently, the book merges three main dimensions, namely M&A, the business models of banks, and those of FinTech, thereby offering a novel and comprehensive perspective within the existing financial economics literature.

6.3 Implications for the Banking Industry, Policymakers, and Stakeholders

The findings of this book offer theoretical and practical implications for the bank's industry, policymakers, and stakeholders.

For banks, the findings suggest the strategic importance of carefully planning M&A with FinTech players, as these business relationships are increasingly recognised as drivers of innovation and competitiveness in the banking industry. As suggested by Zhao et al., (2022), the current IT infrastructure of incumbent banks may present specific challenges in meeting the evolving needs of financial development. Our findings highlight the potential benefits of banks considering strengthening their equity investments in FinTech firms to drive innovation and enhance efficiency in their business models to support their digital transformation. Although the study suggests that FinTech investments are an increasingly affordable option for incumbents, our findings also help banks to increase their advice about FinTech M&As. While these operations offer opportunities for growth, business model reengineering, and enhanced profitability, they also bring complexities and new risks related to integration, operational efficiency, and risk management. Banks should also align their business model with the FinTech firms acquired to ensure the derived synergies can be fully realised. Additionally, banks must develop long-term strategies to manage the short-term challenges that may arise, including increased costs and potential inefficiencies, while remaining focused on achieving longer-term performance improvements. Thus, banks should use their assets to promote a deep integration of technology and the banking industry by vigorously developing their financial technology capabilities.

For practitioners, particularly those engaged in financial advisory and risk management roles, the book emphasises the necessity of adopting a long-term perspective when evaluating the financial effects of bank-FinTech mergers and acquisitions (M&As) in the banking industry. While there are immediate effects on the profitability and efficiency profiles of banks, our analysis demonstrates that benefits such as improvements in ESG performance and risk management take time to materialise. Our findings indicate that bank managers should develop and implement strategies that account for these time lag effects and promote sustainable integration processes that gradually enhance performance across multiple dimensions. Furthermore, the book emphasises the critical role played by banks and FinTech business models, suggesting that bank managers should perform an *ex-ante* evaluation of possible M&As considering the heterogeneity of banks and FinTech firms and the synergies that could arise from their optimal interaction. Substantially, the findings of this book recommended that bank managers respond to the FinTech wave with *"targeted"* typologies of M&As, according to their area of expertise. This evidence could trace incumbent banks' future growth and innovation strategies, which can take the route of equity investment in the financial technology sector, depending on specific players' characteristics and capabilities, expressed by the FinTech firms' business models.

The book provides insights for stakeholders in the FinTech industry regarding the business models of banks that are more inclined to pursue targeted mergers and acquisitions (M&A) in specific FinTech categories. FinTech firms can benefit from our results by identifying the banks most interested in strategic investment based on their business models, thereby increasing the success rate of M&As. In addition, the findings highlight how specific FinTech firms are able to improve banks' profitability and ESG profile, positioning these players as ideal partners for banks focused on digital and green transitions. By aligning their strategies with the identified needs of banks, FinTech firms can better position themselves as M&A targets and for long-term collaborations.

The findings of this book underscore important policy implications for policymakers and supervisory banking authorities. Specifically, our cross-jurisdictional comparison analysis, based on different countries' jurisdictions (IMF, 2021; World Bank, 2020), has emphasised that a flexible and adaptive regulatory framework is essential to fostering innovation without compromising financial stability. Based on this evidence, policymakers and regulators are encouraged to implement guidelines or new frameworks to help acquirers better evaluate the expected synergies and risks of FinTech acquisitions. Banks should strike a balanced and cautious approach when interacting with a new player in the financial environment. Additionally, regulators should foster an environment conducive to innovation and collaboration between traditional financial institutions and FinTech operators; this approach could promote more sustainable and mutually beneficial bank-FinTech relationships in the evolving financial environment.

Moreover, the findings underscore the growing relevance of ESG considerations in the banking sector, revealing a strong interconnection between the digital and ESG/green dimensions (Galeone et al., 2024).

This evidence challenges the conventional wisdom that the digital transition and the green transition are mainly taking place on parallel tracks, converging toward the emerging concept of a "*twin transition*" in the banking industry (BIS, 2022; European Commission, 2022).

Therefore, supervisory banking authorities should ensure that the regulatory framework facilitates technological innovation and aligns with broader sustainability goals, encouraging banks to integrate ESG factors into their strategic planning and operations.

As remarks, the book's theoretical and practical implications could be extended across the financial ecosystem. Incumbent banks should carefully identify their optimal FinTech investment using the novel understanding provided in this book. A clear understanding of the business features (such as BM) that could make a FinTech M&A beneficial for acquiring banks is able to enhance the effectiveness of the bank's investments in innovation.

References

Bank for International Settlements (BIS). (2022). Denis Beau: What role should banks play in the twin digital and climate revolution? Speech by Mr Denis Beau, first deputy governor of the Bank of France, at the conference at the Jean Monnet University, 15 April 2022.

European Commission. (2022). Towards a green and digital future, EUR 31075 EN, publications office of the European Union (by Muench, S., Stoermer, E., Jensen, K., Asikainen, T., Salvi, M. & Scapolo, F.), ISBN 978-92-76-52451-9, https://doi.org/10.2760/977331, JRC129319.

Galeone, G., Ranaldo, S., & Fusco, A. (2024). ESG and fintech: Are they connected? *Research in International Business and Finance, 69*, 102225.

Haddad, C., & Hornuf, L. (2023). How do fintech start-ups affect financial institutions' performance and default risk? *The European Journal of Finance, 29*(15), 1761–1792.

International Monetary Fund (IMF). (2021). *Stay competitive in the digital age: The future of banks*. IMF Working Paper. WP/21/46.

Katsiampa, P., McGuinness, P. B., Serbera, J. P., & Zhao, K. (2022). The financial and prudential performance of Chinese banks and fintech lenders in the era of digitalization. *Review of Quantitative Finance and Accounting, 58*(4), 1451–1503.

Lee, C. C., Li, X., Yu, C. H., & Zhao, J. (2021). Does fintech innovation improve bank efficiency? Evidence from China's banking industry. *International Review of Economics & Finance, 74*, 468–483.

Li, E., Mao, M. Q., Zhang, H. F., & Zheng, H. (2023). Banks' investments in fintech ventures. *Journal of Banking & Finance, 149*, 106754.

Macchiavello, E., & Siri, M. (2022). Sustainable finance and fintech: Can technology contribute to achieving environmental goals? A preliminary assessment of 'green fintech'and 'sustainable digital finance'. *European Company and Financial Law Review, 19*(1), 128–174. https://doi.org/10.1515/ecfr-2022-0005

Wang, Y., Hu, J., & Chen, J. (2023). Does fintech facilitate cross-border M&As? Evidence from Chinese A-share listed firms. *International Review of Financial Analysis, 85*, 102435.

World Bank. (2020). Fintech in Europe and Central Asia: Maximizing benefits and managing risks. Fintech note, no. 4.

Zhao, J., Li, X., Yu, C. H., Chen, S., & Lee, C. C. (2022). Riding the fintech innovation wave: FinTech, patents and bank performance. *Journal of International Money and Finance, 122*, 102552.

Zheng, H., & Mao, M. Q. (2024). Fintech mergers and acquisitions. *Journal of International Money and Finance, 143*, 103076.

Index

G. B. Ferilli, *Bank-FinTech M&As and Banking Innovation*, Palgrave Macmillan Studies in Banking and Financial Institutions, https://doi.org/10.1007/978-3-031-84445-4

The manufacturer's authorised representative in the EU is Springer Nature Customer Service Centre GmbH, Europaplatz 3, 69115 Heidelberg, Germany. If you have any concerns regarding our products, please contact ProductSafety@springernature.com

Printed and bound by CPI Group (UK) Ltd, Croydon, CR0 4YY
16/09/2026
02217784-0001